KOREA
BRIEFING

Asia Society

The Asia Society is a nonprofit, nonpartisan public education organization dedicated to increasing American understanding of Asia and broadening the dialogue between Americans and Asians. Through its programs in contemporary affairs, the fine and performing arts, and elementary and secondary education, the Society reaches audiences across the United States and works closely with colleagues in Asia.

The views expressed in this publication are those of the individual contributors.

KOREA BRIEFING

Toward Reunification

David R. McCann, Editor

Published in Cooperation with the Asia Society
Karen S. Fein, Series Editor

An East Gate Book

M.E. Sharpe

Armonk, New York
London, England

An East Gate Book

Library of Congress ISSN: 1053-4806
ISBN 1-56324-885-9 (hardcover)
ISBN 1-56324-886-7 (softcover)

Printed in the United States of America

The paper used in this publication meets the minimum requirements of the
American National Standard for Information Sciences—
Permanence of Paper for Printed Library Materials,
ANSI Z 39.48-1984.

BM (c)   10   9   8   7   6   5   4   3   2   1
BM (p)   10   9   8   7   6   5   4   3   2

Contents

Preface

Whereas past volumes in the *Korea Briefing* series have focused on developments in the Republic of Korea (ROK), this year's edition provides equal coverage of the Democratic People's Republic of Korea (DPRK). As the immediate impact of the cold war's end recedes into recent history, the question of the divided peninsula remains unresolved. *Korea Briefing: Toward Reunification* presents analysis of both Koreas' politics, economics, and societies in the context of their future relations with each other. It remains to be seen in North Korea whether and when Kim Jong Il will be officially declared president and how the DPRK leadership will steer the country out of economic crisis; the resolution of these two issues will bear directly on the reunification process.

The Asia Society is grateful to David R. McCann for putting together a superb team of authors, carefully editing the chapters, and maintaining a sense of humor throughout, and to the contributors themselves for their diligence and enthusiasm. The Society owes special thanks to Deborah Field Washburn, who, during her five-year tenure as series editor, shaped the series and ensured its distinguished reputation. Karen S. Fein worked hard in honor of that tradition and was assisted by Patricia Loo, who provided useful comments on early drafts; Lili Cole, Allison Ostrer, and Les Baquiran, who helped to prepare and proofread the manuscript; and Patricia Farr and Patricia Emerson, who copyedited, as always, with care. Finally, we wish to express our appreciation to M. E. Sharpe's Douglas Merwin for his support of the project and Angela Piliouras and Mai Shaikhanuar-Cota for their efforts in the volume's production.

Marshall M. Bouton
Executive Vice President
Asia Society

August 1996

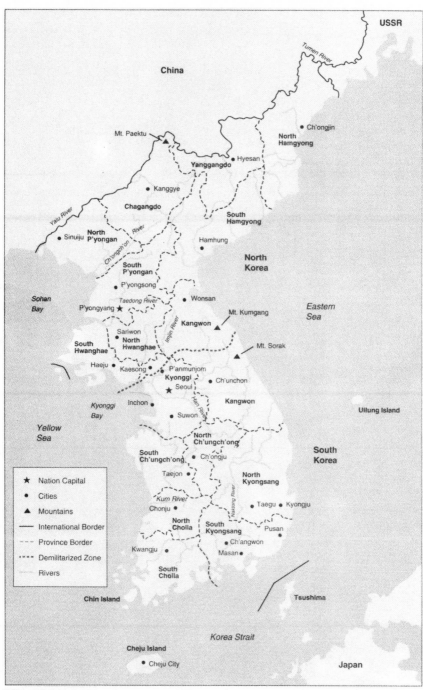

USSR

China

Tumen River

Mt. Paektu ▲

● Ch'ongjin

North
Hamgyong

Yanggangdo ● Hyesan

● Kanggye

Chagangdo

South
Hamgyong

Yalu River

● Sinuiju North
P'yongan

Ch'ongch'on River

● Hamhung

North
Korea

South
P'yongan

● P'yongsong

Sohan
Bay

Taedong River

P'yongyang ★ ● Wonsan

Eastern
Sea

Kangwon ● Mt. Kumgang ▲

Sariwon
● North
Hwanghae

Imjin River

South
Hwanghae

● Mt. Sorak ▲

Haeju ● ● Kaesong

P'anmunjom

Kyonggi
● Seoul ● Ch'unchon

★

Kangwon

Kyonggi
Bay

Inchon ●

Han River

● Suwon

Ullung Island

Yellow
Sea

North
Ch'ungch'ong

South
Ch'ungch'ong ● Ch'ongju

● Taejon

North
Kyongsang

South
Korea

Kum River

Nakdong River

Chonju ●

● Taegu ● Kyongju

North
Cholla

South
Kyongsang ● Pusan

● Ch'angwon

Kwangju ● ● Masan

South
Cholla

Chin Island

Tsushima

Korea Strait

Cheju Island

● Cheju City

Japan

★ Nation Capital
● Cities
▲ Mountains
— International Border
--- Province Border
···· Demilitarized Zone
— Rivers

Korea

Introduction

David R. McCann

In the three-year span covered by the Chronology in this edition of *Korea Briefing*, no other event compares in importance with the death in July 1994 of Kim Il Sung, the leader of the Democratic People's Republic of Korea (DPRK) for nearly half a century. The symbolic significance and practical implications of Kim Il Sung's death are immense, not merely because of the duration of his rule, but also because he managed in that near-50-year interval to turn his personal identity into the body politic.

In the extended moment since the death of the "Great Leader," the rest of the world has tried to peer over and around the walls of secrecy and myth that surround the North, to catch a glimpse of his son and political heir, Kim Jong Il, and reach some assessment of his likely term of office. As in a game of charades, the outside keeps trying out its answers to the inner, the enigma of the son. Still in mourning? Overthrown? Enamored of Western movies? He has already lasted longer than any official Washington spokesperson predicted two years ago.

The more interesting speculative position will be some time in the future, when the present enigmatic obscurity will have been rewritten as the mythological beginnings of the Kim Jong Il regime. Although the apparent desperation of the North, because of the recent floods and famine, has invited the direst predictions of sudden, chaotic collapse, it would be wise to recall that in 1953 the North had been bombed flat and yet survived, its political regime intact. While Russian and Chinese support for the regime have evaporated in political collapse and economic adventuring in the West, respectively, Japanese, United Nations, South Korean, and U.S. aid may yet help to retrieve the situation. In all the murky speculation, one thing is clear: the United States must learn about North Korea, its political leaders, and its people. The Chronology reveals the growing number of U.S. and Republic of Korea (ROK) meetings with DPRK representatives that have taken place over the last few years, and basic information about the contents and results of those meetings may help to displace the cold war characterizations that linger in some quarters. For a bizarre but encouraging example, the exchange between North and South Korean representatives dated November 7, 1994, is instructive.

* * *

Beyond comprehending the personality cult, future efforts to manage the relationship with North Korea must also focus on refashioning a relationship with a Korean nation that is still divided. In the South, a number of current issues point to the same fundamental question of how to work with, past, or through the division of the country. The election of Kim Young Sam was the first direct election of a civilian president in Korea's history. The span of the military regimes of Park Chung Hee and Chun Doo Hwan, the military origins of former president Roh Tae Woo and his close association with Chun, and even the indirect election in 1948 of Syngman Rhee by the South Korean National Assembly were rooted in the early cold war military division of Korea and took their scripts from the anti-communist morality play of post–World War II U.S. foreign policy.

The post–Berlin Wall euphoria at the prospect of reunification has been replaced by an anxious yet realistic concern in South Korea about the economic and social impact of full reunification. Various econometric models produce slightly different pictures of a reunified Korea, but all show the huge impact on the South Korean economy of absorbing the foundering economy of the North.

South Korea confronts challenges of its own creation as well as those originating in the post–Kim Il Sung North. Collapses, explosions, and corruption have shaken the Kim Young Sam administration. The collapse of one of the Han River bridges in October 1994 and one year later of a major department store in which nearly 650 people died were tragedies that have raised agonizing questions about South Korea's rapid-growth consumer economy. The explosion in a subway construction project in Taegu reinforced fears that the integrity of infrastructure, social as well as mechanical, was being sacrificed to the demands of unchecked growth. The bribery and corruption scandal that initially focused on Roh Tae Woo soon led to his predecessor, Chun Doo Hwan, lapped at the feet of opposition leader

Kim Dae Jung, and then threatened to spill onto the Kim Young Sam administration. That investigation has been supplanted in the news—though the Kim administration continues in other quarters to pursue its anti-corruption campaign—by the indictments of Chun and Roh on charges of mutiny and sedition in connection with the December 12, 1979, military putsch, the May 1980 Kwangju uprising, and the uprising's violent aftermath. Both were found guilty.

The trials and convictions of former presidents Chun and Roh mark a major shift in the Korean sociopolitical sphere. The shift is part of the democratization movement that came into the open in the 1970s, in a rapidly changing congeries of groups, issues, and programs, and led straight to the 1987 demonstrations for an open and direct presidential election. In addition to the recent willingness to acknowledge and confront a sometimes violent domestic history, the shift has also been marked by an increasingly skeptical view of U.S. interests in Korea. This skepticism flared up into substantial anti-Americanism at the time of the Kwangju uprising, when U.S. acquiescence if not actual involvement in the planning of the military suppression of the uprising was widely suspected. A U.S. State Department white paper issued in 1989 in response to South Korean National Assembly hearings on the incident flatly denied any U.S. knowledge of South Korean plans to use the military, but a story based on State Department documents obtained under the Freedom of Information Act just as flatly demonstrates that the White House staff was fully aware of the matter. (See reference under Suggestions for Further Reading.) It is safe to predict, under these circumstances, that the South Korean view of the structure of its relationship with the United States, as of its ties with the North, has and will become more realistic. The sense of an emotional connection with the United States and of endless forgiveness for U.S. gaffes will doubtless become attenuated as a result. This has been amply demonstrated in recent protests concerning the Status of Forces Agreement and the trials of U.S. soldiers accused of harming Korean citizens.

* * *

This edition of *Korea Briefing* is in two parts. The three chapters constituting the first part focus on changes related to the Korean state, North and South. Charles K. Armstrong and Kongdan Oh provide overview and analysis of recent events and their implications in chapters on North and South Korean politics and economic relations, respectively. Young Whan Kihl describes the situation of inter-Korean and Korean foreign relations following the end of the cold war and the death of Kim Il Sung. All three suggest that reunification, pushed and pulled by political and economic change within Korea as well as by global political shifts, has become axiomatic. The issue is whether full reunification or some other form of accommodation will be the result, which is in turn related to whether the process will be rapid and disruptive or gradual.

The second part of the *Briefing* begins with two case studies in the recent changes. Sang Duk Yu describes the history of the Korean Teachers Union, from its origins in the Japanese colonial period up to its contemporary accomplishments, setbacks, and agenda. This story is a remarkable interior view of the democratization process that has unfolded in South Korea during the last two decades. Stephen W. Linton, who acted as the interpreter for Jimmy Carter and for Billy Graham in meetings with Kim Il Sung shortly before Kim's death, presents an unusual portrait of the late North Korean leader and of his personality minus the cult. Readers will no doubt be surprised by Linton's assertion that Kim Il Sung did not view the United States as his implacable foe. Finally, and from an unusual perspective, Ross King ties the two interior realms together in his account of the language reform programs in North and South Korea. Reflecting the complexity of its subject, Ross King's article uses the McCune-Reischauer system for romanization. The rest of the *Briefing* follows the practice of the print media in eschewing the use of hyphens in given personal names and of diacritics.

* * *

I am grateful to the authors, first of all, for their contributions to this project. Thanks, as well, to my predecessor, Donald Clark, for his example, encouragement, and tempering advice. Special thanks to Karen S. Fein of the Asia Society, for sound editorial work, attentive but not alarmed concern for the schedule, and throughout, a genuine commitment to the quality of the book.

The Politics of Transition in North and South Korea

Charles K. Armstrong

The first half of the 1990s was a significant period of political transition in both the Republic of Korea (ROK) in the South and the Democratic People's Republic of Korea (DPRK) in the North. In South Korea, the continuation and extension of the democratization process begun in the political upheavals of the late 1980s led to the election of the first civilian president in a generation, local and general elections that were possibly the freest and fairest in the history of the ROK, and a wide-ranging series of economic and political reforms. In the DPRK, the death in July 1994 of President Kim Il Sung, who had ruled the North Korean state for nearly 50 years, led to the apparent but as yet unformalized succession of his son Kim Jong Il.

Beyond the state of transition, however, North and South Korea can hardly be more different. The loss of the Soviet Union as its main trading partner and source of economic assistance, combined with long-term problems of production and distribution in its domestic economy compounded by crop failures and massive flooding in the summer of 1995, has created a deepening economic crisis in North Korea. By some estimates, the DPRK economy shrank by as much as 5 percent per year in the first half of the 1990s. The South Korean economy, on the other hand, performed better than even many optimistic proponents had predicted, reaching 9 percent GNP growth in 1995. The dramatic changes brought about by political reform in the South contrast strikingly with the determined commitment to the political system in the North, despite global and regional trends that appear extremely unfavorable to the DPRK. Whereas the DPRK seems to be committed to continuity with the past regardless of how the world around it is changing, the ROK has been confronting the most sordid and painful elements of its recent history, with a campaign against the corruption and business-government collusion that have been at the heart of the South Korean political economy for decades, and the trial in 1996 of two former military dictators, Roh Tae Woo and Chun Doo Hwan, on charges of mutiny and sedition in the 1979 coup d'état that brought Chun to power.

South Korea: Reform, Recovery, and Regionalism

South Korean politics in the mid-1990s seemed to reaffirm the process that began with the political upheavals of 1987, when widespread protests by workers, students, and the middle class brought to an end the authoritarian rule of President Chun Doo Hwan and forced the new government of Roh Tae Woo to institute democratic reforms. In December 1992 Kim Young Sam became the first democratically elected civilian president in over 30 years, and his government has extended the democratic reform process through electoral reform, anti-corruption drives, and the expansion of social welfare. At the same time, however, South Korean politics has been marked by deepening divisions along regional lines; growth in the power of large conglomerates, or *chaebol* (including the unsuccessful presidential bid of Hyundai chairman Chung Ju Young); the crushing defeat of the ruling party in local elections and the loss of its majority in the National Assembly; and popular disillusionment with President Kim Young Sam. Recovery of high economic growth rates and the prosecution of former political leaders for corruption and anti-democratic acts boosted Kim Young Sam's popularity in mid-decade, but Kim and his party are still deeply unpopular in some areas of South Korean society, and the anti-corruption drive holds the danger of implicating Kim himself.

The Kim Young Sam Government

The 1990s began with the dramatic and unexpected merger of Roh Tae Woo's ruling Democratic Justice Party, Kim Young Sam's opposition Reunification Democratic Party, and Kim Chong Pil's New Democratic Republican Party into the Democratic Liberal Party (DLP). The move apparently was intended to create a grand conservative coalition that would maintain a solid and long-term majority in the National Assembly, analogous to the Liberal Democratic Party (LDP) in Japan,

Table 1

National Assembly Elections, March 1992

	DLP	DP	UPP	Independent	Total
Seoul	16	25	2	1	44
Pusan	15	0	0	1	16
Taegu	8	0	2	1	11
N. Kyongsang	14	0	2	5	21
S. Kyongsang	16	0	3	4	23
Kwangju	0	6	0	0	6
N. Cholla	2	12	0	0	14
S. Cholla	0	19	0	0	19
Taejon	1	2	0	2	5
N. Ch'ungch'ong	6	1	2	0	9
S. Ch'ungch'ong	7	1	4	2	14
Inchon	5	1	0	1	7
Kyonggi	18	8	5	0	31
Kangwon	8	0	4	2	14
Cheju	0	0	0	3	3
Total	116	75	24	22	237

Source: Adapted from Hong Yung Lee, "South Korea in 1992: A Turning Point in Democratization," *Asian Survey,* Vol. 33, no. 1 (January 1993), p. 34.

as well as to isolate opposition leader Kim Dae Jung. In South Korea it was widely believed that, as a condition of the merger, Kim Young Sam had won a secret agreement from Roh that Kim would be the DLP candidate in the following presidential election, scheduled for 1992. Thus, according to this interpretation, Kim had abandoned the opposition and joined the new ruling party in order to realize his presidential aspirations. In December 1992 Kim won the presidency with 42 percent of the vote, compared with 34 percent for Kim Dae Jung and 16 percent for Hyundai chairman Chung Ju Young.[1] The National Assembly elections earlier that year had already given the DLP 116 elected seats, compared with 75 for Kim Dae Jung's Democratic Party (DP) and 24 for Chung's United People's Party (UPP). While the DLP dominated the National Assembly and held the presidency, it did not maintain the solid majority the DLP founders had hoped for.

Kim Young Sam came to power promising a new era of politics,

---

1. Donald S. Macdonald, "South Korea's Politics Since Liberation," *Korea Briefing, 1993,* ed. Donald N. Clark (Boulder, Colo.: Westview Press, 1993), p. 17.

one that would make a clean break with the authoritarian practices of the past, eliminate bribery and corruption in government, improve the popular standard of living, and make government more accessible to the people. These reforms clearly struck a chord with the people of South Korea, and within a few months of his inauguration Kim had achieved a popular approval rating of nearly 90 percent.[2] But by half-way through his presidential term in 1995, Kim's popularity and that of his party had plummeted.

Part of Kim's problem was the popular perception that the South Korean "economic miracle" had peaked and that economic growth was inexorably declining. GNP growth fell from 8.4 percent in 1991 to 4.8 percent in 1992, the lowest in 12 years.[3] There was a widespread sense that South Korea had lost its international competitiveness, with a 17.4 percent increase in wages in 1992, an apparently declining work ethic, and popular aversion to the "Three Ds"—dirty, difficult, and danger-ous work. A series of man-made disasters caused concern that eco-nomic growth had proceeded too quickly, without regard for proper safety measures. Gas mains exploded in Seoul and Taegu, and in Octo-ber 1994 the 15-year-old Songsu Bridge over the Han River in Seoul collapsed, killing 32 commuters. The following June, in the most dev-astating construction disaster in the history of the ROK, the Sampoong Department Store in the affluent Kangnam area of Seoul collapsed, resulting in over 650 deaths. Subsequent investigation into these disas-ters indicated structural deficiencies, lax attention to building codes, and faults that had been deliberately ignored by government inspectors bribed by building companies. While none of this was directly attribut-able to the Kim Young Sam government, the disasters reflected nega-tively on the administration in power.

After 1993 the South Korean economy revived, although it did not reach the double-digit growth rates of the boom years of the 1980s. The Bank of Korea estimated GNP growth rates of 8.2 percent in 1994, 9.3 percent in 1995, and a projected 7 to 7.5 percent in 1996.[4] However,

2. Chong-Sik Lee and Hyuk-Sang Sohn, "South Korea in 1993: The Year of the Great Reform," *Asian Survey*, Vol. 34, no. 1 (January 1994), p. 4.

3. Hong Yung Lee, "South Korea in 1992: A Turning Point in Democratization," *Asian Survey*, Vol. 33, no. 1 (January 1993), p. 39; Victor Cha, "Politics and Democracy Under the Kim Young Sam Government: Something Old, Something New," *Asian Survey*, Vol. 33, no. 9 (Sep-tember 1993), p. 851.

4. L. Gordon Flake, "The Korean Economy in 1995," in *Korea's Economy 1996* (Washing-ton, D.C.: Korea Economic Institute of America, 1996), pp. 6–9.

the trade deficit also increased, and concern over South Korea's long-term loss of international competitiveness remained as businesses shifted to low-wage areas in Southeast Asia and elsewhere. Moreover, the public was dissatisfied with the government's sole aim of economic growth. Demands for greater economic justice, social welfare, and environmental protection were increasing. After decades of rapid industrialization with little regard for the resulting pollution, popular concern about environmental issues surged in the 1990s. Nongovernmental groups addressing such issues as water and air pollution, nuclear power, and industrial waste proliferated and formed an umbrella organization called the Korean Federation of Environmental Movements.

The government responded to these concerns about the environment and social welfare in a number of ways. The Office of the Environment was elevated to the level of a ministry, although government spending on the environment remained extremely low compared to that of advanced industrialized countries.[5] Corporations also began to implement pollution-control devices. In the area of social welfare, unemployment insurance was introduced in 1995, and a pension system begun in 1988 is scheduled to cover all workers by 1998.[6] Although the ROK is far from becoming a Western-style welfare state, the South Korean government began to play an active hand in the physical and social welfare of its citizens rather than merely promote economic growth as an end in itself.

Kim Young Sam promoted liberalization and internationalization of the economy, the latter coming under the slogan *segyehwa,* or globalization. Economic liberalization, including the reduction in government regulation and the opening of financial markets, was presented as a sign that the South Korean economy had matured and that the ROK was ready to join the ranks of advanced industrial economies. The most highly promoted symbol of South Korea's economic ascension in the first half of the Kim Young Sam administration was the ROK's application to enter the Organization of Economic Cooperation and Development in 1996. As part of the increasing separation of the state from the economy, South Korea's Economic Planning Board, the government's main body for economic policy making since the early 1960s, was dissolved.

---

5. Katherine Y. Kim, "Developing Awareness," *Far Eastern Economic Review*, November 16, 1995, p. 72.

6. Mark Clifford, "The Pressures of Winning," *Far Eastern Economic Review*, June 22, 1995, p. 44.

Ironically, some of these liberalization measures helped to concentrate economic power even more in the hands of the *chaebol*. Monetary policies, deregulation, and tightening of bank loans led to the bankruptcy of many small and medium-sized businesses, increasing the economic dominance of large conglomerates. In the 1990s Chung Ju Young and other *chaebol* leaders began to enter politics. The *chaebol* were becoming both more powerful within the economy and more autonomous from the state.

The Kim Young Sam government's political reforms included public distancing of the current administration from the authoritarian governments of the past. The Agency for National Security Planning, formerly the dreaded Korean Central Intelligence Agency under Park Chung Hee, was restructured to reduce its role in domestic surveillance and become more accountable to the public. Political rights were restored to tens of thousands of dissidents. However, the National Security Law, which since 1948 had given the government sweeping rights to arrest and detain without due process individuals suspected of anti-state (and especially pro–North Korean) activities, remained in place.

In his campaign for "clean government" Kim attempted to eliminate the bribery of bureaucrats and elected politicians, enforce strict limits on political fund-raising, and publicly disclose the financial assets of all government officials. In the early months of the Kim government, dozens of high-ranking civil servants and hundreds of public officials were punished for unethical activities. Anti-corruption probes extended to the formerly untouchable military, reflecting the military's loss of power in South Korean politics. Some of the highest-ranking officers under the previous military governments were arrested for taking kickbacks in the purchases of high-tech weaponry, and in 1993 the Hanahoe (Unity Society), a powerful secret society within the military founded in the 1970s of which both Chun Doo Hwan and Roh Tae Woo were members, was disbanded.

Elections and the Rise of Regionalism

Within a little over four years South Korea held four major elections: two National Assembly general elections, in March 1992 and April 1996; a presidential election in December 1992; and an unprecedented set of nationwide elections for local government positions in June 1995. These elections indicated the continued institutionalization of pluralist politics in South Korea as well as the emerging contours of a three-party political dynamic based primarily on regional loyalty and personalized leadership associated with the "Three Kims": Kim Young Sam, Kim Dae Jung, and Kim Chong Pil.

In the mid-1990s, Kim Young Sam and the DLP, which changed its name to the New Korea Party in January 1996, remained dominant in national politics but lost a significant amount of popular support. Kim's party experienced a crushing defeat in the 1995 local elections. Contrary to the hopes of the 1990 three-party merger, the DLP had failed to emulate the LDP's long-term monopoly of power in postwar Japan. South Korea in the 1990s is not like Japan in the 1950s: South Korean political dynamics have never been the same as those of Japan (they tend to be more volatile, with parties splitting into factions based on loyalty to individual leaders), and citizens in the 1990s are more critical of their governments everywhere. South Korea in the 1990s has left behind the polarized politics of authoritarian leadership and anti-government opposition. But the emerging political system is characterized neither by (pre-1993) Japanese-style one-party democracy nor by European-style ideologically oriented political parties. South Korea is becoming increasingly characterized by regionally based, personality-driven politics.

After his third failure to win the presidency in 1992, Kim Dae Jung announced his retirement from politics and left the chairmanship of the Democratic Party to Lee Ki Taek, a native of South Kyongsang. However, on July 18, 1995, following a successful showing for the DP in local government elections, Kim announced that he would return to politics and form a new opposition party. Much to the chagrin of Lee Ki Taek and DP loyalists, 53 members of the National Assembly left the Democratic Party and joined Kim's National Congress for New Politics (NCNP), making the NCNP the largest opposition party in the assembly. Meanwhile, Kim Chong Pil, former head of the Korean Central Intelligence Agency and mastermind of Park Chung Hee's 1961 coup, split from the DLP to form the United Liberal Democrats (ULD). The ULD claimed to represent the conservative forces associated with previous military regimes and had its core constituency in Kim Chong Pil's native province of Ch'ungch'ong. While the DLP retained its majority, the National Assembly had become divided among four competing parties. Eventually the reduced DP was to become the smallest of the four.

Table 2

Local Elections, June 1995

	DLP	DP	ULD	Independent	Total
Heads of large-area autonomous bodies[a]	5	4	4	2	15
Heads of basic-area autonomous bodies[b]	70	84	23	53	230
Members of major city and provincial councils	286	355	83	151	875
Total	361	443	110	206	1,120

Source: Korea Annual 1995 (Seoul: Yonhap, 1995), pp. 58–59; John Kie-Chang Oh, "The 1995 Local Elections in Korea," in *Korea's Economy 1996* (Washington, D.C.: Korea Economic Institute of America, 1996), p. 28.

[a]Mayors of 5 major cities and governors of 10 provinces
[b]Mayors or commissioners of small cities, counties, and major city wards

The Roh Tae Woo government had originally scheduled local elections for 1992, but under Kim Young Sam the elections were postponed until June 27, 1995. These elections were important because they were the first full-scale local elections in the history of the Republic of Korea and because they were widely perceived to be a kind of midterm referendum on the Kim Young Sam presidency. Local election results indicated widespread dissatisfaction with Kim Young Sam and the DLP and demonstrated the strong regional basis of party politics. Ruling party candidates fared disastrously throughout the country, losing to the opposition by a margin of more than two to one overall (see Table 2). Particularly humiliating for the DLP was the loss of 10 of the 15 provincial governorships and mayoralties of major cities, especially the mayoralty of Seoul, in which the ruling party candidate placed only third, after the DP's Cho Soon and the independent candidate Pak Chan Chong. In the roughly 5,500 local government races, the DLP won 33.8 percent of the vote, the DP 30.5 percent, the ULD 10.8 percent, and independents 24.8 percent. Regional biases were pronounced: the DLP won all 62 major local posts in South Kyongsang, the DP won 84 of 85 seats in South Cholla, and the ULD won 64 of 69 seats in Ch'ungch'ong.[7] Local elections belied the

7. John Kie-Chang Oh, "The 1995 Local Elections in Korea," in *Korea's Economy 1996* (Washington, D.C.: Korea Economic Institute of America, 1996), p. 29.

DLP's aspirations to represent a firm national consensus and indicated instead division along regional lines as well as popular disillusionment with the Kim Young Sam government.

The trend toward regionalism in South Korean electoral politics is rooted in the political economy of the past 35 years of South Korean modernization. Since the beginning of the Park Chung Hee regime in the early 1960s, political power and economic development in South Korea have been skewed toward the Kyongsang provinces in the southeast at the expense of the Cholla provinces in the southwest. This imbalance reached its peak during the Fifth Republic under Chun Doo Hwan (1980–88), when the representation of Kyongsang people in high government positions reached proportionately more than double that of Cholla people. The discrimination against Cholla was demonstrated most vividly in the bloody suppression of anti–martial law protesters in Kwangju, the capital of South Cholla Province, in 1980. It is unlikely that the government could have gotten away with such a crackdown in any other part of the country. Economic leadership has also heavily favored Kyongsang: in 1987, 23 of the 50 largest *chaebol* were headed by Kyongsang people and only two by Cholla people.[8] Three successive presidents—Park, Chun, and Roh—were natives of North Kyongsang, and Kim Young Sam is from South Kyongsang.

In the 1970s the association of Kyongsang natives with the status quo and the dissatisfaction of Cholla natives began to take political expression, with Cholla voters rallying around their native son, Kim Dae Jung. During the period of military dictatorship, Kyongsang regionalism was associated with authoritarian politics and Cholla with left-leaning opposition, but after the democratic upheavals of the late 1980s Kim Dae Jung shifted to the right, and the ideological differences between the ruling party and the opposition became negligible. Voter support for political parties became a matter of regional identification pure and simple. In the 1992 National Assembly elections, for example, 100 percent of the seats in South Cholla went to Kim Dae Jung's Democratic Party (see Table 1).

Despite that President Kim Young Sam attempted to address Cholla grievances by appointing a number of Cholla natives to high

---

8. Sallie W. Yea, "Regionalism and Political-Economic Differentiation in Korean Development: Power Maintenance and the State as Hegemonic Power Bloc," *Korea Journal* (Summer 1994), p. 18.

positions in his administration and the DLP was less dominant in Kyongsang than Chun and Roh's Democratic Justice Party had been, results of the 1995 and 1996 elections indicated that regionalism was becoming solidified in voter support. Until the passing of the "Era of the Three Kims" and the rise of individuals and parties with truly national appeal, it seems likely that regionalism will remain endemic to South Korean politics.

Stunned by the results of the 1995 local elections, which did not bode well for the ruling party's chances in the general elections less than a year away and the presidential elections scheduled for 1997, Kim Young Sam and the DLP began to regroup and to distance themselves from Chun and Roh's defunct Democratic Justice Party and its association with authoritarian rule. In October 1995, Roh—who had resigned from politics after Kim Young Sam's election in 1992—admitted before national television that he had amassed a secret slush fund amounting to $650 million between 1988 and 1993.[9] In December the DLP announced that it would change its name to the New Korea Party (NKP) at the beginning of 1996. The NKP began aggressively campaigning under the slogan "Reform Within Stability," hoping to revive support for the government's political reform measures as well as play on popular fears that South Korean democracy remained fragile, vulnerable to internal tendencies toward instability and authoritarianism as well as to the external threat of North Korea. The Kim Young Sam government moved dramatically to draw attention to high-level corruption and South Korea's authoritarian past, bringing to trial heads of business, former military leaders, sitting National Assembly members, and—most spectacularly of all—Kim Young Sam's predecessors, Roh Tae Woo and Chun Doo Hwan.

Buoyed by the popularity of these renewed reform measures, and possibly by the well-publicized incursions of North Korean troops into the demilitarized zone shortly before the general elections, the NKP fared better than expected in the National Assembly elections on April 11, 1996. The NKP won 139 seats, which left the party 11 short of a majority but capable of creating a majority through defections by non-NKP candidates, especially independents.[10] Kim Dae Jung's NCNP

---

9. *Economist*, November 11, 1995, p. 34.

10. Andrew Pollack, "South Korea's Ruling Party Trips but Does Not Fall in Elections," *New York Times*, April 12, 1996, p. A3.

came in a distant second with 79 seats; the ULP won 50 seats; and the DP won 9, fewer than the 16 independents, and effectively disappeared from the political map.

Political Scandals and the Trials of Two Presidents

At his inauguration Kim Young Sam had spoken of leaving the past to the judgment of history and forgiving those who had instigated the military coup of 1979 and the Kwangju massacre of 1980. But in May 1993 Kim reversed course, declaring the 1979 coup illegal and removing four military generals for their parts in it. By October 1995 Kim's anti-corruption drive had reached to his immediate predecessor, Roh Tae Woo. Popular suspicions immediately arose that other politicians were implicated in the Roh Tae Woo slush fund scandal. Kim Dae Jung admitted to accepting some two billion won ($2.5 million) from Roh for his election campaign in 1992, but Kim Young Sam vehemently denied receiving any money from Roh Tae Woo's slush fund. Nevertheless, charges of corruption came dangerously close to President Kim when Chang Hak Ro, one of his top aides, was arrested in March 1996 on charges of accepting millions of dollars in bribes from business leaders while in office. Roh's trial on corruption charges began in December 1995, and suspicions that Kim Young Sam would eventually be implicated in political corruption refused to go away.

In November 1995, apparently in part to deflect attention from his possible involvement in the slush-fund scandal, Kim Young Sam returned to the highly emotional subject of the 1980 Kwangju massacre with special legislation to punish coup leaders responsible for the atrocity. On December 3 Chun Doo Hwan was arrested on charges of mutiny for his role in the "12/12 Incident," the military coup of December 1979, and for ordering the crackdown in Kwangju in May 1980. He was also charged with taking bribes in office, and the separate trials of Chun and Roh on bribery charges began in early 1996. On March 11 the joint trial of Chun and Roh for mutiny and sedition, dubbed the Trial of the Century by the Korean media, began. On August 26 the Seoul District Court sentenced Chun to death and Roh to twenty-two years and six months in prison for mutiny, treason, and corruption in office. Chun and Roh immediately appealed their sentences; an appeals trial was scheduled to begin in October.

Despite widespread support for attacking government corruption and punishing those responsible for the Kwangju massacre, Kim Young Sam's overall popularity remains low. To many it seems that his reform measures and the arrest of Chun and Roh were cynical and politically motivated moves aimed at boosting his popularity and distracting the public from Kim's own involvement in corruption. More fundamentally, Kim and the NKP are no longer at the leading edge of political thinking in South Korea. Going beyond the rejection of authoritarian politics that began in 1987, the people of South Korea in the mid-1990s seem to be questioning the state-centered ideology that has characterized the ROK since the early 1960s, with its emphasis on political centralization and macroeconomic development at the cost of democratic politics, local autonomy, social justice, and consideration for the environment.

North Korea: Succession, Economic Decline, and Uncertainty

Whereas the central concern of South Korean politics is the extent and process of democratization, the North Korean political system seems to many outside observers to be struggling for its very survival. The imminent collapse of the Democratic People's Republic of Korea has been predicted since at least the heady years of 1989 and 1990, when Marxist-Leninist regimes in Eastern Europe and the USSR toppled one after another. North Korea, with its unreformed Stalinist command economy, political isolation, and foreign policy rhetoric of fierce anti-Americanism, is said to be an economic basket case and political dinosaur with no place in an East Asia increasingly characterized by robust market economies, active political and economic ties among neighboring states, and generally pro-Western international relations. One school of thought has held that a German-style absorption of North Korea by the South is inevitable and predicted a collapse of the DPRK as early as 1995.[11] Others have been more cautious in their predictions, suggesting a range of scenarios from limited economic reform (with possible fatal consequences for the political system), to

---

11. See for example Aidan-Foster Carter, "Korea: Sociopolitical Realities of Reuniting a Divided Nation," in *One Korea? Challenges and Prospects for Reunification*, ed. Thomas H. Henrikson and Kyongsoo Lho (Stanford, Calif.: Hoover Institution Press, 1994), pp. 31–47.

attempts at retaining the status quo, to a hard-line military overthrow of Kim Jong Il.[12] More recently, reports of widespread hunger resulting in part from the devastating floods of 1995 have renewed speculation that the DPRK is on the verge of collapse. Trevor Page, head of the UN World Food Programme, visited the North Korean city of Haeju in January 1996 and reported "appalling" conditions of reduced food rations, unheated classrooms, and lack of fuel.[13] Even soldiers, according to some reports, were resorting to desertion and theft in order to survive.[14]

While the economic crisis is indeed serious and the possibility of political collapse cannot be discounted, a close examination of the system in the DPRK reveals greater potential for continued existence than many outside observers are willing to concede. Among the three interdependent factors of economic performance, political institutions, and ideological control, it can be convincingly argued that the last is perceived by the DPRK regime as the most important. The minimal solution, from the perspective of regime survival, would be relief from the current economic crisis, which would allow for the maintenance of ideological control and the corresponding retention of power by the state and party elite. In the long run the DPRK will almost certainly open up and transform itself in some fashion, one hopes, leading to a peaceful and politically unified Korean peninsula. But in the short run collapse can be averted, and it is in the interest of all the states with a direct stake in the region—China, Japan, Russia, the United States, and not least South Korea—to help forestall such a collapse.

Economic Crisis

In the absence of reliable data on the North Korean economy, much of the outside world's understanding of the DPRK's economic situation is

---

12. Nicholas Eberstadt, "North Korea: Reform, Muddling Through, or Collapse," *NBR Analysis*, Vol. 4, no. 3 (Seattle, Wash.: The National Bureau of Asian Research, 1993); Rinn-Sup Shinn, "North Korea: Policy Determinants, Alternative Outcomes, U.S. Policy Approaches," *CRS Report for Congress* (Washington, D.C.: Congressional Research Service, June 24, 1993).

13. Elaine Sciolino, "In North Korea, the Threat Is Total Collapse," *New York Times*, February 18, 1996, p. E5. Ezra Vogel has suggested "the possibility of a collapse within two or three years," in Jim Mann, "U.S. Trying to Prevent Tailspin by North Korea," *Los Angeles Times*, February 11, 1996, p. A1.

14. "Military Going Hungry, Say N. Korean Defectors," *Washington Times*, February 1, 1996, p. A15.

necessarily speculative. What does seem to be clear, however, is that by the early 1990s the North Korean economy, which had out-performed that of South Korea until the early 1970s but had been declining since then, was in serious trouble. The loss of Soviet trade and assistance, an aging physical plant, the lack of foreign exchange, and a series of bad harvests had created mounting economic difficul-ties even before the disastrous summer of 1995. In 1993 the DPRK launched a campaign for eating two meals a day, ostensibly for public health reasons but clearly reflecting a shortage of food. That same year the government admitted that the targets of the Third Seven-Year Plan (1987–93) had not been reached.

The most serious economic problem facing the DPRK by the mid-1990s was simply producing enough food to adequately feed its people. Both natural and man-made factors contributed to the food crisis, including natural soil depletion, the inability to import fertil-izer owing to a lack of foreign exchange, a deteriorating distribution infrastructure, and the reduction of food imports from the former socialist bloc. Even before the 1995 floods, North Korea had re-quested food assistance from a number of countries.[15] With a food crisis already developing in the DPRK, massive floods in July and August 1995 devastated the major grain-producing areas of North Korea. According to a United Nations interagency fact-finding mis-sion in December 1995, the floods had left half a million people displaced and 100,000 families destitute. Grain loss was estimated at 1.5 million tons, putting thousands at risk of starvation. For the first time the DPRK appealed to the international community for emergency assistance, and in January 1996 the World Food Pro-gramme opened an office in P'yongyang, the first international hu-manitarian agency ever to do so. By June 1996 an international relief effort had raised about $15 million in food assistance for the DPRK; nevertheless, the World Food Programme predicts that food supply could remain a problem well into 1997.[16]

Through the first half of the 1990s North Korea's economy shrank by an average 5 percent per annum, according to outside estimates, and by mid-decade its per capita GNP had fallen to one-tenth that of the

15. Food and Agriculture Organization of the United Nations/World Food Programme, "Spe-cial Alert No. 267," May 13, 1996, p. 2.

16. World Food Programme, "News Update," May 13, 1996, p. 2.

South. This has led some outside observers to conclude that economic catastrophe is inevitable without some sort of drastic and far-reaching economic reform. However, there are problems with this estimation of North Korea's economic crisis. First, economic decline may not be as great as these figures suggest. Marcus Noland's careful, balanced analysis of the North Korean economy points out that the Bank of Korea estimates of North Korean output, which are the most widely cited figures on the DPRK economy, are extremely unreliable and are based on classified information that is impossible to check. Furthermore, such economic contraction runs counter to anecdotal evidence of some improvement in living standards in the last few years—at least until the 1995 floods.[17] Second, slow economic growth or even decline does not necessarily translate, in a society as controlled as that of North Korea, into popular discontent and political unrest. And third, North Korea has made several attempts since the mid-1980s toward economic reform, including a new joint venture law in 1984, a series of laws for foreign investment, and, most important, the opening of a Free Economic and Trade Zone in the northeastern region of Rajin and Sonbong in 1991. Although foreign investment is still minimal in the mid-1990s, Japan, South Korea, Germany, and other foreign countries have begun to show interest. North Korea also maintains trade with the outside world, including $310 million in trade with South Korea in 1995, a 34 percent increase over 1994.[18]

In short, North Korea seems to be facing hunger but not widespread starvation; an industrialized if backward economy relative to South Korea, it is certainly better off than many developing nations. International aid to fend off the worst of the food crisis, some degree of heightened foreign investment, and infrastructural improvement might enable the economy to get back on its feet in the near term. Economic and political implosion cannot be ruled out, but neither can "the possibility that the regime might limp along for some significant amount of time."[19]

---

17. Marcus Noland, "The North Korean Economy," in *Economic and Regional Cooperation in Northeast Asia,* Joint U.S.-Korea Academic Studies, Vol. 6 (Washington, D.C.: Korea Economic Institute of America, 1996), p. 144.

18. According to the ROK National Unification Board. See Nautilus Institute, *Northeast Asia Peace and Security Network Daily Report,* March 4, 1996.

19. Noland, "North Korean Economy," p. 158.

Political Institutions

Although some observers have used the term "economic collapse" to describe the possible outcome of the current crisis in the DPRK, the real danger is economic deterioration and political discontent leading to a collapse of the government. In this regard it is important to consider the stability and strength of North Korea's political institutions, the most important of which are the Korean Workers' Party (KWP) and the Korean People's Army (KPA). After the death of Kim Il Sung, some outsiders speculated that elements in the military were unhappy with Kim Jong Il and were blocking his formal accession to power. However, Kim has placed allies in key positions in the military and has attempted to woo the military elites.[20] As yet there are no concrete signs of serious disaffection in the military. It is both a powerful political force and a significant drain on the economy, estimated to consist of some 1.2 million men.[21] Maintaining a political role for the military and ensuring that it benefits from any future economic reform may be important to the continuity of the Kim regime.

North Korea is a highly stratified society controlled from the top down. Growing evidence indicates that the loyalty of parts of the core political elite is shaky. South Korea has reported some 200 defectors from the North in 1994 and 1995, far more than in previous years, including relatives of very prominent political figures—most notably the former wife of Kim Jong Il, Sung Hae Rim. On the other hand, one of the distinctive features of the North Korean political system is that the KWP is a mass party, consisting of three million adults, or one in five adult residents of the DPRK. Thus, there are millions of people in North Korea with a stake in keeping the current political system in place. The KWP's control is weakening in some areas but shows few signs of imminent collapse; there are as yet no alternative forms of political organization, overt or clandestine, that could conceivably replace the party.

---

20. Shim Jae Hoon, "Empty Driver's Seat," *Far Eastern Economic Review,* October 26, 1995. Based on the testimony of Choe Ju Hwal, a lieutenant colonel in the KPA who defected to South Korea.

21. Eberstadt, "North Korea," p. 19.

Ideological Continuity

For decades, the DPRK has put more emphasis on ideological indoctrination and uniformity than probably any other socialist state. The core
concept of North Korean official ideology since the mid-1950s, which
became enshrined as the guiding principle of North Korean politics in
the DPRK constitution of 1972, is expressed in the term *juche*. Often
translated as "self-reliance," especially in economic matters, *juche* is
concerned at heart with political independence and Korean nationalism. Kim Il Sung first used the term in a 1955 speech addressed to
ideological workers, emphasizing the need to know Korea's unique
history, geography, and culture in order "to educate our people in a
way that suits them and to inspire in them an ardent love for their
native place and their motherland."[22] Portrayed as an original Korean
contribution to revolutionary ideology, *juche* gradually supplanted
Marxism-Leninism as the official guiding principle of North Korean
politics. In the most recent DPRK constitution of the 1990s Marxism-
Leninism is not even mentioned, although the DPRK is still referred to
as a socialist state.

The collapse of communism in Eastern Europe and the USSR, the
growth of close economic ties between South Korea and Russia and
South Korea and China, and the economic and diplomatic eclipse of
the DPRK by South Korea have not led North Korea to abandon its
ideological commitment to socialism or to *juche*. On the contrary, in
the 1990s the DPRK's emphasis on ideology has become more pronounced than ever. In his first major political statement since the
death of Kim Il Sung, a treatise entitled "Socialism Is a Science"
published in the official KWP newspaper *Rodong Shinmun* on November 4, 1994, Kim Jong Il reaffirmed North Korea's adherence to
the principles embodied by *juche*, including "independence in politics, self-sufficiency in the economy, and self-reliance in national
defense." These goals would be attainable, according to Kim, only
with the thorough ideological indoctrination of the entire society,
united firmly behind the party and the leader. Thus, "socialist con-

---

22. Kim Il Sung, "On Eliminating Formalism and Establishing *Juche* in Ideological Work,"
Works, Vol. 9 (P'yongyang: Foreign Languages Publishing House, 1981), p. 396.

struction" must always give "priority to ideological transformation and political work."[23]

Far from conceding that socialism has certain shortcomings that led to its downfall in the Soviet bloc, the DPRK attributes the collapse of East European socialist states and the USSR to those societies' insufficient adherence to socialist principles, especially as a result of poorly educating young people in the ideals of socialism. "History teaches us," according to another *Rodong Shinmun* article by Kim Jong Il, that if a society that considers itself socialist "does not properly educate its youth, they cannot grow up believing in revolution and cannot maintain socialism."[24]

North Korea continues to assert that the tide of history is leading to the global victory of socialism, despite "difficulties" in some parts of the world. The DPRK insists that it will follow the path of *juche* regardless of events beyond its borders, adhering to what North Korea has come increasingly to call "Korean-style socialism" or "socialism of our own style." Exactly what "socialism of our own style" means in concrete terms remains somewhat vague, except that it is associated with political independence, the primacy of ideology over all other factors, and the unquestionable leadership of Kim Jong Il. For example, a North Korean editorial statement declares that "the socialism of our style centered upon the masses is developing fully under the refined leadership of Comrade Kim Jong Il by imbuing the whole society with the *juche* idea. . . . The ideal of socialism, the people's ideal of independence, can never be suppressed or destroyed."[25]

However, the vagueness of concrete content in North Korean *juche* may give the regime a certain degree of flexibility, as it can claim to remain true to Korean-style socialism while engaging in a certain degree of actual reform, especially in the economic realm. Alongside articles denouncing U.S. imperialism and extolling the eternal virtues of socialism, the North Korean media give extensive coverage to foreign investment in the DPRK and report enthusiastically on developments in the new Rajin-Sonbong Free Economic and Trade Zone in the far northeast. This seems in part to reflect tension within the leadership

23. Kim Jong Il, "Socialism Is a Science," *P'yongyang Times*, November 12, 1994, pp. 4–5.

24. Kim Jong Il, "Respect for Revolutionary Elders Is the Sublime Moral Duty of Revolutionaries," *Rodong Shinmun*, December 25, 1995, p. 2.

25. Choe Chol Nam, "Socialism Unites People with One Mind and Will," *Korea Today*, January 1993, p. 5.

between hard-liners and reformers, but on the other hand a certain degree of economic flexibility is not inconsistent with North Korea's long-standing emphasis on political and ideological concerns over economics. In a typically North Korean reversal of the traditional Marxist primacy of economic base over ideological superstructure, one recent DPRK article states that "the decisive factor in the victory of the revolution is not objective material and economic conditions. . . . The decisive guarantee for the victory of socialism is giving precedence to the enhancement of the independent ideological consciousness of the popular masses."[26]

Thus, one way to interpret political statements emanating from the DPRK since Kim Il Sung's death is that the North Korean regime is searching for a way to retain the ideological legitimacy of the current leadership while justifying a certain degree of economic flexibility and foreign capitalist penetration. Like China since the late 1970s, North Korea may be moving in the direction of geographically limited experiments in economic reform while keeping the political system intact, with the Rajin-Sonbong Free Economic and Trade Zone representing the initial step in this direction. Abandoning *juche* as a basic political principle would fatally undermine the authority of Kim Jong Il, whose legitimacy depends on carrying on the legacy of his father; on the other hand, the DPRK cannot emerge from its economic morass without reforming its economy and linking itself more closely with the West, departing from the path on which Kim Il Sung led the country for decades.

Conclusion

By the mid-1990s, the result of 50 years of competition between North and South Korea is, in the eyes of most of the world, the clear victory of the South. The economic viability, international recognition, and deepening democracy of the ROK contrast sharply with the economic crisis, political uncertainty, and archaic authoritarianism north of the DMZ. South Korea has its political problems, in particular the persistence of regionalism and personalism in party politics and the uncertain effects of the anti-corruption drive. But to many outside observers and many within South Korea, it seems that the strength and legiti-

---

26. Son Hyon Sok, "*Juche* Revolutionary Cause Continues," *Korea Today*, February 1995, p. 15.

macy of the South Korean system and the fragility of the DPRK make it all but inevitable that a unification will soon take place, essentially as an extension of the southern system over the entire peninsula.

Yet the DPRK may have more staying power than many observers think. However anachronistic its politics may appear, the North Korean regime has been remarkably tenacious over the years, surviving the devastation of the Korean War and outliving nearly every other socialist state. Left to its own devices, the DPRK could conceivably follow the path of its Asian neighbors China and Vietnam, opening up to foreign trade and market reform in the economic realm while maintaining the political primacy of the ruling party. However, the proximity of South Korea makes such a scenario more problematic for the DPRK, as the possibility of absorption by the ROK puts North Korea in a more vulnerable position than China or Vietnam. In the event of a sudden collapse of the DPRK government, whether or not the ROK would be economically or politically prepared for such a merger may be a moot point. But if the DPRK manages to survive and reform and the ROK continues to develop a more affluent, equitable, and politically stable society, the two may come together in a more peaceful and less disruptive manner than sudden absorption, gradually moving toward a single nation-state.

The Problem and Promise of Inter-Korean Economic Cooperation

Kongdan Oh

The German unification of October 1990 profoundly affected the two Koreas. Citizens of the Republic of Korea (ROK), or South Korea, began to believe that Korean unification was no longer an impossible dream, and the South Korean government saw an opportunity to eliminate its greatest security threat by effecting a post–cold war reconciliation with North Korea. To the extent that the citizens of the Democratic People's Republic of Korea (DPRK), or North Korea, learned anything about German unification, the news was presented as a warning that the South Korean puppets of U.S. imperialism were intent on defeating socialism in North Korea and bringing them misery. The leaders of North Korea must have feared that if Korea followed in Germany's footsteps their government would be destroyed and their days numbered.

In terms of the process of unification the German case was instructive, teaching that the path to political unification must be paved by years of economic and social cooperation. Even though German unification was triggered by larger events in Europe, the Germans' preparations enabled them to seize the opportunity. South Korea acted on this example by renewing its proposal for social, political, and economic contacts with the North. North Korea in turn adopted a defensive posture by insisting that political and military agreements must precede social and economic reconciliation, with an initial political step being the adoption of a unification framework that would provide for a Korean confederation guaranteeing the continued existence of separate political and economic systems on the Korean peninsula.

The author would like to thank Ralph C. Hassig for his assistance in the preparation of this chapter.

Long before German unification each Korea had, at times, made proposals for unification, most notably North Korea's 1980 proposal for the formation of a Democratic Confederal Republic of Koryo and South Korea's 1982 proposal for a somewhat different Unified Democratic Republic of Korea; but in the context of the cold war these initiatives had greater propaganda value than practical significance. Not until cracks began to appear in the communist facade did Koreans in the South begin to think that unification under democracy might actually be possible within their lifetime. South Korea's reunification initiative was taken by President Roh Tae Woo when he adopted a Northern Policy (*Nordpolitik*) in 1987, in imitation of West Germany's Eastern Policy (*Ostpolitik*) of the mid-1960s. Roh's grand political strategy was to proceed on two tracks: the international and the inter-Korean. In the international community South Korea would pursue diplomatic relations with the East European governments, then with the Soviet Union, and finally with China.

The international strategic environment was truly favorable for the success of *Nordpolitik*. The reforming Soviet Union was interested both in obtaining investment from South Korea and in reducing tensions on the Korean peninsula. Moscow's dealings with P'yongyang were declining: a traditionally generous trade-and-aid relationship was being put on a trade-for-cash footing. The military alliance, marked primarily by the Soviet Union's provision of weapons to North Korea on extremely favorable terms, was also downgraded. The diplomatic temperature between Moscow and P'yongyang cooled measurably when President Gorbachev met President Roh informally in San Francisco in June 1990, three months before their governments established diplomatic relations.

China continued to conduct a careful two-Korea policy even after normalizing relations with Seoul in August 1992, but China's trade with South Korea quickly surpassed its trade with North Korea and China particularly welcomed investment from South Korea's conglomerates. As it became clear that North Korea had little interest in taking China's advice to institute gradual economic reform, the Chinese became increasingly impatient with their communist neighbors on the Korean peninsula. The nuclear confrontation between North Korea and the international community also worried the Chinese, who wanted neither a nuclear North Korea on their border nor an international embargo of North Korea.

The breakup of the communist political and economic bloc and with it the socialist market that had benefited North Korea for so many years prompted P'yongyang to revise its political and economic policies and to try to carve out for itself a place in the changing international environment. In September 1991 the North Koreans applied for separate membership in the United Nations when it became clear that China would no longer veto South Korea's separate admission.

South Korea's initial expectation was that *Nordpolitik* would lead to cross-recognition of the two Koreas by all the major powers, with China and the Soviet Union recognizing South Korea in return for U.S. and Japanese recognition of North Korea. In fact, *Nordpolitik* was in a sense too successful: Seoul rapidly succeeded in establishing diplomatic and trade relations with virtually all the communist governments, but P'yongyang was unable to achieve its half of cross-recognition, given the decline of communism in general and the DPRK's increasingly weak political and economic situation in particular. P'yongyang's response was to adopt a defensive position against South Korea's offers of reconciliation and against the post-cold war realignment of powers that produced a world of capitalists and quasi capitalists, none of whom had any interest in the economics of socialism.

With little success in its approaches to Japan and the United States, North Korea decided it must deal with South Korea as a stepping-stone to the big powers. P'yongyang's paramount goal was to secure agreements that would reduce security threats. The North and South staged a series of high-level meetings between September 1990 and September 1992, the highlight of which was the signing of two important agreements in the final days of 1991. With these agreements in place many South Koreans were optimistic that their strategy of *Nordpolitik* had brought an end to confrontation on the Korean peninsula and that Koreans could together reap the benefits of the end of the cold war. Unfortunately, reduced tensions and increased inter-Korean exchange did not materialize on the scale most people envisioned, and the basic reason for this failure is quite simple. While South Korea and its political and economic allies saw the reconciliation of the two Koreas in the context of the collapse of communism as a first step in North Korea's abandonment of communism, absorption into South Korea, and participation in the new world order, North Korea's hope was that South Korea and the rest of the international community would accept its

totalitarian political system and its socialist economic system as legitimate alternatives to liberal democratic capitalism and permit the regime in P'yongyang to continue business as usual.

In this political context the promise of inter-Korean economic cooperation has not been fulfilled, although a prototypical form of cooperation has been achieved. An examination of North Korea's external
economy, the history of its economic relations with South Korea, and
the domestic politics and perceptions of the two Koreas can provide at
least a partial understanding of the problem and promise of economic
cooperation on the Korean peninsula.

Inter-Korean Economic Cooperation

North-South Dialogue

From 1988 to 1992 government representatives of the two Koreas met
at least 160 times. Seventy meetings related to the high-level talks, 25
to the nuclear issue, and 23 to sports exchanges, and at least 18 meetings of Red Cross representatives were convened to discuss visits of
separated family members.[1] This level of contact compares with only
30 meetings from 1980 to 1987. The most significant of these meetings were the eight high-level meetings attended by South Korea's
prime minister and North Korea's premier between 1990 and
1992. The two documents they negotiated in late 1991 provided for a
nuclear-free Korean peninsula and set forth terms of a Basic Agreement between the two governments.

The provisions of the Basic Agreement are embodied in three main
chapters dealing respectively with reconciliation, nonaggression, and
exchanges and cooperation. The two governments agreed to "recognize and respect each other's system" and not to "use force against
each other." As to their economic relationship, in order to "promote an
integrated and balanced development of the national economy and the
welfare of the entire people, the sides shall engage in economic exchanges and cooperation, including the joint development of resources,
the trade of goods as domestic commerce, and joint ventures." To
support these reconciliation and cooperation goals, both sides promised

---

1. *Tongil Paekso 1995* (Unification White Paper 1995) (Seoul: National Unification Board,
December 1995), p. 183.

to permit inter-Korean travel, correspondence, reunions, and visits for separated families as well as to reconnect roads, railroads, and postal and telecommunication links. To implement the agreement, joint committees on political affairs, military affairs, and South-North exchanges and cooperation were to be formed. Unfortunately these committees never met, and the promises for exchanges and cooperation have never been fulfilled.

The failure of the Basic Agreement should not come as a complete surprise. After all, the agreement was signed in an atmosphere of deep-rooted and long-standing mistrust, with little in the way of goodwill to lubricate its implementation and smooth over disagreements and no experience between the two Koreas in working together. The two Germanys, on the other hand, had begun working toward reconciliation in the late 1960s and signed a Basic Treaty in 1973, long before reunification. Moreover, the two Koreas remained involved in political relationships with their respective big-power supporters. North Korea was gradually losing the support of the former Soviet Union but could still count on China for political if not military support. South Korea maintained a security alliance with the United States, which had over 35,000 troops on Korean soil. One of Washington's primary goals was to maintain and strengthen the global nuclear nonproliferation regime, and North Korea's challenge to that regime meant that the United States was closely involved in Korean affairs. In fact, the nuclear issue was an important reason that the Basic Agreement failed so dramatically, as inter-Korean cooperation became linked to the nuclear issue.

Another reason for the failure of Korean détente was that inter-Korean relations were inextricably bound up with the domestic politics of the two Koreas. In North Korea the supreme political consideration was the maintenance and enhancement of the Kim Il Sung regime and preparation for the succession of Kim's son Kim Jong Il. In South Korea Kim Young Sam, a stranger to foreign policy, replaced President Roh in 1992 and presided over a wavering North Korea policy, sometimes talking peace and sometimes taking offense at North Korea's personal attacks against him, attacks that became more severe after he refused to offer condolences on the death of Kim Il Sung in July 1994. In short, the period from 1990 through 1992 saw an unparalleled degree of inter-Korean dialogue, but this dialogue could not be sustained under the circumstances; the two Koreas were still displaying a cold war mentality, and the North Koreans were unwilling to contemplate a significant change in their political and economic policies to bring them into line with current international realities.

North Korea's External Economic Relations

Given South Korea's status as one of the successful Asian economies, its external economic relations require no comment other than to say that they remain protectionist by U.S. standards. But North Korea has hardly begun to adapt to international commerce. Thus, little can be expected in the way of inter-Korean economic cooperation until the DPRK adopts the necessary economic policies. In fact, North Korea's external economic relations have deteriorated markedly since the communist states began moving toward a market economy in the late 1980s. In theory this economic decline should be favorable for South-North economic cooperation in the sense that, to use an old Korean expression, North Korea does not have many hills to rub against as a socialist cow and thus should be tempted to rub against South Korea. But the logic of this proverb has not been accepted in P'yongyang.

External Economic Organizations and Business Laws

South Korean companies interested in doing business in North Korea must first negotiate entry into the country. Even though P'yongyang began soliciting foreign investments in 1984 with the passage of its Foreign Joint Venture Law, there is still no systematic or transparent process by which foreign investors can enter the country. Until recent years North Korea had virtually no contact with the foreign business community, and what contacts it had were made on an ad hoc basis with various individuals, both inside and outside the government, who had the right connections in P'yongyang. In 1992 an attempt was made to consolidate external economic contacts under the control of the Administrative Council's External Economic Committee (EEC), chaired by Yi Song Tae. Two organizations under this committee were the Committee for the Promotion of External Economic Cooperation (CPEEC), under the direction of Yi Song Nok, and the External Economic Cooperation Committee, under Kim Chong U, but prospective investors and traders continued to rely on personal connections, and reports routinely surfaced of large bribes being paid to North Korean officials for permission to enter the country. In 1994 the external economic window was reorganized, with the EEC overseeing both the CPEEC and an Industrial Trade Promotion Committee in charge of North Korea's major (government-owned) trading companies.[2] Under the CPEEC an External Economic Cooperation Bureau took charge of four sub-bureaus: the Nation Development Guiding Bureau, the Rajin-Sonbong Bureau, the Foreign Joint Venture Bureau, and the International Cooperation Bureau. In principle these organizations have different functions, but it remains to be seen whether this reorganization has any practical significance for prospective investors.

North Korea officially opened its economy to investment from foreign companies with the passage of the 1984 Foreign Joint Venture Law, modeled on China's successful 1979 joint venture law. Previous to this the only measurable investment was provided by Japanese companies run by members of Chosen Soren, the association of North Korean residents of Japan, but most of the Chosen Soren investments were small. The international response to the 1984 joint venture law was insignificant: between 1984 and 1993 only 144 joint ventures were established, mostly by small North Korean companies in Japan, with total investment estimated at only $150 million.[3] As the DPRK's trade relations with the former Soviet Union contracted, P'yongyang passed a flurry of new business laws in 1991–92 designed to attract investors from the market economies, who under the new laws could establish either joint or wholly owned ventures. In order to reduce the impact that foreign companies would have on the protected North Korean society, the isolated Rajin-Sonbong Free Economic and Trade Zone (FETZ) was established in 1991 and virtually all investors were pointed in that direction.

These business laws helped clarify the North Korean business environment, but they fell short of the level of transparency that most foreign investors desired. Of particular concern to South Korean companies is their nationality status: are they to be treated as foreign nationals and thus covered by the same protections as other foreign

2. Doowon Lee, "The North Korean Economic System: Historical Analysis and Future Prospects," presented at the conference A Comparative Study of the System of Market Economy and Land Ownership/Use, East-West Center, Honolulu, Hawaii, August 7–12, 1995, pp. 17–18.

3. Joint venture figures from KOTRA as reported by Yonhap news service, September 28, 1994; cited in Foreign Broadcast Information Service, *Daily Report, East Asia* (hereafter FBIS-EAS), No. 94–188, September 28, 1994, p. 54.

investors, or are they a special category of business with no country? Since the promulgation of these new business laws has done little to attract foreign investment to North Korea, there has been no opportunity to test the adequacy of these laws.

Economic Relations with the Socialist and Transforming Economies

The demise of communism and the gradual adoption of a market economy in the Soviet Union were severe blows to North Korea. In the late 1980s, 55 percent of P'yongyang's trade was with the Soviets. In December 1990 Moscow announced its intention to begin conducting trade with North Korea on a hard-currency basis at world-market prices, a policy that was phased in gradually over the next few years. In 1991 North Korea's imports from the Soviet Union fell by two-thirds from the 1987–90 level, and by 1993 imports were only a tenth of their former level.[4] The blow to North Korea fell particularly hard on the energy sector. Compared with the period from 1987 to 1990, in 1992 the Soviet Union shipped only a tenth as much coal and coke and a tenth as much oil to North Korea. Another important impact, although one that we know less about, was the reduction in deliveries of military equipment.

China did not require that trade be conducted on a cash basis until 1993, and this requirement has apparently been implemented gradually over a period of several years. The revision of trade terms meant not only that North Korea had to pay considerably more for its imports of oil and coal but also that grain imports began falling as China's growing domestic consumption left little room for exports. China was North Korea's last hope for socialist trade, and as this source dried up the North Koreans had to tighten their belts as their economy slowly collapsed for want of energy and food.

Economic Relations with the Market Economies

As the DPRK's trade with the former Soviet Union and China declined, trade with Japan, which by 1991 had become P'yongyang's second-largest trading partner, took on greater importance. But this

---

4. Nicholas Eberstadt et al., "The Collapse of Soviet and Russian Trade with the DPRK, 1989–1993," *Korean Journal of National Unification*, Vol. 4, 1995, pp. 87–104.

trade, which continued to be almost exclusively with Chosen Soren companies, was only a fraction of the trade North Korea had conducted with the socialist economies. Even the Chosen Soren trade declined as a new generation of Korean Japanese, less loyal to a North Korea they had never known, took over management of these companies. North Korea was unable to develop trade with non–Chosen Soren Japanese companies, some of which had lost money in the 1970s when North Korea defaulted on hundreds of millions of dollars' worth of loans used to buy Japanese capital goods. P'yongyang's only hope for renewed commerce with Japan seemed to be to establish diplomatic relations with Tokyo, at which time reparations payments of several billion dollars would be made available to stimulate North Korea–Japan trade. But for a variety of reasons diplomatic progress stalled and trade with Japan has remained stagnant, although by 1995 Japan had become North Korea's largest trading partner as P'yongyang's trade with China and the rest of the world continued to decline.

The North Koreans realize that no country can thrive in the international economy unless it has diplomatic and economic relations with the United States. Washington imposed a tight embargo on trade with North Korea at the beginning of the Korean War, and these trade restrictions were lifted only partially after the signing of a U.S.-DPRK nuclear agreement in October 1994. As part of that deal, however, the United States promised to provide North Korea with 500,000 tons of heavy oil per year while construction of two nuclear reactors was under way. These oil shipments began in late 1994 (with 50,000 tons that year), and if they continue as specified in the nuclear agreement, they will become a primary source of oil for North Korea. North Korea has also invited U.S. companies to visit its Rajin-Sonbong FETZ, but the Americans are no more interested than the Japanese in investing in a bankrupt, unreformed communist state.

Inter-Korean Economic Relations

History and Current Situation

Inter-Korean trade did not exist during the cold war, unlike the situation between East and West Germany, and when North Korea drafted its Foreign Joint Venture Law in 1984, it was not targeted at companies in South Korea. South Korea took the initiative in inter-Korean

Table 1

ROK Trade with the DPRK (in thousands of dollars)

Year	Imports to ROK	Exports to DPRK	Total
1989	18,655	69	18,724
1990	12,278	1,187	13,465
1991	105,722	5,547	111,269
1992	162,863	10,563	173,426
1993	178,166	8,425	186,591
1994	176,298	18,248	194,546
1995*	177,329	48,619	225,948

Source: Unification White Paper 1995, p. 291.
*First nine months

trade by announcing an open-door policy toward the North in October 1988 in line with President Roh's July 1988 declaration that "trade between the two Koreas will be open and be regarded as domestic transactions."[5] This policy stimulated a small amount of indirect trade, primarily of North Korean imports to South Korea (see Table 1). In 1989 South Korea imported $19 million in North Korean goods and sold $70,000 in goods to the North. Seoul's 1988 inter-Korean economic policy was elaborated in a series of laws passed in the 1990–92 period known collectively as the Law on South-North Exchange and Cooperation. The climax of economic exchange in this period was Daewoo Corporation's decision to invest $5 million in the construction of several clothing plants in the port city of Nampo.

Despite the signing of the Basic Agreement at the end of 1991, by late 1992 relations between North and South Korea had cooled to such an extent that no new economic initiatives were possible. The main reason the economic initiative died an early death was that South Korea linked trade to North Korea's resolution of the nuclear issue, although this was not the only stumbling block. None of the initiatives set forth in the Basic Agreement had been implemented, and it appeared that North Korea wanted to abrogate the agreement. In the first months of 1993 the situation worsened as the United States and South Korea resumed their annual Team Spirit military exercise (canceled in 1992) and

5. *South-North Dialogue in Korea*, no. 46 (Seoul: International Cultural Society of Korea, December 1988), p. 63.

Table 2

ROK Processing-on-Commission Trade with the DPRK
(in thousands of dollars)

Year	Imports to ROK	Exports to DPRK	Total	Goods
1991	23	13	36	bags
1992	556	414	970	bags, clothing, shoes
1993	4,385	3,611	7,996	clothing, toys
1994	16,598	11,966	28,564	clothing, shoes
1995*	22,243	16,328	38,571	clothing, shoes, color televisions, fashion accessories

Source: Unification White Paper 1995, p. 307.
*First nine months

North Korea announced its intention to withdraw from the International Atomic Energy Agency's (IAEA) Nuclear Nonproliferation Treaty. The nuclear standoff lasted until October 1994, when the United States and North Korea signed a bilateral agreement in which P'yongyang promised to stop operating its nuclear reactors and eventually accept full IAEA inspections if the United States would lead a consortium to provide the North with two modern nuclear reactors and an interim supply of fuel oil, with South Korea paying at least 60 percent of the bill.

Even though no new inter-Korean trade initiatives were launched during this nuclear standoff, indirect inter-Korean trade continued to expand, and the number of South-North business contacts (mostly made in third countries) increased from 105 cases in 1991 to 219 cases in 1992, 230 cases in 1993, and 196 cases through September 1994, just before political relations improved.[6] By 1994 North-South trade had reached about $200 million annually, most of it in the form of North Korean raw-material exports to South Korea and processing-on-commission trade in which South Korea sent cloth or product components to the North to be processed into goods which were then shipped back to South Korea. By 1994 this processing trade had reached about $30 million (see Table 2).

---

6. Yonhap news service report, September 26, 1994; cited in FBIS-EAS-94–187, September 27, 1994, pp. 50–51.

On November 7, 1994, the South Korean government lifted its ban on direct business contacts with North Korea. Despite their hostile attitude toward the Kim Young Sam government, the North Koreans were eager for South Korean conglomerates to invest in the North, with one of their top external economic affairs officials, Kim Chong U, extending an invitation to several *chaebol* (conglomerates) as well as to U.S. corporations to invest in Rajin-Sonbong.

The Kim Young Sam government was ambivalent about permitting extensive business contacts with the North. On the one hand inter-Korean economic cooperation would facilitate eventual reunification by opening North Korea's society. Private investment would also reduce the eventual cost to the South Korean government of integrating the impoverished northern economy into South Korea at the time of unification. On the other hand the North Koreans were clearly trying to bypass the Seoul government by dealing with nongovernment organizations in the South such as businesses. As one astute South Korean commentator put it, the North Koreans wanted to propagandize the companies as "national capitalists" beyond the control of the government in Seoul.[7] Consequently, the South Korean government would at times veto business contacts when it feared that its companies were becoming too enthusiastic about doing business in North Korea.

The North Korean government was also sensitive to North-South business contacts, especially any that appeared to be sponsored by the South Korean government. When President Kim lifted the business ban in November 1994 and offered to provide economic aid to the North, P'yongyang responded with harsh rhetoric:

> The fact that the traitor Kim Young Sam raved about North-South economic cooperation and made a gesture for reconciliation was a mere drama aimed at tiding over [the ROK's] internal and external isolation and crisis and a self-admission that the policy of confrontation he has pursued so far has been a failure.[8]

---

7. "What Is North Korea's Ulterior Motive?" *Dong-A Ilbo* editorial, November 12, 1994, p. 3; translated by FBIS-EAS-94–219, November 14, 1994, p. 72.

8. (North) Korean Central Broadcasting Network, November 10, 1994, 2100 GMT; translated by FBIS-EAS-94–219, November 14, 1994, p. 51.

The Leading Role of South Korea's Chaebol

The South Korean *chaebol* have taken the lead in exploring business opportunities in North Korea, just as they have taken the lead in developing the ROK's domestic economy (although historically with more government support than they enjoy for their North Korean endeavors). While *chaebol* leadership in economic affairs—under government guidance—has been the ROK's economic policy ever since the era of President Park Chung Hee, the *chaebol*'s entry into North Korea poses a dilemma for the South Korean government. President Kim's domestic economic policy has been to reduce the power of the *chaebol* and provide greater opportunity for middle-sized businesses, which are underdeveloped in the ROK. Moreover, the *chaebol*, with their financial resources and extensive global business networks, are more difficult to control than smaller businesses, and the government wants to control all contacts with North Korea. Finally, evidence of massive *chaebol* bribery of former South Korean presidents provides a reason for Kim Young Sam to show no favoritism toward the *chaebol*.

This is not to say that the *chaebol* are all that eager to invest in the North or that the North Korean government is opening its borders to unlimited investment. Hyundai and Daewoo were the first into the North. Hyundai chairman Chung Ju Young visited North Korea in January 1989 and agreed to develop the Mt. Kumgang resort area and build port facilities at Wonsan. Daewoo chairman Kim U Chung visited the North in 1992 and agreed to build apparel and toy factories in the port city of Nampo. The Hyundai investment plans never materialized, but the Daewoo clothing factories were built after a delay of several years. A number of the other *chaebol*, including Samsung, LG (Lucky-Goldstar), Ssangyong, Sunkyong, Kolon, Dongyang, Hanhwa, Hyosung, Kohap, Lotte, Jinro, and Hanil, have either conducted processing-on-commission trade with North Korea or made modest investment plans.

The *chaebol* rarely make their investment plans or North Korean contacts public. This secrecy can be attributed to a desire to keep information out of the hands of the competition, keep the trust of their North Korean contacts, and preserve as much independence as possible from the South Korean government. The *chaebol*'s motivations for investing in the North are varied. For one, investment demonstrates a patriotic spirit that is popular with the Korean people. The *chaebol* also do not want to miss out on any business opportunities on their doorstep, even if the profit potential of those opportunities has yet to manifest itself. Of particular concern is that Japanese corporations might enter North Korea on the back of reparations payments made to P'yongyang by the Japanese government when it normalizes relations.

Although most of the top *chaebol* have made some contacts with North Korea, the size of the business ventures is small. The South Korean government imposed a limit of $5 million on investments, but few companies have invested even that much. Compared to the billion-dollar investments of Korean companies in China and Vietnam, the move into North Korea is only exploratory.

Problems of Doing Business in North Korea

The success of inter-Korean cooperation will depend both on political decisions made in Seoul and P'yongyang and on business decisions made by potential South Korean investors. Although the political constraints on economic cooperation currently pose the most obvious stumbling block, the business barriers should not go unnoticed.

North Korea has insisted that foreign investment be limited almost entirely to the remote Rajin-Sonbong FETZ, which they refer to as the "Golden Delta" and the "Rotterdam of the East." Potential investors tend to describe Rajin as a wild plain. Since the South Korean government permitted its businesses to contact the North, several studies have surveyed the attitudes of South Korean businessmen toward doing business there. In January 1995 the Korean Trade and Investment Promotion Agency (KOTRA) contacted 550 South Korean firms interested in doing business in the North.[9] The majority of the firms indicated that they were cautious about making North Korean investments, with over 50 percent planning to invest less than half a million dollars and only 5 percent considering an investment of as much as $5 million. About half the firms were contemplating a joint venture and half preferred a wholly owned venture. The goals of the prospective investors varied. Thirty-five percent planned to produce

---

9. Yonhap news service report, January 24, 1995; cited in FBIS-EAS-95–015, January 24, 1995, pp. 35–36.

products in North Korea for export to third countries; 31 percent would produce for the South Korean market; 18 percent hoped to market their products in North Korea, although there appear to be no provisions for such domestic sales; and the remaining 16 percent of the investors planned to extract North Korean natural resources. Companies' motives for investing in the North included establishing a bridgehead ahead of the competition, taking advantage of the duty-free status of inter-Korean trade, and procuring cheap labor and natural resources.

At about the same time as the KOTRA survey the government's Ministry of National Unification (MNU) polled 107 South Korean companies already having business contacts in North Korea.[10] Only 17 percent of the companies said they were interested in immediate investment, compared to 34 percent who had shown interest in a November 1994 survey just after the South Korean government relaxed restrictions on South-North business contacts. Only 21 percent of the companies wanted to invest in the Rajin-Sonbong area, with the rest preferring one of the larger and more accessible North Korean cities such as Nampo or P'yongyang. Perceived obstacles to doing business included uncertainty about the DPRK's political situation (57 percent), poor inter-Korean relations (14 percent), the lack of market mechanisms in the North (9 percent), P'yongyang's poor credit rating (6 percent), and the North's poor infrastructure (6 percent).

In February 1996 the MNU released another survey of 33 large and 66 smaller companies with North Korean contacts. Concerning obstacles to trade and investment, 52 percent cited North Korea's continued political instability, 18 percent its bad credit rating, 16 percent poor infrastructure, and 6 percent lack of legal and institutional instruments to facilitate South-North trade. Most companies were still skeptical about investing in Rajin-Sonbong: only 27 percent wanted to invest in the area; 38 percent predicted that without a radical change in the DPRK's economic policies the Rajin-Sonbong trade zone would not succeed; and another 27 percent expressed skepticism based on the North's poor infrastructure. In fact, only 9 percent of the businesses predicted that Rajin-Sonbong would be a success. Considering alternative investment sites, 46 percent believed that China and Vietnam offered better investment opportunities than North

---

10. Yonhap news service report, March 7, 1995; cited in FBIS-EAS-95-044, March 7, 1995, pp. 42–43.

Korea, 10 percent said that North Korea was equally attractive, and 33 percent considered North Korea more attractive, citing labor quality (48 percent), ease of communication (33 percent), and geographical proximity (11 percent).[11]

The Complementarity of the Two Korean Economies

In many respects the resources of the two Koreas complement each other, constituting a strong argument for increased economic cooperation. This complementarity can be considered from the viewpoint of the absolute and comparative advantages of South and North Korea as well as from the viewpoint of the advantages that the two would share as a consequence of economic cooperation.[12]

South Korea's relatively flat topography (compared with the North) makes it a better agricultural producer, especially for wet rice. This advantage is magnified by better agricultural technology and farm machinery. In industry, South Korea surpasses North Korea in practically all sectors by virtue of its superior technology and management expertise, but the comparative advantage probably lies in light industry, which is poorly developed in the North. The South also has the capital and credit that are sorely needed in the bankrupt North. Although the ROK lags behind the major world economies in terms of marketing expertise, it is learning fast, and if its recent "globalization" campaign succeeds it could become a world-class marketer.

Mountainous North Korea has relatively more mineral resources, and with only half the population of the South it also has more land available for factories. Since its founding the DPRK has stressed heavy industry and for many years surpassed the ROK in this sector. Unfortunately, the North's factories are now technologically outdated, but an infusion of capital and technology could make them competitive, given

11. "South Korean Companies Prefer Nampo to Rajin, Sonbong for Investment," COMLINE News Tokyo Financial Wire, February 8, 1996.

12. For recent discussions of the complementarity of the North and South Korean economies, see Jang-Hee Yoo, "South-North Economic Relations in the Korean Peninsula: A Complementary Hypothesis," *Korea and World Affairs*, Vol. 14, no. 3 (Fall 1995), and reproduced in the Ministry of National Unification's *Information Service*, Vol. 5, October 31, 1995, pp. 30–42; Namkoong Young, "A Comparative Study on North and South Korean Economic Capability," *Journal of East Asian Affairs*, Vol. 9, no. 1 (Winter/Spring 1995), pp. 1–43; for a pessimistic take on complementarity as seen from a political viewpoint: Nicholas Eberstadt, "Inter-Korean Economic Cooperation: Rapprochement Through Trade?" *Korea and World Affairs*, Vol. 18, no. 4 (Winter 1994), pp. 642–661.

the availability of raw materials and cheap labor. But perhaps the greatest advantage of the North lies in its workforce, which is well educated for basic tasks, well disciplined, and poorly paid. Not only are the workers disciplined, but the entire society is also so well controlled that random crime and corruption of the sort now found in Russia and China are apparently rare, although institutional corruption is presumably widespread. Of course, all workers are employed by the state (or allocated to organizations at the behest of the state). This can create problems for foreign businesses in terms of worker-management negotiations. Another potentially troublesome issue involves the human rights of workers who have no freedom of movement in the labor market.

A unified Korean industry and market would confer multiple advantages on both Koreas. A larger domestic market would provide for domestic economies of scale, and larger industries would be more competitive on the international market. The improved relations which would necessarily accompany economic cooperation would permit both governments to reduce their defense expenditures (estimated to be 25 percent of GNP in the North and 5 percent in the South) and concentrate on providing for a nonredundant military capability designed for defense against Korea's traditional rivals, China and Japan.

Once the political barriers to economic cooperation are overcome the many similarities of North and South Koreans will make cooperation easier. They live in close proximity, share a common culture, and speak the same language. Moreover, they share a 5,000-year heritage as a homogeneous people. But before these complementary Korean resources can be harnessed by this homogeneous people, difficult political divisions must be surmounted.

Political Obstacles to Economic Cooperation

Despite a gradual increase in trade over the last several years, inter-Korean economic cooperation remains at a pitifully low level. While part of the problem lies in the economic backwardness of North Korea, the primary stumbling block is the political barrier between the two states and the nature of their domestic politics. Three aspects of the political situation are particularly relevant to the issue of economic cooperation: the question of regime legitimacy, especially on the part of the North Korean government; continued military threat perceptions, especially on the part of the South Korean government; and unsettled domestic political situations in both Seoul and P'yongyang.

North Korea's Domestic Politics and Struggle to Survive

The DPRK's domestic politics appear to be unsettled since the death of Kim Il Sung in July 1994, lending credence to long-standing doubts (at least among foreign observers) about the ability of Kim Jong Il to fill his father's shoes. Not only has the junior Kim failed to address successfully economic problems that his father left unsolved, but North Korea's economy has also been shaken by a devastating flood in the summer of 1995, which in a society given to reading omens is a particularly inauspicious sign for Kim Jong Il. Although Kim appears to be at the top of the political heap in P'yongyang, it is likely that he is sharing power to some degree with others, particularly with hard-line military leaders who reject any form of reconciliation with South Korea. In a culture in which seniority is a virtual prerequisite for position, Kim, at age 54, is a generation younger than the other top leaders, which must place a strain on their collective relationship. Despite the fact that the North Korean hard-liners appear to have no solution to North Korea's economic problems or its decline in political and military power, they can exert influence in the name of their dead leader, who in life showed few signs of compromise. Whether or not Kim Jong Il is the reformer that some claim him to be, his position is most likely not secure enough to allow him to initiate economic reforms without the consent of other political players. Given that in the first two years after his father's death the son has not even officially taken over the top positions in the government or party, it would seem unlikely that anything in the way of bold initiatives can be expected from P'yongyang in the foreseeable future.

As the rest of the world abandons communism, the burden rests on the DPRK to prove that totalitarian socialism is still a viable option. North Korea's response to communism's decline has been to soldier on with "socialism in our own style." For any nation an important source of regime legitimacy and national security is economic strength. For North Korea the prospect of economic success rests largely on securing foreign investments while controlling the impact of those investments on its tightly closed social system. "Foreign pollution" is a threat to the peculiar worldview that the North Korean government has inculcated in its people, and the greatest pollution threat is perceived to come from South Korea, which has uniformly been depicted as a bankrupt slave state under U.S. domination. Consequently, all economic contacts with South Korean companies are strictly controlled, and investments are largely relegated to the isolated Rajin-Sonbong trade zone.

An example of the lengths to which the DPRK must go to defend its system is P'yongyang's resistance to offers of economic aid from South Korea. P'yongyang has even been reluctant to accept rice from the South to alleviate a very serious food shortage. The North Koreans have at least two concerns. First, they do not wish to establish intergovernmental links, which would constitute a recognition of the legitimacy of the South Korean government. Second, they do not want to admit that they are experiencing economic difficulties, especially difficulties attributable to weaknesses inherent in their economic system. Comments from international aid donors, including South Korea, to the effect that the North's food problems will be solved only when its economic system has been reformed are interpreted by P'yongyang as an attack on the government's sovereignty. Consequently, the North Koreans showed little gratitude for the 150,000 tons of rice provided by South Korea in 1994, and this lack of gratitude in turn fueled hostility in the ROK toward any more inter-Korean cooperation. Instead of serving as a link between the two Koreas, the rice aid has further separated them.

South Korea's Domestic Politics and Threat Perceptions

President Kim Young Sam is a skillful politician; he is particularly sensitive to the way the political winds are blowing. He also has little command of foreign policy. Consequently, his administration's policy toward North Korea has shifted with public opinion. Public opinion in turn is both monitored and influenced by the major South Korean newspapers. The four big dailies in Korean are *Chosun, Dong-A, Han'guk,* and *Chungang,* but the conservative *Chosun Ilbo* (Daily) has become the most widely read and influential of the four, and its hardline stance against North Korea influences both its readers and Kim Young Sam. When North Korea responded to South Korea's rice donation with ingratitude, the conservative media urged the government not to deal with North Korea, and President Kim accordingly adopted a hard line toward P'yongyang.

Threat perceptions remain high in the minds of many South Koreans, who are not likely to forget the day of June 25, 1950, when the North Koreans launched an attack across the DMZ and came close to overrunning all of the South. Memories of the Korean War are particularly vivid for the older generations. A survey of generational attitudes toward the North found that people in their 20s regarded North Koreans more as a society that needed South Korea's assistance and cooperation (67 percent) than as a country to watch with alarm (25 percent). The comparable views for the 30s age group were 63 percent and 29 percent; for those in their 40s, 54 percent and 33 percent; and for those in their 50s, 40 percent and 39 percent. Even this older generation views North Korea more as a people needing assistance and cooperation than as posing a threat.[13]

The South Korean military, with its responsibility for national defense, continued to warn in its 1994–95 and 1995–96 defense white papers of the threat of North Korean provocations and potential for domestic chaos in North Korea if the economic situation worsened, but disagreement exists as to whether South Korea is inferior, equal, or superior to North Korea in terms of military strength. Given the juxtaposition of the two military forces and the range of battle scenarios, the question of relative military strength is not easily answered. South Korea clearly suffers from at least four military disadvantages. First, the location of Seoul, the heart of South Korean government, business, and society, is within easy striking distance of North Korean forces. Second, South Korea has relied heavily on the United States for the more technological aspects of its defense, i.e., command, control, communication, and intelligence, and in these capabilities the South Koreans still feel vulnerable. Third, as the aggressor North Korea could choose the time and place of an attack, so the South must be prepared for a wide range of eventualities. Fourth, South Korea's high-technology economy is more vulnerable to disruption than is the North's more primitive economy.

As North Korea has watched its diplomatic and economic positions erode with the loss of its communist allies, it has adopted an increas-

---

13. Woo-Young Lee, *To Resolve Generational Conflicts Toward Unification* (Seoul: Research Institute for National Unification, 1995), pp. 35–45.

ingly belligerent tone toward South Korea as a warning not to take advantage of its weakened position. Statements from P'yongyang to the effect that the two governments are on the brink of war continue to be made. The most memorable such statement in recent years was the warning, uttered by a North Korean official in a March 1994 meeting with his South Korean counterparts, that North Korea would turn Seoul into a "sea of fire."

North Korea has repeatedly offered to engage in arms control talks, proposing that each side eventually reduce its forces to 100,000 (down from 1.1 million in the North and 600,000 in the South). But the South Koreans, remembering the North Korean surprise attack that began the Korean War and cognizant of the militarized nature of the entire North Korean society, insist on political, economic, and social confidence-building measures before letting down their military guard. Rather than reducing troop strength, North Korea has reportedly been moving more troops, artillery, and planes toward the front, where they would seem to be better positioned for offense than for defense. Whether this movement should be interpreted as a defensive bluff or as preparation for the possible last-ditch suicidal attack of a dying regime is a matter of conjecture. The former scenario certainly seems to be the more plausible. But in the opinion of the more conservative groups in South Korea—especially the troika of *chong, kun,* and *chongbo* (government, military, and intelligence)—the two Koreas remain locked in a struggle for political legitimacy and survival.

Two schools of thought exist on how best to respond to the perceived North Korean threat. The engagement school believes that economic cooperation will not only reduce tensions but will also improve North Korea's economic position so that when unification is finally achieved South Korea's financial burden will be lightened. The confrontation school believes that any help North Korea receives, either in terms of foreign investment or humanitarian aid, will simply prop up a hostile regime and provide it with greater resources to use against the South. Unable to decide on a North Korea policy, the South Korean government has taken the precaution of trying to control all contacts— political, social, and economic—with North Korea. This attempt at control extends beyond South Korea's borders to contacts that other countries, especially the United States and Japan, have with North Korea. The justification that the South Korean government gives for its attempts to control foreign contacts with North Korea is that such contacts may strengthen hostile elements in the North, thus interfering with the process of Korean reunification.

Prospects for Inter-Korean Economic Cooperation

Even in the face of a dismal economic situation in North Korea and strict measures taken by both the North and South Korean governments to control inter-Korean trade, South Korean businesses continue to show interest in North Korea, and trade and investment continue to increase. By 1994 cumulative inter-Korean trade initiated in 1988 had reached $1 billion.

Over the last several years South Koreans have learned valuable lessons about economic exchange. First, patience with North Korea is more than a virtue: it is a necessity. The North Koreans have deep and legitimate political fears, and they have little notion of how a market economy operates. Second, even though some North Korean business and economic technocrats work diligently to open their economy, the government bureaucracy makes postponements and delays a part of doing business, and bureaucratic corruption is endemic. Third, telecommunication links between North Korea and the outside world are primitive. When ships enter a North Korean port, they lose touch with the home company until they leave North Korean waters. South Korean companies that send raw materials to the North for processing lose control over the manufacturing process and must wait until the finished goods arrive back in South Korea to see how they are made. Fourth, payment for goods is difficult to arrange, since the two countries use different currencies and lack a clearing system for payments. North Korean payment for what few goods it purchases is usually made in barter.

The conventional wisdom is that inter-Korean economic cooperation will benefit only North Korea. Certainly the South Korean government seems to believe this, controlling business contacts with North Korea as leverage to try to force P'yongyang to establish intergovernmental contacts. But in fact without the North, South Korea's economic future is limited in terms of the strength of both its domestic economy and its position in the international market. Domestically, South Korean workers are moving into the middle class. Work that is "dirty, difficult, dull, or dangerous" is avoided. Land and labor are scarce, wages have risen above those in China and Southeast Asia, and the domestic market is not large enough to support capital-intensive industries. Moreover, the government still has to bear the burden of large expenditures to protect its border with North Korea and prepare for the eventuality of a North Korean social and economic collapse.

In the international market Japan continues to enjoy a substantial lead over South Korea in the high-tech field. China, which is in a sense a South Korea 30 times larger and only a few years behind, is muscling its way into the international market with the help of overseas Chinese, including those in Taiwan. Without a distinctive advantage such as those the Japanese have developed in technology and the Chinese in size, South Korea will have trouble competing successfully with its larger neighbors.

It would seem that the politics-first approach toward inter-Korean economic cooperation that has been adopted by both the South and North Korean governments is lacking in vision. Seoul considers the North to be a backward, imprisoned part of South Korean territory, to be strangled into submission or offered small charity as a political gesture to remind the North Koreans that they have lost the economic contest. The insults that North Korea routinely heaps on the South Korean government are, not surprisingly, taken very badly. In short, Seoul is still fighting the cold war with the governing elite in P'yongyang. Inadequate consideration has been given to the advantages of a bold economic opening to the North Korean people. A business-led opening would have the potential to reform the North Korean political and economic systems and effect a gradual reconciliation of the two Koreas. It seems unlikely that South Korean business investment would make the North Korean regime more antagonistic to South Korea. It is true that massive foreign investment might prevent the regime from collapsing, but only the least thoughtful and most hostile of South Koreans believe that a political collapse in the North, which would likely trigger a more general social collapse, would be in South Korea's best interest.

As a result of South Korea's democratization, domestic politics now play an important role in the formulation of inter-Korean policy. Kim Young Sam's primary goal is to position the government party for a win in the 1997 presidential election. Politicians tend to play it safe and err on the side of conservatism, and Kim is overseeing a hawkish inter-Korean policy that will please the conservative elements in the South Korean electorate and media.

For its part, the North Korean government's control of its people's contact with South Korea makes the Kim Young Sam government look like a laissez-faire administration. Yet it must be clear to the North Korean leaders that there is no saving their economic system. The choice is between making a change under relatively favorable conditions and waiting for a collapse. Under its gerontocratic leadership (including the relatively youthful Kim Jong Il because in a sense he is only an agent of his dead father) the North Koreans have done little more than muddle through, making minor adjustments with the hope that the future will bring more favorable conditions.[14] What these conditions might be is hard to guess. Perhaps the starving North Korean people will make a herculean effort as repeatedly called for by the party. Or perhaps world socialism will return, or the market economies, led by Japan and the United States, will begin pouring massive investments into North Korea while allowing it to preserve its capitalist-hostile economy.

It is probably too much to expect that North Korea will be an agent for peaceful change on the Korean peninsula, because the North Korean economy is run for the benefit of the political elite, who can live relatively well even if their economy is moribund and who presumably have their escape routes planned in the unlikely event of a people's uprising. This puts the burden of achieving reconciliation and economic cooperation on the shoulders of the leaders of South Korea, who are accountable to their people and in a broader sense to the masses of common people in the North.

---

14. Nicholas Eberstadt, "North Korea: Reform, Muddling Through, or Collapse?" in the series *NBR Analysis*, National Bureau of Asian Research, Vol. 4, no. 3, September 1993.

Why the Cold War Persists in Korea: Inter-Korean and Foreign Relations

Young Whan Kihl

Following the demise of the Soviet Union in 1992, there was an upsurge of optimism that the Korean cold war system would also come to an end. In the mid-1990s, however, this anticipation of a Korean endgame has proven to be either premature or inaccurate. While the Korean security system will certainly undergo radical shifts in the long run, the peninsula remains frozen in a state of cold war tension for the time being.

The failed transformation of the Korean peninsula can be attributed to three factors: the lack of sincere reconciliation and restoration of mutual trust between North and South, complicated by domestic political change within each Korean state; the widening gap in power and capability—both military and economic—between North and South Korea owing to differential rates of economic growth and modernization; and the external policy orientation of the respective Korean states, including North Korea's nuclear brinkmanship. Each of these elements underlies the failed normalization of inter-Korean relations; together they have propelled a cold war rivalry into the mid-1990s. This chapter will address the issue of the persisting tensions in Korea and the reasons for the prolongation of Korea's status as a divided nation-state in terms of both the stalemated inter-Korean dialogue and of each regime's foreign relations. To place the current debate in a broader context, it begins with a brief overview of Korea's geopolitics and recent history.

Korea's Geopolitical Situation

Through the ages Korea has had "a strategic importance far out of proportion to its size."[1] Korea's status has been determined largely

---

1. Norman D. Levin and Richard L. Sneider, "Korea in Postwar U.S. Security Policy," RAND Corporation, P-3775 (June 1982).

by its geography. The Korean peninsula lies at the intersection of major powers in Northeast Asia; it has been a bone of contention among China, Russia, and Japan. Korea is not only a land bridge connecting China and Russia, but also a "dagger," as the saying goes, "pointing at the heart of Japan." Since the end of World War II, Japan, which had expansionist designs on Korea in the past, and the United States have acted to check Chinese and Russian expansionism. Not surprisingly, Korea has been viewed as a strategic asset by these major powers, which hoped to have a stable Korea act as a buffer zone in the balance of global- and regional-power politics.

During the cold war the security of the Korean peninsula was an integral part of the global strategic calculus of the United States and the Soviet Union. President Harry Truman's containment policy, for instance, was put into effect and tested in Korea. In the Korean War (1950–53), which almost ignited World War III, Stalin's Soviet Union avoided direct involvement in armed conflict by engaging Kim Il Sung's North Korea and Mao Zedong's China to carry out the war for international communism by proxy.[2]

The fall of the Soviet empire in 1992 fundamentally altered the security dynamics and strategic environment surrounding the Korean peninsula. John Mearsheimer, in a 1990 article entitled "Back to the Future," warned of the possible dangers accompanying the end of bipolarity in Europe.[3] As he noted, "the next decades in Europe without the superpowers would probably not be as violent as the first 45 years of this century, but would probably be substantially more prone to violence than the past 45 years."[4] What transpired in Central and Eastern Europe has implications for what may come about strategically in Northeast Asia as well. North Korea lost its superpower patron and other allies, although it was quick to recognize the Commonwealth of Independent

---

2. See, for instance, Sergei N. Goncharov, John W. Lewis, and Litai Xue, *Uncertain Partners: Stalin, Mao and the Korean War* (Stanford, Calif.: Stanford University Press, 1993). According to this study, "the invasion of June 25, 1950, was pre-planned, blessed, and directly assisted by Stalin and his generals, and reluctantly backed by Mao at Stalin's insistence" (p. 213). This study also reveals that "Kim began lobbying for a Soviet-backed invasion of the South as early as March 1949" and that Stalin wanted to avoid a war against the United States for at least 15 to 20 years and therefore did not want a war in Korea in 1950. Also see William Stueck, *The Korean War: An International History* (Princeton, N.J.: Princeton University Press, 1995).

3. John Mearsheimer, "Back to the Future: Instability in Europe After the Cold War," *International Security*, Vol. 15 (Summer 1990), pp. 5–56; "Why We Will Soon Miss the Cold War," *Atlantic Monthly,* Vol. 269, no. 8 (August 1990), pp. 35–50.

4. Mearsheimer, "Back to the Future," p. 6.

States and the newly constituted East European countries. It lost valuable foreign trade access to the former communist bloc countries.

Whether the disappearance of bipolarity will destabilize the Korean peninsula in the years ahead is not clear at this point. However, one can argue that the danger of instability in the future security environment in Asia does linger in such chronic regional conflicts as Korea's protracted division.

The Promises and Disappointments of a Negotiated Settlement

Since Korea was partitioned in 1945 by foreign powers, it is important to many Koreans that they achieve reunification on their own. In the South-North Joint Communiqué of July 4, 1972, the two regimes agreed on three "principles for unification of the fatherland." The first is that "unification shall be achieved through independent efforts without being subject to external imposition or interference"; the second that "unification shall be achieved through peaceful means and not through use of force against one another"; and the third, that "a great national unity, as a homogeneous people, shall be sought first, transcending differences in ideas, ideologies, and systems."[5]

Despite the great promise of the communiqué, North and South Korean dialogue has been sporadic at best. Prior to 1972 inter-Korean relations had passed from violent contact during the Korean War to a period of estrangement and occasional border clashes, including North Korean commando raids across the demilitarized zone (DMZ). The period of dialogue following the 1972 communiqué did not last beyond 1974, and the next phase of inter-Korean dialogue was also brief, lasting for just one year from 1984 to 1985. An exchange of visits did take place in 1985 between a few separated family members and some artist troupes.

The dramatic end of the cold war era presented a new occasion for resuming inter-Korean dialogue and negotiation.[6] When the impact of German reunification reached the Korean peninsula, the leaders of the

---

5. For an analysis of the July 4, 1972, joint communiqué, see Young Whan Kihl, *Politics and Policies in Divided Korea: Regimes in Contest* (Boulder, Colo.: Westview Press, 1984), pp. 55–59.

6. Young Whan Kihl, "The Politics of Inter-Korean Relations: Co-existence or Reunification?" in *Korea and the World: Beyond the Cold War,* ed. Young Whan Kihl (Boulder, Colo.: Westview Press, 1994), pp. 133–152.

two Korean states responded by initiating high-level talks between their prime ministers. These efforts resulted in the signing of the two historic agreements of December 1991, the Agreement on Reconciliation, Non-aggression, and Exchanges and Cooperation Between the South and the North was signed on December 13, and the Joint Declaration of De-nuclearization of the Korean Peninsula on December 31. The inter-Korean agreement, effective February 19, 1992, stipulates in its preamble that "in keeping with the yearning of the entire Korean people for the peaceful unification of the divided land," both sides are deter-mined to "remove the state of political and military confrontation and achieve national reconciliation, . . . avoid armed aggression and hostili-ties, reduce tension, and ensure the peace," and "realize multifaceted exchanges and cooperation to advance common national interests and prosperity." Both sides agreed that their "relations, not being a relation-ship between states, constitute a special interim relationship stemming from the process toward unification." North and South Korea pledged together "to exert joint efforts to achieve peaceful unification." In the Joint Declaration both sides promised to "not test, manufacture, pro-duce, receive, possess, store, deploy, or use nuclear weapons . . . use nuclear energy solely for peaceful purposes . . . not possess nuclear reprocessing and uranium enrichment facilities . . . conduct inspection of the objects selected by the other side and agreed upon between the two sides," and for such purposes "establish and operate a South-North Joint Nuclear Control Commission within one month of the effectuation of this joint declaration."

However, the dialogue on Korean peace and reunification did not last long. Kim Il Sung's death on July 8, 1994, three weeks before his scheduled first summit with Kim Young Sam, was most untimely in terms of normalizing relations. The international controversy in 1992–94 regarding North Korea's nuclear weapons program also increased ten-sions by raising the specter of renewed danger and insecurity on the peninsula.

The Immovable Obstacle: Politicization of Inter-Korean Relations

As of the mid-1990s the leadership of both the ROK and the DPRK have failed to implement the terms of the 1991 agreements.[7] This is

---

7. For the text of these agreements, see *Korea and the World*, pp. 343–348.

partly attributable to the fact that both Koreas have been too preoccupied with political transition and the consolidation of power at home to focus on implementing "exchanges and cooperation."[8] But their failure is also largely due to the fact that since their establishment in 1948 the governments of the two Koreas have been competing for political legitimacy. The Republic of Korea was proclaimed on August 15, 1948, following the UN-monitored general elections on May 10, and was subsequently recognized as the lawful government south of the 38th parallel. The Democratic People's Republic of Korea came into existence on September 9, 1948. The inter-Korean rivalry was originally a microcosm of the U.S.-USSR hegemonic conflict in global politics. This mutual animosity has continued into the 1990s. South Korea typically derides the post–Kim Il Sung regime as a personal dictatorship, a dynasty, and a government ready to collapse in the near future. North Korea in turn demonizes the South as a "puppet" and "colony" of the United States. The antagonistic atmosphere created by this mutual vituperation blocks constructive progress between the two Koreas.

The primary reason for the poor state of inter-Korean relations is the failure to reach a genuine reconciliation and restoration of mutual trust between North and South Korea. For example, South Korea's delivery of food relief to North Korea in the fall of 1995 was not received by North Korea as a brotherly, humanitarian gesture. The South's shipment of rice to North Korea was abruptly suspended, in fact, when the crew of the cargo ship was detained and charged with espionage for taking pictures of the Ch'ongjin harbor facilities.[9] Seoul, in turn, insisted that P'yongyang formally request food aid through official government channels rather than informal routes, so as to gain maximum publicity of the superiority of the South Korean system over the North's failed economic system.

Korea's rival regimes have obstructed rather than fostered reunification. Nonetheless, the Korean people, sharing a sense of national identity, are pushing the two regimes toward unification. Owing to their demands, the inter-Korean dialogue initiated in 1972 has been intermittently resumed. Paradoxically, the ethnonationalism that fuels North and South Koreans' desire for unification is exploited by each political

---

8. For coverage of domestic political issues, see the chapter by Charles K. Armstrong in this volume.

9. See Samuel S. Kim, "North Korea in 1995," *Asian Survey*, Vol. 36, no. 1 (January 1996), p. 70.

regime in order to enhance its claim of legitimacy. Each depicts the other as betraying the cause of a genuine national Korean community.

The two regimes are fighting for control of the interpretation of Korean ethnonationalism. Korean nationalism began as a modernization movement during the Choson dynasty in the late 19th century. Modernization ideas and nationalism were intertwined in the Korean context. As in many Asian and other non-Western countries, the Korean nationalist movement has been accompanied by a tendency to focus on the ethnic origin and identity of population.[10] The 1993 claim that North Korea had uncovered the tomb of Tan'gun, the mythological progenitor of the Korean race some 4,000 years ago, is a manifestation of this conscious attempt by the regime to reassert ethnicity. The theme of common origin and ancestry of the Korean people is deliberately promoted and accentuated by the political leadership of the DPRK.[11]

According to one Western scholar, North Korea's discovery of Tan'gun's tomb represents P'yongyang's "competition for legitimacy in ethnic nationalism" and is the DPRK's "response to crises of identity in Korean history."[12] It is no coincidence that a skeleton claimed to be that of Tan'gun, dated 5,011 years before 1993, was unearthed from a tomb at Kangdong, northwest of P'yongyang. According to the DPRK, since Tan'gun chose P'yongyang as the capital of the first Korean state of Old Chosun, P'yongyang must be the "true, eternal capital of the nation and people."[13] This "elaborate and costly exercise," according to John Jorgenson, has been "used to legitimate the North Korean Kim dynasty, for the entire discovery and elucidation of that *volk* history was due to *juche,* the autarkist or 'subjectivist' ideology of Kim Il Sung."[14]

Another obstacle to the implementation of the 1991 agreements has been the DPRK's isolation. Whereas the South hoped for reunifica-

---

10. Gunnar Myrdal, *Asian Drama,* Vol. 1 (New York: Pantheon, 1968), pp. 54–57.

11. North Korea's party organ, *Rodong Shinmun,* carried 15 conference papers presented at the conference "Tan'gun and Old Chosun" held in the People's Great Study Hall in P'yongyang on October 12–13, 1993. *Rodong Shinmun,* October 13, 14, 15, 1993.

12. John Jorgenson, "Tan'gun and the Legitimization of a Threatened Dynasty: North Korea's Rediscovery of Tan'gun," *Korea Observer,* Vol. 27, no. 2 (Summer 1996), pp. 273–306.

13. Jorgenson, p. 274.

14. Ibid. For more on Tan'gun, see Stephen W. Linton's chapter in this volume.

tion with the fall of the Berlin Wall, the North was apprehensive about its potential absorption. In any case, the German situation was different from the Korean. The two sides in Germany had been actively involved in economic exchanges and cooperation, but not the two Koreas. East Germans also had much greater exposure to the outside world, through the mass media, travel, and direct contact, than have the North Koreans. Substantially more isolated than East Germany, North Korea has held true to the traditional image of Korea as the Hermit Kingdom. The DPRK's survival as one of the last Leninist-Stalinist states may be due in part to the tight control and isolation deliberately imposed upon the people by the dictatorial elite.

Barring the collapse of one side and its absorption by the other, the reunification of Korea is most likely to be attained through peaceful dialogue and negotiation. But full political reunification by peaceful means will not come about without the two Koreas' first instituting peaceful coexistence between themselves. Without the institutionalization of peaceful coexistence and coactivity, no system of integration is likely to be successful. The basic French-German shift from conflict to cooperation in building the European Union should serve as a lesson for Korean leaders. In the absence of mutual toleration and acceptance, public pledges to reunite by peaceful means amount to little more than empty rhetoric and propaganda. However, this simple logic of cooperation has not been put into practice because of the political ambitions and the arrogance of ruling elites in both Koreas.

Consequences of Asymmetry Between
North and South Korea

Whereas the capitalist, market-oriented policies of the South have brought about an economic miracle, the centrally planned, autarkic policies of the North have resulted in slow growth and have yet to yield a socialist "paradise on earth." Under these circumstances North Korea is understandably reluctant to engage with South Korea in "exchanges and cooperation."

The primary goal of statecraft is to enhance national power and wealth. This is the greatest challenge to the political leadership of both Koreas. The history of the rise and fall of great powers, according to historian Paul Kennedy, indicates that a nation must learn to balance the twin requirements of strategy and economics in order to remain a viable, strong, and hegemonic power.[15] Clearly, the leadership of North and South Korea must learn to grapple with the challenge of relating national economic means to national strategic ends.

In terms of the dynamics of inter-Korean relations, it is evident that North Korea is a power in relative decline, whereas South Korea is a power on the rise due to its expanding economic wealth. What is significant in the Korean context is not so much the absolute and aggregate size of the economies of North and South Korea as the relative balance and distribution of wealth between the two. The latter factor will shape the character and process of inter-Korean relations and interaction.

The history of inter-Korean relations shows an economic imbalance between North and South Korea over time; the South Korean economy since around 1974 has continued to outpace the North's. Moreover, a noticeable time lag exists between the trajectory of a state's relative economic strength and that of its military and territorial influence. The widening gap in wealth between the two Koreas in recent years will have military and strategic consequences in the years to come. Whereas South Korea is capable of sustaining the cost of modernizing its 650,000-strong armed forces with increases in defense expenditure, North Korea will be hard pressed to keep its 1.1-million-strong armed forces in combat readiness. In the arms race between the two sides, North Korea can least afford to pay for military defense because its economy will continue to suffer.

Contrasting Diplomacy and Foreign Relations

In addition to the internal competition for political legitimacy and the consequences of the imbalance of wealth and power, the frozen state of affairs on the peninsula derives from the contrasting external policy orientations of the two Korean states. Each regime's foreign policy affects its management of the economy and diplomacy. While South Korea's diplomatic open-door policy fosters an ambitious and highly successful policy of export-led growth and industrialization, North Korea is unable to energize and overcome economic

15. Paul Kennedy, *The Rise and Fall of the Great Powers: Economic Change and Military Conflict from 1500 to 2000* (New York: Random House, 1987).

stagnation under its inward-oriented *juche,* or self-reliance, political philosophy. The North's economy has basically been kept in isolation from the outside world. Its latest initiative toward establishing a Free Economic and Trade Zone (FETZ) in the Rajin-Sonbong area on the northeast coast is a belated acknowledgment that its faltering economy desperately needs an infusion of new blood. The diplomatic status of Seoul is far ahead of that of P'yongyang in terms of generating international recognition and support. North Korea's nuclear ambition has impeded the achievement of its policy objectives of normalizing diplomatic relations with the Western countries and Japan.

South Korea's Foreign Policy

As long as tension along the DMZ remains high, the U.S.-ROK security alliance will remain intact. The existing armistice has been upheld since July 1953, although North Korea unilaterally declared in April 1996 that it would no longer abide by the terms of the armistice agreement but would instead seek a newly negotiated framework. The stationing of 37,000 U.S. ground forces acts as a deterrent to North Korea's possible invasion, providing a trip wire along the DMZ. The UN Command has been reconstituted as the U.S.-Korea Combined Forces Command under a South Korean general and a U.S. general who are responsible for overall strategy and operations.

With an improvement in South Korea's defense preparedness vis-à-vis North Korea and the eventual normalization of inter-Korean relations, the security alliance will be reexamined and readjusted. A recent RAND-KIDA (Korea Institute of Defense Analysis) joint study group has come up with a set of four alternative paths and scenarios for the future U.S.-ROK alliance. Depending on how successfully the alliance and security cooperation are managed in the altered post–cold war security environment, there are four possibilities: a robust peninsula alliance, a reconfigured peninsula alliance, a regional security alliance, and a political alliance.[16] A robust peninsula alliance will be maintained "so long as North Korea continues its hostility and offensive military deployments against the ROK," while a reconfigured

---

16. Jonathan D. Pollack and Young Koo Cha, *A New Alliance for the Next Century: The Future of U.S.-Korean Security Cooperation* (Santa Monica, Calif.: RAND, 1995), p. xvi.

peninsula alliance would entail "the United States ... provid[ing] principally a rapid-reinforcement capability if a crisis with North Korea recurs." A regional security alliance, on the other hand, will materialize if "political and military conditions in Korea move in a more positive direction," and a political alliance may also result "in which the United States and the ROK would be restricted to largely symbolic forms of security cooperation (such as high-level political consultations)."[17]

In more recent policy initiatives away from the historic confines of the post-1953 security framework, the administration of South Korean president Kim Young Sam has emphasized the theme of a new path toward globalization. The nation has realized a diplomatic triumph from its implementation of *Nordpolitik*, a foreign policy aimed at normalizing relations with the former socialist bloc countries. Diplomatic relations were established between Seoul and Moscow in 1991, followed by the establishment of ties with Beijing in 1993. The hosting of the 1988 Olympic Games in Seoul and the political transition toward democracy have led to an enhanced global image of South Korea. It enjoys a reputation as one of the most rapidly developing countries, both economically and democratically.

Seoul has been an active participant in the affairs of many international agencies and organizations, both public and nongovernmental. South Korea is committed to the free-trade program of the newly inaugurated World Trade Organization. In December 1995 the ROK was elected to the UN Security Council as a nonpermanent member by an overwhelming majority, despite P'yongyang's strong objection. South Korea was elected as executive committee member of several UN agencies, including the International Atomic Energy Agency (IAEA) and the International Labor Organization. Seoul has also hosted numerous international conferences of both intergovernmental and nongovernmental international organizations, such as the Inter-Parliamentary Union and the World Advertisement Congress.

North Korea's Foreign Policy

Kim Il Sung had reportedly presided at an important meeting two days before his death in 1994 on the plans for the summit meeting with

---

17. Ibid., pp. xvii–xviii.

South Korean president Kim Young Sam scheduled for July 28, 1994. Although plans had been completed for such matters as the meeting place, the itinerary, and the number of delegates and press corps to accompany South Korea's visiting team, no substantive discussion had been held on the agenda. A third round of high-level talks began in Geneva on July 8, 1994, but was suspended on July 9 upon the announcement of Kim Il Sung's death. Although the talks were resumed on August 5, North Korea did not begin to show signs of recovering from the shock of Kim's untimely death until mid-October 1994, when the two sides reached a breakthrough agreement at Geneva on steps to ease nuclear tensions in Korea.

The controversy over North Korea's nuclear weapons program was triggered in the early 1990s by satellite disclosure of extensive site preparation for nuclear reprocessing facilities in Yongbyon, 60 miles north of P'yongyang. This center comprises not only facilities to fabricate nuclear fuel consisting of a 5-megawatt research reactor to produce irradiated fuel rods, but also a reprocessing facility to extract weapons-grade plutonium from irradiated fuel. In addition, North Korea was building a 50-megawatt reactor at Yongbyon and a 200-megawatt electric-power reactor at Tae-chon, slated to be completed in 1995 and 1996, respectively.[18]

World attention was focused on Korean security issues on March 12, 1993, when P'yongyang announced it would withdraw from the Nuclear Nonproliferation Treaty (NPT). On June 11, one day before it was to take effect, the DPRK rescinded the withdrawal. The next day, the second round of high-level talks took place in Geneva between the United States and the DPRK about ways in which the nuclear controversy could be settled by diplomatic means. The IAEA on-site inspections of North Korea's declared nuclear facilities in 1993, however, led to certain discrepancies between what was reported and what the inspectors discovered. To clear this discrepancy the IAEA demanded to inspect two undeclared sites, which North Korea refused on the ground that they were military bases.[19]

---

18. Michael J. Mazarr, *North Korea and the Bomb: A Case Study in Nonproliferation* (New York: St. Martin's Press, 1995); Kongdan Oh and Ralph C. Hassig, "North Korea's Nuclear Program," in *Korea and the World,* pp. 233–250.

19. Young Whan Kihl, "Confrontation or Compromise on the Korean Peninsula: The North Korean Nuclear Issue," in *Korean Journal of Defense Analysis,* Vol. 6, no. 2 (Winter 1994), pp. 101–129.

On May 14, 1994, North Korea announced that it had begun replacing fuel rods at the Yongbyon experimental nuclear reactor without IAEA inspectors present to determine whether plutonium had been extracted from the spent fuel. On May 17 U.S. defense secretary William Perry warned that North Korea was diverting fuel rods into enriched plutonium and that unless IAEA inspectors interceded, North Korea would be able to build five or six new nuclear bombs over the next two years. On June 13 North Korea withdrew from the IAEA in an act of defiance over the agency's report to the UN Security Council that its inspectors were unable to verify the DPRK's continued compliance with NPT safeguards. The report cleared the way for UN Security Council deliberations regarding the possibility of imposing sanctions on North Korea.

The North Korean nuclear controversy has been capped, temporarily, by the formula adopted by the Geneva Agreed Framework between the United States and the DPRK of October 21, 1994. According to the agreement, North Korea will be given two light-water reactors by the year 2004 and 50,000 tons of heavy oil in 1995 and 500,000 tons annually thereafter as compensation for its projected energy losses under the agreement. In exchange North Korea has agreed to freeze and terminate, in due course, its nuclear facilities subject to verification by the IAEA. It has also agreed that 8,000 fuel rods separated from the spent fuel and removed from the 5-megawatt reactor at Yongbyon will be stored and eventually shipped out of the country. The Korean Energy Development Organization (KEDO) was subsequently established to implement the terms of the agreement relating to the construction of the two light-water reactors and the delivery of heavy oil to North Korea.[20]

P'yongyang has yet to establish diplomatic relations with either Washington or Tokyo. Despite the progress made with the signing of the Geneva agreement, it will take some time before North Korea is able to fully regain its credibility and repair its reputation. A partial lifting of trade barriers in place since the Korean War is in

---

20. For further details of the nuclear issue, see *Peace and Security in Northeast Asia: The Nuclear Issue and the Korean Peninsula,* ed. Young Whan Kihl and Peter Hayes (Armonk, N.Y.: M. E. Sharpe, 1997).

effect, and negotiations for an exchange of liaison offices are under way between North Korea and the United States.

P'yongyang's foreign policy alternatives are limited in the security environment of the mid-1990s. The DPRK has lost its diplomatic leverage that had been grounded in ties with communist bloc nations. P'yongyang's relations with its traditional allies, Moscow and Beijing, are in fact not as smooth and cordial as they have been in the past.[21] The anniversary of the Treaty of Friendship, Cooperation, and Mutual Assistance made with Moscow on July 6, 1961, was not observed in P'yongyang in 1995. In fact the Russian defense minister Pavel Grachev said during a visit to Seoul in May 1995 that the Moscow-P'yongyang defense treaty was outdated and his country was reviewing it. The treaty, which provides for mutual defense, is likely to expire in September 1996 unless a provision for a five-year advance notice of renewal is invoked by either side. According to a Radio Russia report of September 7, 1995, the Russian government officially notified P'yongyang of its decision to negotiate a new treaty. A modified version worked out by Russia has been sent to North Korea, but P'yongyang has yet to respond.

North Korea–China relations have been strained since Beijing and Seoul established diplomatic relations in August 1992. The Chinese leader Jiang Zemin paid an official state visit to South Korea in 1995, although he has yet to do likewise to North Korea. Jiang stopped in Seoul en route to the Osaka APEC summit in exchange for an earlier state visit by South Korean president Kim Young Sam. Since 1992 Sino–North Korean trade has been settled in hard currencies, which North Korea lacks. Beijing is also reluctant to provide economic assistance to P'yongyang either in kind or on credit for such basic commodities as food and oil (Beijing agreed to deliver relief goods and food, including corn, to North Korea in the summer of 1996). A number of North Korea's high-level delegations were dispatched to China for the purpose of increasing economic exchanges. One such visit in 1996 was led by vice foreign minister Choe U Jin, who was assured by China's foreign minister Qian Qichen that China would expand its economic

---

21. Alexander Zhebin, "Russia and North Korea: An Emerging, Uneasy Partnership," *Asian Survey,* Vol. 35, no. 8 (August 1995), pp. 726–739.

support of North Korea. At the same time Qian asked that P'yongyang suspend exchanges with Taiwan. Taiwan in any case rejected the North Korean plan to issue sight-seeing visas in Taipei in the absence of an overall agreement between the two countries.[22] The 35th anniversary of the signing of the mutual defense treaty between China and North Korea in July 1961 was celebrated both in Beijing and in P'yongyang.

North Korea's desire to negotiate a diplomatic normalization treaty with Japan has not been realized. Talks were suspended in November 1992 because of several issues, including the North Korean nuclear controversy.[23] Other pending bilateral issues that have slowed the progress of normalization talks between P'yongyang and Tokyo include human rights, compensation for Japan's colonial rule of Korea, and Japan's request for information concerning a missing Japanese woman believed to have been abducted by North Korea.

North Korea is seeking a peace treaty with the United States, and the establishment of official relations with the United States is foremost on P'yongyang's diplomatic agenda. Progress hinges upon the successful implementation of the nuclear agreement as well as such issues as missile-technology control and the return of the remains of U.S. servicemen killed in the Korean War.

To achieve its diplomatic objective, P'yongyang is exerting pressure on the United States to replace the armistice agreement signed at the end of the Korean War in July 1953. This is behind recent North Korean actions to change the existing structure of the Military Armistice Commission (MAC) by violating provisions of the armistice agreement. P'yongyang has not only boycotted regular MAC meetings in P'anmunjom but has also acted to expel the Polish and Czech members of the Neutral Nations Supervisory Commission (NNSC). The NNSC, established in 1953 to monitor the armistice agreement, consists of four neutral nations: Switzerland, Sweden, the Czech Republic (then Czechoslovakia), and Poland. Although North Korea had recommended the latter two countries, it expelled the delegations of Czechoslovakia in April 1993 and Poland in May 1995 after those states rejected communism.

---

22. AFP, from Taipei, April 30, 1996.

23. Hong-Nack Kim, "Japan and North Korea: Normalization Talks Between P'yongyang and Tokyo," in *Korea and the World,* pp. 111–131.

In late February 1996 North Korea announced that it would no longer follow the rules of the 1953 armistice. In its place P'yongyang proposed a tentative agreement with the United States until a permanent peace agreement could be concluded and a joint DPRK-U.S. military body could be established to replace the Military Armistice Commission. In a violation of the armistice, North Korea sent scores of armed troops into the joint security area at P'anmunjom. They remained there from April 5 to April 7.

At the Cheju Island summit on April 16, 1996, U.S. president Bill Clinton and South Korean president Kim Young Sam announced a new peace initiative that called for four-party talks among South Korea, North Korea, the United States, and China. This meeting would seek to establish permanent peace in Korea by defusing the tensions that had resulted from the North Korean demands for changing the armistice regime.

On matters of Korean security, North Korea is opposed to a multilateral security forum in lieu of bilateral, direct negotiations with the United States, and the DPRK has yet to announce its acceptance of the four-party peace talks proposed by Bill Clinton and Kim Young Sam. North Korea had voiced opposition to the idea of collective security talks for Northeast Asia involving North and South Korea, China, Japan, Russia, and the United States. A spokesman for the DPRK Foreign Ministry stated on January 23, 1995, "We oppose the appearance of any forum of multilateral security dialogue in this region," adding that the move was an "attempt to divide security affairs into subregional spheres." It is hoped that this rigid stance will not be applied to the four-party peace initiative. Because the security forum idea was proposed by Tokuichiro Tamazawa, director-general of Japan's Defense Agency, North Korea charged that the move was "aimed at expanding Japan's sphere of influence in Northeast Asia and justifying her conversion into a military power."[24] This anti-Japanese sentiment seems to be derived from the pre–World War II legacy of Japan's colonial domination.

---

24. DPRK Foreign Ministry statement, January 23, 1995, as cited in *Vantage Point,* Vol. 18, no. 2 (February 1995), p. 23.

Despite these negative views, P'yongyang has been an active participant in the United Nations and other multilateral organizations. In a
clear reversal of its long-standing policy of opposing separate UN
membership in favor of "joint" membership with South Korea as a
single entity, North Korea acted to join the United Nations on September 17, 1991. Since then, P'yongyang has used the United Nations not
only as a forum to articulate its foreign policy but also as a source of
technical assistance.[25]

In September 1995, in an unprecedented appeal, the DPRK turned
to the World Food Programme, the food-aid arm of the United Nations. The agency responded with a series of emergency shipments to
North Korea in 1995 and 1996. A UN interagency fact-finding mission, comprising the World Food Programme, UNICEF, the UN Department of Humanitarian Affairs, the Food and Agriculture
Organization, and the World Health Organization, was dispatched in
September 1995 to carry out an on-the-spot assessment of the flood
damage that had brought about the food shortage. Other nongovernmental organizations, such as the International Red Cross, were also
drawn into the field operation.

As P'yongyang's attitude toward multilateral institutions is changing, North Korea has been actively courting and relying on UN Development Program (UNDP) support for technical assistance in building
new infrastructure and modernizing existing facilities such as telecommunications and a regional development program. For example,
P'yongyang's appeal for UNDP assistance resulted in a comprehensive
survey of North Korea's energy and electricity needs.[26] However,
P'yongyang's nonaligned-nations, third world diplomacy is also en-
countering resistance and lack of support in the 1990s, in a marked
contrast to past years. With the end of bipolarity the nonaligned-
nations movement has lost its broad appeal and raison d'être.
P'yongyang's cultivation of ties with Cuba and Laos is the only remaining legacy of this now-defunct diplomatic practice.

---

25. Young Whan Kihl, "North Korea and the United Nations," prepared for presentation at
the conference "North Korea's Foreign Policy," Columbia University, May 31–June 1, 1996.

26. As an example of such a UNDP-sponsored project, see Peter Hayes and D. Von Hippel,
"Engaging North Korea on Energy Efficiency," in *Peace and Security in Northeast Asia,* pp.
142–177.

Conclusion: Counter-Stasis and the Force of Popular Ethnonationalism

As the 20th century draws to a close, no nation—large or small—can afford to remain isolated from the rest of the world. The animosity in inter-Korean relations is a microcosm of the broader picture of international relations. The world has become tense with an increasing degree of interdependency of nations and complexity in agenda setting. That the situation on the Korean peninsula remains uncertain is in many ways a reflection of North Korea's continued *juche* ideology and policy of self-imposed isolation and autarky. Korean reunification, if achieved, may result from a lack of adaptation by either or both Korean states, especially if North Korea fails to make an orderly and smooth transition into the post–cold war world. According to Young C. Kim, there are three possible pathways to Korean reunification: war, mutual consent, and default.[27] Mutual consent is the official reunification policy line of both North and South Korea. The two official reunification plans differ only in method and approach, not in objective. Whereas South Korea advocates a gradualist approach, the North Korean approach is more direct and immediate. North Korea proposes the formation of the Democratic Confederal Republic of Koryo, and South Korea has advocated the establishment of the Unified Democratic Republic of Korea.[28] North Korea's plan calls for "one nation, one state, and two regional governments" wherein each political system will be kept intact within a single unified nation-state. The ROK plan advocates the building of a Korean National Community as an intermediary stage toward eventual reunification.

Post–Kim Il Sung North Korea is undergoing the stress of transition and consolidation as well as economic stagnation. The difficulty is compounded by the food shortage brought on by the devastating floods of 1995. Under these circumstances, reunification by default is the

---

27. Young C. Kim, "Prospects for Korean Reunification: An Assessment," in *Korea and the World,* pp. 253–260.

28. For discussion on varied approaches to Korean reunification, see B. C. Koh, "A Comparison of Unification Policies," in *Korea and the World,* pp. 153–166; Kihl, *Politics and Policies,* pp. 205–230; Kihl, *Korea and the World,* pp. 133–152.

most realistic scenario. If the North Korean regime collapses, the rational response for other countries, including South Korea, would be to ensure the smooth landing of the DPRK state in order to manage and minimize the negative fallout and impact of the collapse on the surrounding countries. Managing the flood of refugees from the North, for instance, should be planned well in advance.

Unless efforts are made to coordinate divergent international efforts to bring about North Korea's successful transition, the implementation of the terms of the Agreed Framework, including the construction of two light-water reactors by KEDO, will become unhinged. Perhaps the proposed four-power peace initiative will incorporate plans to cope with such contingencies. Or the UN Security Council may step in to monitor unfolding situations and possible security crises.

In response to the May 1996 appeal for emergency assistance by the UN Department of Humanitarian Affairs, the United States and Japan each donated $6 million; South Korea came forward with $3 million. This will make up part of the $43.6 million in emergency assistance that the UN announced it intended to raise. Other nongovernmental organizations, such as the International Appeal for North Korean Flood Victims, based in Tokyo, have also made generous donations. The organization's chairman, Bernard Krisher, made several trips to North Korea with his son Joseph. On March 5 through 12, 1996, they unloaded 260 metric tons of rice in the port city of Nampo. Then they assembled a convoy of trucks to deliver and distribute rice to three flood-afflicted counties. These international humanitarian efforts will ease the change of the regime and prevent North Korea from crash-landing into the post–cold war era.

The possibility of North Korea's overcoming the current crisis largely by its own efforts, however, also should be considered. The nation seems to have survived a worst-case scenario of system implosion similar to that of the East European communist states following the dismantling of the Berlin Wall. If internal stress, such as mass starvation and food riots, continues, North Korea could undergo system implosion. Since North Korea does not want to be absorbed by the South, the alternative is to carry out a bold program of economic reform. Understandably, South Korea does not wish to rush into reunification, which would mean inheriting the economic woes of the North.

The future of inter-Korean relations will require the two states to take the intermediary step toward peaceful coexistence prior to eventual unification. Yet, for political reasons, neither side is prepared to accept the other's official reunification policy plans and formula. The politicization of inter-Korean relations and the battle for hegemony reflect Korea's ethnic nationalism. But as long as there is a reservoir of desire for peace and reunification among the Korean people, the prospect will not be out of reach. Reunification is the lodestar of Korean nationalism, and reaching it is the goal of people both in the North and the South.

South Korean Teachers' Struggle for Education Reform

Sang Duk Yu

Teachers have traditionally held a respected position in Korea and most other Asian societies, as the saying "never even step on the shadow of a teacher" suggests. But as the modern capitalist way of life has gradually spread in South Korea, it seems to have changed the way people view teachers and their profession. While the number of teachers in the Republic of Korea (ROK) has increased significantly, from about 30,000 in 1945 to about 320,000 in 1985, their socioeconomic status has declined, and the traditional perception of their profession as almost a sacred calling has drastically changed.

The change in the status of teachers began in the 1930s, when Korea's modern public education system was first set in place by the Japanese colonial government in order to train the lower-level officers needed to rule the colony and to maintain the ideology of the regime. After Korea's liberation from Japan, the system came to be viewed as the norm. Since then each South Korean government, from the U.S. military government on through the various regimes, has used the public education system in order to maintain the division of Korea and to strengthen and legitimate a weak government. South Korean teachers are legally classified as public servants—even those who teach in private schools. Under these circumstances, they have had to obey, even if unwillingly, the dictates of the political powers.

Public servants must be politically neutral if they are to maintain their professional integrity and properly serve society; however, most ruling parties in South Korea have attempted to use public servants to implement their political objectives. In a society like South Korea's, which does not have a tradition of political rivalry to adjudicate competing interests among disparate groups, public servants—teachers, in the case of this chapter—have had an especially difficult time maintaining a politically neutral position.

Teachers established their own organization, the Chosun (Korean) Educators Association, for the first time in 1945. This association worked against the U.S. military government, which had its own objectives in wanting to direct the ROK education system, but the early association failed in that initial effort to influence policy.

During the Syngman Rhee, Park Chung Hee, and Chun Doo Hwan administrations, teachers were not permitted to organize and were required to serve the dictatorial administration. But during the periods of change between those administrations, teachers gathered and worked for their right to assemble independently in order to reform the abused education system. It was this movement for education reform, initiated not by the government but from the grass roots, that led ultimately to the founding of the Korean Teachers and Educational Workers Union in 1989.

On May 31, 1995, the Kim Young Sam administration announced its "Education Reform Project" and explained that it would completely change the education system, its contents, and its methods. But the administration also stated that all reform would be executed from the upper levels of government. There was a great deal of skepticism about this project because many governments before Kim Young Sam's had tried to reform the education system from the top down, and all had failed. The governments made no changes whatsoever, not even in the classrooms, which continue to be overcrowded and in poor condition.

This chapter describes how South Korean teachers have sought to change the education system themselves and how they have struggled against a series of dictatorial administrations. Among their efforts, it focuses on the work of Chunkyojo, the Korean Teachers and Educational Workers Union, which has become the center of South Korea's education reform movement.

Government and Education: Historical Background

Modern Korean history has a cyclical pattern characterized by long periods of political stability alternating with comparatively short periods of popular expression of dissatisfaction. Popular movements have been progressively more explosive. They have accompanied the political transitions following the period of Japanese colonial occupation

(1910–45) and the presidencies of Syngman Rhee (1948–60), Park Chung Hee (1963–79), Chun Doo Hwan (1980–88), and Roh Tae Woo (1988–93). The period between 1945, the year of Liberation, and 1948, the year in which UN-sponsored elections led to the permanent establishment of the two regimes in North and South Korea, is referred to as the Liberation Interval. The subsequent period between the end of the Syngman Rhee regime and the beginning of the Park Chung Hee regime is called the Era of the April 19 Student Revolution. The interval between Park's death and the beginning of the Chun Doo Hwan regime is known as Seoul Spring. Since the election of Kim Young Sam as president, South Korea has been experiencing another period of political transition.

The organizational movements of South Korean teachers have been closely related to the cyclical character of ROK history. Before Korea was liberated in 1945, its teachers were the tools of Japanese colonialism, even going to the extreme during World War II of persuading their students to go to war. Korean teachers became active participants in the Japanese colonial education system, which was designed primarily to subject the Korean people to Japanese imperialism.

Immediately after liberation from Japanese control, teachers organized a group called the Chosun Educators Association in order to examine their past role and commit themselves to participation in the building of a new nation. However, this movement was blocked by the U.S. military government and the pro-Japanese officials employed by the Syngman Rhee government, which had a different agenda for South Korea. Some 10 percent of working teachers were dismissed. Most of those were active members of the Chosun Educators Association. Moreover, many progressive teachers died or disappeared during the Korean War.

Under the Syngman Rhee government, teachers once again came to play the role of servants of the regime's political agenda. Furthermore, toward the end of the Rhee administration, a dictatorship sustained by corruption, some teachers became involved in the rigged election of 1959–60. Even those teachers who did not actively support the political regime nonetheless failed to criticize its political injustices. The Rhee regime was overthrown during the April 19 Student Revolution.

"Thus, we establish the teachers union with a wretched and abject heart"—as shown in the April 19 Teachers Union Declaration of Formation, the union members launched an explicitly self-critical movement. It progressed with such energy that only three months after the revolution nearly half the teachers in South Korea had become union members. Despite this momentum, under the Ch'ang Myun government (1960–61) the Teachers Union was subject to official constraint. The Ministry of Justice ruled that there was no reason to prohibit the union, but the Ministry of Education refused to approve any union other than the Korean Federation of Education Association (KFEA), which was led by principals and education bureaucrats who showed little interest in teachers and which had been backed initially by the Rhee government. Nonetheless, the Teachers Union played a vital role in the escalating popular movement for democratization and reunification, but it was suppressed and nearly destroyed following the military coup d'état led by General Park Chung Hee on May 16, 1961. About 2,000 teachers were dismissed, while the core members of the union's executive committee were sentenced to prison terms lasting from five to ten years. They suffered excruciatingly from suppression at the hands of the military government. As a result teachers were unable to develop a systematic, sustained movement and were thus forced to continue to serve the political regime.

The government's two main educational objectives during the 1960s and 1970s were to indoctrinate citizens against communism, with an emphasis on the North-South axis of political antagonism, and to train laborers for the industries supported by the government's export-driven economic policies. The curriculum was established and administered by the state. The principal textbooks were written and published by the state through a strict bureaucracy. Even though an autonomous education system had been legislated by the National Assembly, its implementation was deferred for 20 years by the Emergency Order of Park Chung Hee. The government continued to recognize the KFEA as the only legitimate organization of educators.

As dissatisfaction with Park Chung Hee's dictatorship gradually escalated and the *minjung* movement expanded through the late 1970s, the teaching profession, which had become quiescent because of the government's suppression of the April 19 Teachers Union, began to show new signs of life.

The *minjung* movement was characterized by its anti-military dictatorship and anti-imperialist program. Many parts of the broader social movement were given the name *minjung*, a term that means "the people" with the connotation of "the oppressed." The movement permeated literature, music, arts, theology, and education, as well as labor and farming.

During this period night schools attended by blue-collar workers who lacked secondary education became an important part of a voluntary educators' movement led by college students and a number of teaching professionals. At first these night schools were intended to prepare young laborers for the higher-education entrance examinations, but gradually, as part of the minjung movement's activist agenda, the focus shifted to labor rights and the history of the labor movement in order to prepare laborers to join the broader labor movement.

The Teachers Movement in the 1980s and the Establishment of Chunkyojo

Seoul Spring, the brief period in 1980 of rekindled democratization, ended violently in the Kwangju Incident in May. The tragic, violent end of Seoul Spring made it clear that a movement led by young intellectuals and an assortment of progressive labor activists, similar to the *minjung* movement in the 1970s, could not bring about social change. In the field of education, activists decided to redirect their attention from such projects as labor night schools to institutional public education. Despite the threat of dismissal to its members, the small education movement eventually expanded to include the major cities throughout the nation. To evade the attacks that depicted their organization as leftist, members associated themselves with the YMCA, a religious youth organization, and openly expanded their group at the national level. The movement focused on developing teaching and learning activities using folk songs, folk-mask dances and dramas, and students' real-life experiences.

In the mid-1980s, with the expansion of the democratization movement among students, blue-collar workers, and the agricultural sector, the teachers movement gained considerable momentum. Two events in particular stand out as indicators: the *Minjung Kyoyuk* (People's Education) Magazine Incident in 1985 and the Declaration of Educational Democratization in May 1986, in which approximately 800 teachers participated. In 1985 some 50,000 copies of *Minjung Kyoyuk* magazine were sold despite a government ban. Approximately 20 teachers, writers, and editors of the new magazine were dismissed by the authorities, in response to which a movement was organized to reinstate the dismissed teachers and to disseminate the contents of the magazine. The Declaration of Educational Democratization was a collective request for the fuller democratization of education through such measures as a guarantee of professional autonomy from the government. Leaders of the movement were suppressed by arrest or dismissal on the grounds that the declaration was a so-called collective action, which was prohibited to teachers because they were government workers. Through these and other events in the 1980s, the factional and somewhat sporadic efforts of the teachers movement began to turn into a more sustained and unified program of action.

In 1987, in the major clash between the Chun Doo Hwan regime and the minority political parties led by Kim Dae Jung and Kim Young Sam, all the various groups that had participated in the *minjung* movement of the 1970s took part in pressing for a constitutional amendment to permit a direct presidential election. Following the large-scale demonstration that took place in Seoul on June 10, the people of South Korea obtained the right to elect their president for the first time in 15 years. A series of strikes throughout July and August in the major industrial cities marked the labor movement's success in establishing several thousand new democratic labor unions. Under these positive conditions, the teachers movement continued to focus its efforts on specific issues, such as the elimination of corruption, and to expand its membership on the national level. As a result of these projects, teachers established the Korean Teachers Association (KTA) in September.

The newly formed association confronted a number of tasks. Curricula and textbooks had been designed to maintain the divisional and dictatorial political regime; the educational administrative structure was based on a bureaucracy reminiscent of the military chain of command; the autonomy of the education system was still deferred; the educational environment, with its unbalanced emphasis on preparation for college entrance examinations, led students to identify their classmates as competitors and opponents, not as companions; classes were large, with a legal minimum of 60 students; and, in part because of the unhealthy, overcompetitive environment, more than 100 students continued to commit suicide each year. In the overcrowded, poorly supported system, teachers endured low wages and extra mandatory duties. These problems were the results of three key factors: the policy to maintain the divisional regime; the export-driven economic policy; and the general lack of support and funds for education. However, there was no route by which the association's requests for remedies could be turned into educational policies because the educational administrative structure was a top-down, command-oriented system, and the only legally recognized teachers organization remained an obstacle. Furthermore, the KTA had no real authority or method to accomplish its goals. All it could do was voice the educators' concerns in the form of official declarations and inform the public through demonstrations, and there was no response to either its declarations or its demonstrations from the government. The KTA leadership came to realize that if the association was to begin to make changes, it needed the right and the power of collective bargaining.

As previously noted, according to ROK law public servants were prohibited from participating in the labor movement and collective action. The Trade Union Act did not grant labor rights to organizations that were not legally registered as labor unions. Furthermore, education law allowed recognition of only one teachers organization in each province. During the first two years after its formation, the KTA began to campaign to amend these laws. As a result, and in the favorable political climate of a National Assembly majority of opposition party members in February 1989 a law was passed in a special session of the Assembly permitting public servants below level six, which included teachers, to form trade unions. But difficult times lay ahead. Elected as a result of division in the opposition parties, President Roh Tae Woo exercised his veto power over various democratic reforms, including the 1989 law. Furthermore, Roh showed no intention of changing existing education policies.

The 20,000 teachers who had by this time become members of the association spent several nights debating what they should do. After long discussions about whether to reorganize the association as a union regardless of the government's response, the members decided to follow the historical principles of labor movements. In the history of the world labor movement, a labor union is formed by the laborers acting independently, with legal recognition of the union being granted by the national government afterward. The formation of a labor union is not brought about by the passage of a law. On May 28, 1989, despite heavy opposition and interference by the authorities, the union was formed—truly an historic event.

The four general principles of Chunkyojo, the Korean Teachers and Educational Workers Union, are as follows: Chunkyojo is firmly united to establish the full autonomy of education and to realize democracy in education; Chunkyojo will strive to improve the socioeconomic status of teachers and to secure the civil rights of all teachers so as to improve the educational environment; Chunkyojo stands in the vanguard of realizing a "true education"—one that is nationalist, democratic, and humanist—for all students so they can lead their lives as independent citizens of a democratic society; Chunkyojo will cooperate with any organization in Korea and with any worldwide teachers organization that supports liberty, peace, and democracy.

Among these principles, the most significant is the concept of a "true education." What is this true education, and why is it important in the South Korea of the mid-1990s?

The Definition of "True Education"

The term "true education" has become popularized in South Korea since the establishment of Chunkyojo, and the union has striven to realize the values it embodies and to overcome the problems that afflict the system of education. The ideology of education is intended to reflect that of the nation as well as the hopes and objectives of the social movements involved in the process of changing the old society to a new one. True education has three objectives: to build nationalism, to establish democracy, and to promote humanism.

True education strives to overcome the anti-national elements in the earlier curriculum—especially the previous acceptance of a divided state as natural—and to create an appropriate nationalist education for the eventual reunification of Korea. This need became evident after the Kwangju massacre. With the completely unexpected revelation of U.S. involvement, the South Korean people realized that U.S. foreign policy did not necessarily support them. Anti-U.S. sentiment began to appear among members of the anti-imperialist and anti-monopoly movements. First articulated by students and young intellectuals, this stance was eventually adopted by most social movements.

In accordance with the tenet of true education to create a nationalist society, Korean students should study the spirit of the Tonghak Revolution of the 1890s, which was led by intellectuals and farmers against foreign powers such as the Japanese, French, and others who had begun to attack Korea and its weak feudalistic government; they should follow the example of the Righteous Army's armed struggle against Japanese attack in the 1910s; and they should learn from the nationalist movement, which protested against Japanese colonialism and advocated liberation in the past and favors reunification in the present, to build a truly independent country. These historic movements established a tradition of striving for independence from foreign powers, but most of their participants' names have been erased from the record. South Koreans should acknowledge their ancestors' achievements. In the post-1945 period, those who tried to establish a reunified country peacefully and those who fought against the military dictatorship supported by foreign powers were imprisoned and suffered severe torture. In contrast, those who served the Japanese received high positions after Liberation in the U.S. military government and the Syngman Rhee administration. They continued to receive benefits after the collapse of the Rhee administration because of the protection of the Park regime. In short, those who have sacrificed their lives for the Korean nation have suffered, whereas those who have served the ruling class have prospered throughout ROK history.

According to Chunkyojo, students must learn how Korean nationalists have struggled so that they will have a basis to reunify the nation and make it truly independent. This is particularly important in the mid-1990s, for in order to globalize in the future, South Koreans must reflect upon their true past and, through an accurate view of history, find a way to take their rightful places in the world.

True education is also democratic. Democratic education means teaching students that the people are the proper masters of society and history. In modern Korean history the worst examples of undemocratic education have been the bits and pieces of the military and bureaucratic curriculum inherited from the Japanese colonial period reinforced during 30 years of military dictatorship. A number of anti-democratic traditions in South Korean society remain, including the Confucian concepts of loyalty and filial piety, the practical inequality of the sexes, patriarchal familial relationships, religious authoritarianism, and feudalistic industrial labor relations. Schools have remained wedded to bureaucratic authority, the use of corporal punishment, violence, and standardization. None of these authoritarian remnants were removed or much altered by the so-called modernization policy after Liberation; rather, they were sustained and strengthened by a government that needed them to maintain its hegemonic political power and its support by foreign powers.

True education, finally, is humanist education. Whereas other social movements have focused solely on nationalist and democratic goals, Chunkyojo has added the objective of humanism. South Korean schools have become fields of fierce competition, where students refuse even to lend their notes to their classmates. Furthermore, the overall size of the public education system has continued to increase, and students commit suicide at the rate of over 100 per year under the burden of college entrance tests and other examinations. It has become imperative for the field of education to recover a human dimension. This goal cannot be achieved simply by changing the entrance examination system for college. Because South Korean society is dominated by individualism and materialism within a highly industrialized economic matrix, serious environmental problems have been allowed to develop that are endangering human life itself. Thus another aspect of humanist education calls for attention to the environment. Although it is difficult to determine where the beginning point for rebuilding a humanized society is located, South Korea must nevertheless try to create a community in which its citizens can live together on a rationalized, stable basis rather than in a state of ceaseless competition. Humanist education is a start.

The Uncompleted Struggle for Legalization

Chung Won Sik, an extreme right-wing anti-communist and a former Seoul National University professor, was the minister of education in 1989. He viewed the efforts of the teachers described above as a challenge to the political system and persuaded the officials of the military regime to carry out a so-called education massacre. He threatened the 20,000 teachers who participated in Chunkyojo, telling them to either withdraw from the organization or lose their jobs. Teachers did not want to abandon the union, but because of the persuasiveness of threats from education officials and principals and the concerns of relatives, the majority withdrew. About 1,500 teachers who were determined to stay with the union were dismissed over the summer of 1989. In August about 600 teachers who still refused to withdraw took part in an 11-day hunger strike. Following the strike, core group of about 20 teachers were either arrested or pursued by the police. Protests against the government's extreme policies were in vain. The government used the rightist media to portray the teachers as anti-establishment leftists. In response, the union used donations from all over the country for advertisements in the major daily newspapers to explain its position.

Democratic activists at all levels joined the union's Joint Countermeasure Committee to handle the crisis. The president of the committee was the president of the Korean Federation of Women, Lee U Jung, a former professor at Seoul Women's College. The principal organizations on the committee included the Korean Federation of University Students, the Council of Korean Labor Unions, the Federation of Korean Farmers Associations, and the Korean Federation of Women. A total of 20 organizations with a combined membership of two million joined the effort. In 1989 and 1990, teachers, youth, students, intellectuals, and parents conducted more than ten mass demonstrations involving tens of thousands of people.

During these demonstrations, participants spoke out on behalf of the union and in favor of changes in the government's hard-line policies, but the government did not budge. At the orders of the Blue House—that is, the chief secretary of the president—the government formed an interdepartmental committee composed of the South Korean CIA security council, the Ministry of Home Affairs, the Ministry of Justice, the Office of Supreme Public Prosecutors, the Ministry of Education, and the Public Information Bureau. The committee met every week, monitoring the union and taking steps to keep it suppressed. During the 1989–90 gatherings and demonstrations, over 107 participating teachers, students of secondary schools, and parents were arrested, and hundreds of additional teachers were dismissed. In the same year the government changed the name of the Korean Federation of Education Association to the Korean Federation of Teachers Association (KFTA) and granted it the right of negotiation and consultation, that is, the right to advise the government on education. In addition, the government affiliated the KFTA with the International Federation of Free Teachers Union. The government also sought to convey a negative image of Chunkyojo by lobbying and sending publications to foreign countries.

As the legal struggle continued, many of the dismissed teachers petitioned for relief from the unfair dismissal, but none of their petitions were accepted; as a result, they sued in order to recover their rights. The majority of those seeking legal redress lost their lawsuits or gave up during trial, realizing that they had no chance. In December 1989, however, one brave judge of a district court in Koch'ang, Kyongnam Province, issued a finding on two private schoolteachers that directed, "since they had no intention of damaging the social order or education, reinstate them." But even this verdict was stayed because of the anti-union campaign waged by government education officials.

The union requested a ruling by the constitutional court on the constitutionality of the Public Servants Law and the Private School Law, but because a majority of the nine constitutional court justices was appointed by the president and his party, the court's finding was against the union. The union thereupon appealed to an international body. According to the Unesco Recommendation on the Status of Teachers, the rights of teachers include the right to assemble, the right to collective bargaining, and the right to strike. The union also asserted that the international community recognized the right of assembly. Chunkyojo joined the newly emerged Education International in 1993 and brought a lawsuit against the ROK government, which did not change its attitude.

In 1993 the new government combined the minority Kim Young Sam faction with a majority faction of conservative politicians from the previous military government. Thus, although the civilian administration proclaimed "reform" as its motto from the start, it did not have the resources to implement that reform. Furthermore, although Kim had been a vocal advocate of low-level public servants' right to assemble and had even participated in demonstrations when the union was being repressed by the government, his stand changed when he joined the conservatives. Because of the broad support of the people and the steady pressure from international organizations, Kim had no choice but to reinstate the dismissed teachers, but he has not yet recognized the right of teachers to assemble. In fact, when the government announced its willingness to reinstate the dismissed teachers, it did so only under the condition of "new employment," that is, in exchange for the teachers' withdrawal from the union and promise not to participate in any union-related activities.

After numerous discussions within the union and negotiations with the government, the union realized that it had no alternatives; it decided to accept the government's offer, allowing reinstatement of most of the teachers. Among the 1,700 who had been dismissed, about 1,500 returned to classrooms within five years. Among the reinstated teachers, no one has actually withdrawn from the union, which remains active. The union continues to grow. When it was first formed, it had about 20,000 members. As of 1996, the union was made up of about 15,000 regular and about 30,000 associate members or approximately 12 percent of the South Korean teacher population. It is the only independent teachers organization in South Korea, with 157 local branches in 15 provinces.

The Task Ahead

It will be a significant landmark when teachers obtain collective bargaining rights in South Korea, for it will mean that they have overcome their role as government agents and have achieved the right to act as the main representative body for education professionals. The history of the South Korean teachers union has been rocky but indicates clear progress. However, as the only independent organization of teachers in the ROK, Chunkyojo has a long road to travel. While the Kim Young Sam government does not directly suppress the nationalist-democratic movement, it obstructs it by other methods (refusing legal recognition, for example), which means that social movements in South Korea continue to confront new strategic challenges. Chunkyojo has not yet been guaranteed a legal position in South Korean society, and although there are no longer grounds for dismissal or arrest associated with membership, there continue to be many cases of interference and surveillance by principals and administrative officials. The government still has no plans to recognize the legal status of Chunkyojo. Moreover, in contrast to the visibility of organized protests under a directly repressive military government, it is difficult to get the kind of public attention that can vitalize an organization under a civil government that does not recognize the official and legal position of the union. Chunkyojo must encourage many more teachers to join so they can prepare for the task of educational reform in this changing society.

Early in 1996 President Kim Young Sam announced an education reform program as part of his plan for an "Open Education and Lifelong Learning Society." However, the program contains many directives that are in line with Kim's economic globalization policy. The content of the program reflects the interests of conservatives and monopolistic corporations and would open the way for the privatization of public education and the subjection of education to the economy. In addition, there is no concrete program to finance or to put into practice the positive elements of the project. In the absence of strong government policies and programs, therefore, Chunkyojo must continue to support an education reform movement that will lead to true education. Chunkyojo will continue to work for the independent formation of curricula and publication of textbooks, the democratization of educational administration, the realization of autonomy for educators, the right of teachers to establish an organization, the right of students to learn, and the preservation of the civil rights of students, teachers, and parents. For these purposes, Chunkyojo needs professionals to develop policies and programs that will promote the educational reform movement at a nationwide level.

Finally, Chunkyojo has to devote itself to creating nationalist-democratic-humanist education in Korea's coming era of reunification. Along with all of the democratic-nationalist groups, it will endeavor to remove from the field of education the remains of Japanese colonialism, of far-right anti-communist ideology, and of military customs and nondemocratic bureaucracy. Free of these traces of foreign domination and its domestic military-bureaucratic counterpart, the field of education would no longer prevent but would instead prepare for the full realization of political, cultural, and human autonomy by the Korean people.

Life After Death in North Korea

Stephen W. Linton

The black Mercedes-Benz slipped down a broad avenue in P'yongyang in the early morning light, carrying my guide and me toward the new center of North Korea's universe, the mausoleum of the "Great Leader," Kim Il Sung.

The driver, in a gray, loose-fitting civilian uniform similar to a Mao jacket, went about his business with an expressionless professionalism. Aside from obligatory pleasantries, we two passengers made no effort to converse. I had arrived the day before from Beijing, where I had picked up my visa at the new consular annex behind the massive North Korean embassy in the diplomatic section. The car stopped at the bottom of a short flight of stairs leading to a broad plaza surrounding what had been the Kumsusan Assembly Hall. President Kim used to live and work here when in P'yongyang. At the direction of his eldest son and successor, Kim Jong Il, the former administrative building has been renamed the Kumsusan Palace and converted into a final resting place for the Great Leader.

As we crossed the wide open space toward another set of stairs leading to the main door of the mausoleum, the guide told me that President Kim used to keep a garden on the grounds for developing new varieties of agricultural produce "uniquely suited to the climate and soil of Korea." According to one story, the peripatetic Great Leader once placed a long-distance telephone call to his staff at the residence because he was worried that a heavy monsoon rain might wash away his corn patch. Not surprisingly, this anecdote contains most of the main points of North Korea's ideology of *juche* (self-reliance): the essential uniqueness of Korea; the bright new historical era that began when Kim Il Sung broke Korea's harmful dependence on foreign powers; the need to develop Korean solutions to Korean problems; economic self-sufficiency; and absolute loyalty to the Leader. A frequent visitor to North Korea, I had heard similar speeches numerous times. With remarkable consistency, almost everyone I had ever met in North Korea had testified that President Kim embodied this principle in everything he said and did during his career as a freedom fighter in the 1930s and 1940s and later as the founder and defender of the Democratic People's Republic of Korea (DPRK).

The story of the corn and the rainstorm sounds more realistic than the stories in children's books in which Kim Il Sung becomes invisible, travels vast distances in a single night, and appears in two different places at the same time, like a master of the secret arts of Taoist immortals. It was easier to imagine the late president making that phone call than to envision the garden that had once been. The plaza surrounding the Kumsusan Palace is now paved with large blocks of tightly fitted granite. I marveled at the painstaking craftsmanship that had gone into giving the grounds surrounding the mausoleum a perfect slope. Times have certainly changed, I thought; rainwater would never puddle here again.

As we walked up a final set of stairs to the entrance of the mausoleum, two soldiers stationed on opposite sides of the thick, oversized doors snapped to attention in synchronization, their nickel-plated AK-47s glinting in the early morning sun. These tough, fierce-looking specimens of North Korea's million-man army stared past us. As I stepped gingerly between them, I could just see a long line of middle-aged women patiently waiting their turn to enter the building through another entrance around the corner.

At the end of a dimly lit vestibule stood a particularly large version of the squarish, pearly white statue of the late president found in North Korean government buildings, schools, and auditoriums. A group of Korean residents from Japan, who had arrived in a tour bus moments before my guide and I had, marched past the statue in single file. Each man paused to bow deeply from the waist before shuffling up the steps toward a reception room separated from the inner sanctum by three air doors. The line of women factory workers also wound its way into this room before passing between the blowers into the presence of the Great Leader. Somewhat discomfited by the rush of air, I too stepped into North Korea's Holy of Holies. In the center of the windowless inner sanctum, lit by dim reddish lights recessed in the ceiling, lay the body of President Kim Il Sung in a glass sarcophagus on a waist-high stone pedestal.

Despite the struggle of uniformed guards to funnel the columns of women into an orderly clockwise orbit around the corpse, they refused to be regimented even in this most disciplined of societies. The sharp cries of the distraught women who bowed, stumbled, and staggered around their dead leader blended into a constant high-pitched wail. Although Korean custom dictates that each mourner pause at the points of the compass to pay homage to the deceased, many were too overcome with emotion to move forward. Groups of women, clasping each other for balance, prostrated themselves again and again until escorted out by the guards, oblivious to the men who wound their way around the corpse toward an exit at the far end of the building.

We blinked back the sunlight as we emerged from the mausoleum into a new day. My most important meeting in P'yongyang, an encounter with the deceased founder of North Korea, was over in less than 30 minutes.

An Enigmatic Nation

Before I stepped up to the microphone to speak at a recent conference on North Korea, the moderator introduced me as someone "who has visited North Korea more times than any other American, except for an SR 71 pilot." Although this good-natured compliment is not completely accurate (I know several Korean Americans who have traveled to P'yongyang many more times than me), it reflects an unfortunate truth: the United States has far too few direct contacts with the Democratic People's Republic of Korea.

An agreed framework detailing a plan to retire North Korea's nuclear program was signed by Washington and P'yongyang on October 21, 1994. Since that time, the brainchild of the accord, the Korean Energy Development Organization (KEDO), a U.S.-led international consortium in which South Korea and Japan play major roles, has made slow but steady progress toward replacing North Korea's graphite-moderated nuclear reactors with two safer light-water-moderated generating plants at a cost of more than $5 billion. The United States and North Korea are holding high-level talks on missiles and MIAs from the Korean War, while the United States continues to contribute more to North Korea's food emergency than any other nation.

This level of official engagement should have caught the public's attention and sparked a national debate over improving relations with the DPRK. After all, North Korea has been an enemy of the United States longer than any other nation in its history. But except for an occasional incident (usually an unpleasant one) that forces the public to focus momentarily on the northern half of the Korean peninsula, Americans continue to show little interest in connecting with North Korea. True, in the mid-1990s the United States and the DPRK have yet to exchange embassies (or even to open interest sections in each other's capitals), but a similar problem did not stop Vietnam from forging relations with the U.S. private sector. More than anything else, the lack of normal contacts (academic, business, religious, and so forth) has kept North Korea an enigma to most Americans, a mystery few wish to solve.

Diplomats assigned to missions in P'yongyang are permitted to reside in the capital city, but this privilege is still denied all but a handful of foreign civilians. None of them are American. While U.S. delegations have been invited to North Korea since the early 1970s, only rarely does the trip last longer than a couple of weeks. The fortunate few who do make the journey, furthermore, are accorded the attentions usually reserved for visiting officials. As hosts, North Koreans embody Korea's long tradition of warm hospitality, paying careful attention to their guests' needs, often at great trouble and expense to themselves. Still, by insisting on treating Americans like shielded, pampered royalty, P'yongyang stifles serious engagement with the society.

Whatever P'yongyang may have gained through its highly selective visa screening process and careful handling of American visitors, it has paid a heavy price for making it difficult for Americans to experience North Korea for themselves. Until P'yongyang eases restrictions on access for American civilians, the U.S. government will not be pressured by its public to lift the economic embargo, and P'yongyang, consequently, will not gain the economic and other advantages it seeks from better relations with Washington.

Restricted access also affects North Korea's international image. Unable to travel freely to the DPRK (and turned off by the harsh anti-U.S. rhetoric in P'yongyang's English-language press), most Americans glean their impressions of North Korea from imaginative reports originating in South Korea, which are picked up and amplified by the media. While the U.S. government may benefit from state-of-the-art intelligence technology in assessing North Korea's military capability, ignorance about the human factor, particularly the character of

North Korea's leadership, makes decision makers understandably cautious in dealing with the DPRK.

In this chapter I have tried to sketch North Korea from the missing human perspective. Based on 16 visits to the North as a student, researcher, interpreter, consultant, and foundation representative (including three meetings with President Kim Il Sung), I have tried to improve understanding of the DPRK by filling in some of the lacking firsthand knowledge. I have also tried to pique the reader's curiosity about what, God willing, may soon be a far more accessible (and less threatening) Democratic People's Republic of Korea.

Leadership

The Charismatic Kim Il Sung

Before he passed away from a heart attack in July 1994, Kim Il Sung would keep visiting dignitaries in suspense. Not until the end of a hectic schedule of protocol meetings and sight-seeing would a guest learn whether he or she was destined to meet the Great Leader. These meetings usually took place in the late president's pleasant country estate located a dozen miles from the capital in a heavily wooded valley filled with chestnut trees and ring-necked pheasants. He used to meet his guests at the door with a hearty greeting and a Russian bear hug. He would then escort them in for a photo-op before a wall-sized painting of Korea's world-famous Diamond Mountains. Reflecting the Great Leader's characteristically optimistic disposition, these meetings were light and cheerful and usually ended with the best eight-course lunch in P'yongyang, served to perfection by the president's personal staff.

In his later years Kim Il Sung suffered from physical problems frequently associated with advanced age. He often had trouble rising to his feet after long meetings and looked exhausted after entertaining foreign dignitaries. He was also hard of hearing, which made conversations somewhat difficult, even though he used a hearing aid wired directly to the interpreter's microphone. But despite these physical handicaps, Kim Il Sung never lost his enthusiasm for life. According to local legend, he always preferred being out among the people to living luxuriously in the capital city. For a half century he traveled the length and breadth of North Korea, giving guidance on the spot to factory and farm workers, who, according to official propaganda, could then double production overnight. Outside observers who scoffed at this ritual missed its deeper significance: Kim may not have been omniscient as the official media claimed, but his peripatetic life-style made him the North Korean equivalent of a Renaissance man without equal in a society characterized by a high degree of compartmentalization.

President Kim had a grasp of detail almost equal to that described in the accolades of the official press. In conversations with his foreign friends he related how he liked to solve problems and enjoyed matching wits with scientists and technicians, particularly those trained overseas. He was naturally suspicious of foreign ideas and taught his people not to accept anything as truth until it had proven to be valid for Korea and Koreans. A visitor never knew what he would say next. Neither apparently did his staff, who poised breathlessly, pen and paper ready, for when he began to speak. So revered was the late president that even the highest North Korean officials would rise to their feet to answer his questions.

Kim Il Sung was imbued with a particularly Korean sense of loyalty. As soon as he was firmly in power after the liberation, Kim sent representatives to Manchuria to find those who had helped him during his years as an anti-Japanese guerrilla fighter. Not only were his former benefactors invited on VIP visits to P'yongyang, but their children still enjoy a special place in the institutional memory of the DPRK.

Kim's parents came from Christian families. In his autobiography, *With the Century*, he admitted that his father attended Sungsil High School, which was founded by Presbyterian missionaries. Not only did the future president begin his education in a mission primary school, but his mother and uncle also ensured that he attended church regularly as a young boy. By way of explanation, Kim also wrote that his father associated with religious people in order to revolutionize their thinking, while his mother only attended services to rest from her busy schedule. Kim Il Sung rejected his Christian heritage when he became convinced that the only way to free Korea from Japanese colonialism was through violent struggle.

Later, when Kim came to power in the Soviet zone of occupation after the peninsula was liberated in 1945, his government gradually increased pressure on the Christian community. The church in North Korea was decimated by persecution and mass migrations to the South during the Korean War. The few believers who remained were relegated to the margins of society. Not until relatively late in his life did Kim Il Sung's policy toward Christians soften. The late president devoted an entire chapter of his autobiography to the Reverend Son Jong Do, who saved his life when he was a young man. In his later years the founder of North Korea found his country's tiny Christian community useful as a conduit to the outside world.

President Kim Il Sung's friendship with the Reverend Billy Graham, who traveled to P'yongyang in 1992 and 1994, symbolizes North Korea's evolving policy toward religious believers. Although he founded the world's most atheistic state, Kim Il Sung retained a certain sympathy for religious believers, particularly Christians. Ecclesiastical ties to the outside world continue to be somewhat suspect in North Korea (a particular problem for Catholics), but members of the official Korean Protestant Federation and Korean Catholic Association are emerging from under the cloud of suspicion that darkened their first decades under communism.

Eager to prove themselves loyal members of society, religious leaders are some of North Korea's most aggressive and vociferous proponents of *juche* philosophy, a stance that has led many outsiders to question their religious convictions. Until Billy Graham visited the DPRK, few North Koreans had ever met a minister who believed that religion should transcend politics. Unlike the liberal Protestant leaders who had preceded him to P'yongyang, Graham did not disparage South Korea or U.S. policy toward the Korean peninsula. Had he done so, he might have won approval from his hosts, but he would have confirmed what they have long feared—that Christians make socially unreliable citizens. Although he carried short messages from U.S. presidents both times he visited, Graham refused to debate sensitive political issues, while his disarming openness, warm respect, and frank offer of friendship won the affection of everyone he met. On Graham's second visit, President Kim paid the evangelist and his son (Reverend Nelson E. Graham accompanied his father on both trips) his highest compliment by insisting that they were "not just friends but just like family."

Even when he entertained foreign visitors, President Kim's mind was never far from Korea. As he approached the end of his life, Kim Il Sung returned not only to his childhood memories of church but also to ancient Korean traditions, particularly legends that served to legitimate political dynasties. His favorite was the story of Tan'gun.

Tan'gun's Tomb

According to Korean tradition, there once lived a bear and a tiger who petitioned Heaven to change them into human beings. Heaven agreed to grant their request if the two animals would confine themselves to a cave and eat only garlic for 100 days. After a while the tiger grew weary and gave up, but the bear persisted. In due time, it was changed into a beautiful young woman who became the wife of the Son of Heaven. She later gave birth to Tan'gun, the founder of the Korean race.

When Koreans speak of 5,000 years of Korean history, they are referring to 4322 B.C., when Tan'gun supposedly founded the first Korean state. Some Western students of Korean history have suggested that the story of Tan'gun reflects a struggle for ascendancy between two rival totemistic tribes (tiger and bear) and an attempt by Koreans to place the origins of their culture and society on an equal chronological footing with China's mythical sage-kings. But while most South Korean scholars admit that the Tan'gun story is myth, North Korea insists that Tan'gun was a real man whose historical identity has been shrouded in fiction by Korea's enemies.

The debate attracted little interest until North Korea "discovered" Tan'gun's tomb. Reactions to the North's claim in the Korean studies community have been predictably diverse. Few took North Korea's discovery seriously, some were embarrassed, and many South Korean historians (not to mention the South Korean government) were furious. Finding Tan'gun's bones (as well as those of his young consort) in the Taedong River Basin bolstered P'yongyang's claim to being the mother of Korean civilization and the true capital of the peninsula. Furthermore, the announcement was made as Seoul was gearing up to celebrate its 500th anniversary.

Whatever archaeological value the site may have held in the beginning, it has probably fallen permanent hostage to the politics of inter-Korean rivalry. While North Koreans were reconstructing the tomb (Kim Il Sung is said to have provided on-site supervision over 40 times), South Koreans were prosecuting the nonagenarian leader of the Tan'gun religion (a small cult centered in the South) for not resisting the temptation to sneak into the North for a peek at the bones of his god. Meanwhile, Seoul's community of North Korea watchers, insisting that P'yongyang had faked the discovery for its own political advantage, speculated that Kim Il Sung might have been building his own tomb, like an ancient Egyptian pharaoh. Some experts still predict that Kim's body will eventually be moved to the tomb he built for Tan'gun.

Tan'gun's new tomb, located on the top of a little hill southeast of P'yongyang, is in fact a small stone pyramid. It is "an exact replica of the original structural ruins discovered at the site," according to the official guide to the premises. Access to the tomb can only be gained by walking up several hundred stairs flanked by new stone statuary. By the time visitors reach the base of the pyramid, they will have been introduced to all of Tan'gun's cabinet as well as four of his sons, one of whom succeeded him as king. The inside of Tan'gun's stone pyramid is off-limits to the public.

The tomb provides a rare perspective on the evolution of ideology in North Korea. Like other communist societies, North Korea has had an uncomfortable relationship with tradition. Trying to identify class heroes in historical records that focus primarily on the exploits of aristocrats is difficult at best. P'yongyang's earliest attempts to rewrite Korean history from a revolutionary perspective reflected this fundamental structural dilemma.

That was until Kim Il Sung picked his son Kim Jong Il (also known as the Dear Leader) as his successor. This solution to the succession question (which has dominated North Korean historiography for the past quarter century) has initiated a partial rehabilitation of Korea's past. The "new thinking" in North Korea is reflected not only in the attempt to identify Tan'gun as a historical figure who, P'yongyang claims, "so successfully solved the question of succession that Korea enjoyed political stability and prosperity for a thousand years," but also in a sympathetic look at Korea's aristocratic history.

Asked whether the traditional stone altar in front of Tan'gun's pyramid was ever used for religious rites, a young interpreter laughed and responded, "we North Koreans believe in scientific socialism and not in ancient superstitions." But Tan'gun's tomb is, in fact, an active shrine. An official guide thought that the North Korean Buddhist Association was responsible for conducting ritual observances; actually, they are carried out by the Chondogyo, who practice a nativistic Korean religion founded in the late 19th century. The guide's confusion is characteristic of a rising generation in North Korea that, for the most part, has not learned to distinguish among different religious faiths.

This does not mean, however, that North Koreans are not proud of their newfound spiritual continuity with Korea's distant past. One can only wonder which prominent personages from the world's most avowedly atheistic nation may have privately witnessed ancestral rites at Tan'gun's tomb.

According to official accounts of the excavation, the bones of Korea's legendary first ruler were discovered some distance to the southeast. But the tomb was not reconstructed where the remains were found. "The original site was inconvenient and not suitable," according to the guide. This vague answer masks the most fascinating thing about the whole construction project: Kim Il Sung moved Tan'gun's grave.

Moving an ancestor's grave is one of the most important decisions one can possibly make in Korean tradition. Because the final resting place of the dead is believed to influence the fate of future descendants, ancestral remains are sometimes moved to a more propitious location several years after initial interment. This is especially true if a lack of preparation (or lack of financial resources) mandated a less than suitable arrangement at the time of death. In this case, reburial in an elaborately landscaped, auspicious location can provide an occasion for the family to display newfound wealth or influence as well as filial piety. This variety of grave moving is almost routine.

Once an ancestor's remains have been established in a particular location for an extended period, however, grave moving becomes a more significant undertaking. The decision to relocate a grave is taken only after concluding that something has gone seriously wrong as the result of a bad choice of an original burial site. The new site of Tan'gun's tomb has been selected with meticulous care, not only to emphasize the importance of P'yongyang but also from the perspective of East Asia's ancient art of geomancy. True to the requirements for an auspicious interment, Tan'gun's pyramid faces south, with an open plain in the foreground and mountains in the background. Water (a must) is also present in the form of a small creek that winds its way around the base of the hill.

Although bad grave sites can be responsible for a family's falling on hard times, moving an ancestor's bones requires great courage. Disturbing the bones of an ancestor is to take one's (and one's descendants') fate into one's hands. So why did Kim Il Sung move Tan'gun's grave?

According to North Korea's official ideology, Koreans have suffered for millennia because of a tendency to rely on "big powers" instead of their own resources. Kim Il Sung, according to this view, changed the flow of history by teaching about *juche* and the need for absolute loyalty to the Leader. Thus mourners at Kim Il Sung's funeral were told that the Great Leader's death was "the worst thing that had happened in our 5,000 years of history." Moving Tan'gun's grave may have been one of Kim's last attempts to seize fate by the throat and to bend Korean history to his will. If so, the Great Leader may have been a much more traditional Korean than anyone knew.

The Mysterious Kim Jong Il

Stunned by the orgy of grief I witnessed at Kim's mausoleum, I could not help wondering about the future of this enigmatic nation where a dead leader is more accessible than his living successor. As our heels clicked against the paving blocks on our way back to the limousine, my guide began a long and fervent monologue extolling the virtues of Secretary Kim Jong Il. The Dear Leader, according to the young man, was "just like his father in every way," a phrase that would be repeated at almost every meeting during my visit.

Secretary Kim Jong Il has not made it easy for people to get to know him. Even though the second anniversary of his father's death (July 8, 1996) has passed, Kim continues to avoid major public appearances and has rejected requests for an audience from a long list of foreign dignitaries, including the president of China, North Korea's most important ally. He has also passed up several opportunities to take official charge of the Korean Workers' Party and to declare himself president, leading many outside observers to wonder who, if anyone, is really in charge in P'yongyang. In North Korea, meanwhile, the people are being indoctrinated into believing that a future without Kim Jong Il is unthinkable.

According to one theory, Kim Jong Il's apparent shyness (which led one helpful foreign reporter to send the Dear Leader a bottle of stage fright medicine) has helped to cloak him in his father's mantle of legitimacy. By his reluctance to assume the titles that are his by inheritance, Kim has made himself a paragon of filial piety in the eyes of the public, cemented the loyalty of P'yongyang's old revolutionary guard, and sent a clear message to young hopefuls that loyalty to the Leader (rather than raw ambition) is the surest route to power in due time.

U.S. analysts who are not convinced that Kim Jong Il's silence is voluntary speculate about power struggles within North Korea's elite, while South Koreans still write articles claiming Kim Jong Il is afflicted with a wide variety of physical or mental conditions that make him unfit for public office.

Despite tensions with the United States, a campaign by South Korea to isolate North Korea diplomatically, and a series of natural disasters that have precipitated a major food emergency, North Korea's elite still believe that Kim Jong Il is their and their children's best hope for a brighter future. Rather than weakening him, challenges from abroad seem to have helped solidify Kim Jong Il's hold on power. The United States' continued concerns about North Korea's clandestine nuclear program, not to mention U.S. irritation at being pummeled nonstop in P'yongyang's official press, have made North Koreans painfully aware that they cannot depend on support from the world's only remaining superpower. Should a crisis arise, neither China nor Russia would be much help to P'yongyang. Not only are Beijing and Moscow hard-pressed to control social unrest unleashed by economic reforms, but as one North Korean diplomat has stated remorsefully, "China and Russia are far more interested in making money than honoring friendship among friends."

When North Korean officials are questioned about why Kim Jong Il has refused to meet with foreigners (or even to attend his own birthday party in 1996), they usually make vague references to Korea's traditional mourning period. According to them, the world will have to wait until at least August 1997 for a good look at North Korea's new ruler. Unless North Korea is able to resolve its worsening food crisis, however, the official succession could be postponed even longer.

Members of the international media are competing to be the first to interview Kim Jong Il. Aware of the potential windfall (but also of the dangers inherent in this kind of once-in-a-generation publicity), the Dear Leader is in no hurry to clinch a deal. P'yongyang also knows, nevertheless, that it cannot postpone Kim Jong Il's debut much longer. Unless the Dear Leader soon emerges from his self-imposed exile, he may lose the support of the late president's supporters who live overseas.

The Chosen Soren, Japan's pro-P'yongyang Korean residents' association, is getting restless. The future existence of this beleaguered expatriate community is bleak regardless of the unresolved succession question. Enrollment in Chosen Soren schools (whose Korean language curriculum is modeled after North Korea's) continues to plummet, partly because a Japanese education is considered more prestigious but also because ties to North Korea are wearing thin after three generations of life in Japan. The Chosen Soren's biggest challenge is convincing young Korean residents of Japan that Kim Jong Il cares for them as much as his father did, a difficult assignment given Kim's reluctance to meet with Chosen Soren officials who make the pilgrimage to P'yongyang.

Unless he comes out of mourning soon, Kim Jong Il also runs the risk of alienating the foreign dignitaries who were charmed by the late president's deft practice of personal diplomacy. During his later years, the buoyant, charismatic Great Leader gained many influential friends whose support helped to counterbalance North Korea's aggressive rhetoric. Now that Kim Il Sung is gone, and Kim Jong Il has shrouded himself in a cloud of mystery, North Korea is in danger of losing its human face.

Economic Difficulties

For almost a decade a tall, slender new hotel has been under construction on a small islet in P'yongyang's Taedong River. Proportionally smaller, it is similar in shape and location to the 63-story Yuksam Building on Yoido Island in the middle of Seoul's Han River. The new building was originally a joint French-DPRK project but ran into difficulties and opened in 1995 despite being only partially completed. Intended to accommodate Western business interests in North Korea, the new hotel has a checkered history that is symbolic of the challenges faced by foreigners who attempt to do business with P'yongyang.

The Taedong River's gently meandering riverbed and carefully planned riverside parks give North Korea's capital city a friendly, more intimate feel than the South's. The northern capital has its share of drab buildings, but many of its edifices are impressive, especially compared with the brute ugliness of most socialist construction elsewhere. The learning curve of P'yongyang's stable, highly centralized urban planners is clearly evident in its skyline. Unlike architecturally older cities (North Korea's capital was leveled during the Korean War), where newer does not necessarily mean more beautiful, each succeeding generation of P'yongyang's buildings is an improvement on its predecessors in every way.

P'yongyang, nevertheless, has had a hard time competing with Seoul, its robust rival sibling to the south. For almost a decade, the massive concrete pyramidal shell of the Yugyong Building (built to resemble the Diamond Mountains) has loomed over the capital's horizon like a windowless haunted house on a hill. Even in its present state, the 105-story skyscraper dwarfs anything in South Korea, fulfilling its major design requirement. Still, North Korea's grandest monument to native ingenuity (and sheer willpower) is also a mute reminder of how rapidly P'yongyang's economy is falling behind Seoul's.

Food Shortages

North Koreans do not need the Yugyong Building to remind them of their precarious economic predicament. The unseasonably cold weather of 1994, which reduced harvests all over East Asia, was followed in North Korea in 1995 by the worst flood in a hundred years. The 1996 growing season is off to a poor start, delayed by ten days of cold weather and a mild drought in June. This year's harvests will also be affected by a chronic shortage of agricultural plastic sheeting (North Korean farmers like to start rice and corn seedlings under plastic to extend the growing season), fertilizer, pesticides, and fuel. In a good year North Korea can grow 60 percent of what it needs to provide its citizens with a spartan diet (South Korea produces 40 percent of its needs). Because only 20 percent of North Korea is arable, and because of a short growing season (110–120 days), growing this much food requires a herculean effort. At particularly busy times of the year (like transplanting season), even city dwellers are mobilized for agricultural work, while almost every possible square meter of land is tilled to the maximum.

North Koreans sometimes push too hard to increase harvests. Inevitably, erosion and soil exhaustion take their toll as slopes as steep as 50 to 60 degrees are sometimes cultivated year after year. The dikes between rice fields, the banks of irrigation ditches and railroad beds, not to mention low hills, are put under the plow in an unending struggle to feed the population. The collapse of socialism elsewhere has turned what was at best an uphill fight into a grim struggle for survival. P'yongyang used to count on food subsidies from its socialist allies and grain purchases from abroad paid for by trade with Eastern Europe to supplement agricultural shortfalls. That was until the Soviet bloc collapsed and China took the capitalist road. Now Moscow wants hard currency for grain purchases, while Beijing has outlawed the export of rice and corn to its most loyal ally.

Even before the August floods that washed away more than a third of the 1995 harvest, the food situation in North Korea was so bad that P'yongyang felt obligated to make an unprecedented appeal to its enemies for assistance. South Korea and Japan initially responded, hoping their generosity would lead to an end to the cold war in East Asia. But when P'yongyang disappointed Seoul by locking up the crew of a ship carrying part of South Korea's 150,000-ton contribution, and a highly placed North Korean suggested that the 500,000 tons of rice Tokyo promised was a down payment on war reparations and not charity, North Korea's neighbors grew reluctant to provide more assistance.

So far, most of what North Korea has received for flood assistance since August 1995 has come from the United States and Europe, the majority funneled through the United Nation's World Food Programme. Despite a successful second UN appeal announced in June 1996, the combined efforts of the international community fell far short of the 750,000 tons experts calculated North Korea needed before the 1996 harvest. While some Washington-based North Korea watchers brace for what many predict will be a famine-induced collapse, frequent travelers to P'yongyang still report no sign of political instability.

Careful students of the collapse of communism elsewhere, North Korea's leadership is reluctant to follow the Chinese model for economic development, particularly in agriculture, for fear of injecting capitalism into its peasant class. As one well-placed official commented, "We do not have China's large agricultural population, nor is our land particularly suited to agriculture anyway. We have to look elsewhere to solve our food situation. China is a very big country which has chosen to risk social chaos for the sake of making money, while we are a small country which cannot afford to gamble with its national existence."

Instead of experimenting with privatization of land, North Korea's stated goal is eventually to bring all farming cooperatives under direct state management (presently farmers receive a portion of what their cooperative produces), extending the state distribution system to every citizen. This plan makes better political than economic sense, buttressing North Korea's claim to be a unique family-state under a paternalistic Leader. Still, North Korea is not a stranger to pragmatism. "We know we have to change our economy," said another official, "we just don't want to reduce our people to beggars like what happened in Eastern Europe."

Foreign Investment

The fact that the uncompleted Yugyong Building is being offered as an investment opportunity to foreign businesspeople is symbolic of a growing awareness within the capital city that more business ties to the outside world may be the best way to jump start North Korea's faltering economy.

As far as anyone knows, however, the leadership has no plans to translate new thinking on the economy into steel, glass, and concrete by building something similar to Seoul's World Trade Center. For the time being, the majority of foreign investments will be limited to the Rajin-Sonbong area, North Korea's "Golden Triangle" located in the far northeast of the peninsula in an area contiguous with both China and Russia. Whether the foreign business community will ever really find a home in North Korea's capital, however, remains to be seen.

For the time being, foreign residents in P'yongyang will have to be content with the Koryo Hotel, the present center of business life in the capital city. Only a few blocks from the railway station in P'yongyang's restaurant district, the Koryo is the social hub of North Korea's tiny but growing population of expatriates.

The salmon-colored tiled twin towers of the Koryo Hotel are replete with a revolving restaurant (the best steak in town), a barbershop, a bathhouse, a hard-currency store, and souvenir shops. The second floor, which boasts a variety of eating establishments, several bars, and three pool tables, is one of the favorite watering holes for P'yongyang's resident foreign (and domestic) community of lounge lizards. The dim main lobby, where visitors interact with a small army of chain-smoking North Koreans carrying leather portfolios and wearing locally made Western-style suits, is North Korea's main economic interface with the outside world.

In theory, delegations visiting P'yongyang are required to follow a highly structured schedule dictated by their sponsoring organizations, which usually includes protocol functions and working-level meetings interspersed with free but obligatory sight-seeing tours to historical sites, massive construction projects, theaters, museums, sports stadiums, and monuments. For this reason visitors rarely run into each other while conducting business and almost never have an opportunity to share impressions and observations.

North Korean officials prefer to isolate delegations from each other, not simply because they are afraid of being spied upon but because they are accustomed to a society that is tightly compartmentalized. The host government prefers its foreign guests to travel up and down a particular spoke from rim to center without trying to move laterally between institutions. The practice of treating all visitors as members of official delegations can be a source of immense frustration for first-time business travelers to P'yongyang who are impatient to get on with the job. They resent a schedule in which large blocks of time are sacrificed for activities that have little or nothing to do with business. Some potential investors also lose interest when they learn how dependent business is on politics in North Korea.

Politics, in fact, is the primary reason that North Korea lags far behind other East Asian nations in attracting foreign investments. P'yongyang has not repaid billions of dollars of loans dating from the early seventies. As a result North Korea has one of the worst credit ratings in the world. Not surprisingly, this has had a chilling effect on entrepreneurs who might otherwise have been willing to take a risk. North Korea also suffers from what amounts to an economic embargo by the United States and its allies, who hope to use economic pressure to promote reforms that would bring the cold war to an end on the Korean peninsula. Since Kim Il Sung's death Washington has eased some of the restrictions. To date, however, these initiatives have made little impact on P'yongyang's faltering economy, convincing some North Korean leaders that, despite the thaw in U.S.-DPRK relations, the United States is plotting with South Korea to bring one of the world's last socialist strongholds to its knees. Until the remaining restrictions are lifted, North Korea will continue to think that its economic problems can be solved through diplomacy. It is unlikely that North Korea will make a serious attempt to reform its economic system until it is able to compete without restrictions for foreign investments.

P'yongyang's concern for security, moreover, has meant that potential investors have been steered toward the Rajin-Sonbong Free Economic and Trade Zone. Experts argue that North Korea's Golden Triangle is strategically located but will need billions of dollars in infrastructure development before its potential can be fully realized. Clearly, this is not a place for the timid investor.

International Relations

Hardy souls intrigued by the challenge of working in one of the world's truly unique societies find in the Koryo Hotel a social oasis where lonely foreigners gather to swap stories. A Scandinavian who had lived at the Koryo for several months once remarked that despite his people's tolerance for loneliness, "even we suffer because we have so few personal contacts with the people here."

Because of its friendly ambiance, more name cards are traded in the Koryo than anywhere else in the country. At the Koryo one can meet a fantastic variety of characters, including PLO "trainees," British socialists, German capitalists, Hong Kong merchants, Chinese businesspeople, American academics, and a wide assortment of diplomats (primarily from third world countries). Each spring the Koryo Hotel is filled to capacity with delegations from all over the world who have been invited to North Korea to celebrate the anniversary of Kim Il Sung's birth on April 15.

Korean Americans and U.S.-DPRK Relations

Up until several years ago, Korean Americans visiting P'yongyang to meet their relatives living in North Korea made up a large portion of the Koryo Hotel's population. This is no longer the case. The flow of Korean Americans receiving visas to visit family has dwindled to a trickle, in part because visitors allowed to travel to their home villages in the countryside fed the South Korean media's insatiable appetite for bad news about the North but also because of an even more restrictive policy toward family visits since Kim Il Sung's death.

Kim Il Sung had a lifelong love-hate relationship with the United States. Even though he converted to Marxism at an early age, Kim not only spoke English but even taught it to his associates in the early days of his revolutionary activities. To the day he died, Kim held fast to the hope that his nation would eventually be reconciled with the United States. Even though the United States was technically at war with his government for most of his life, President Kim looked forward to a time when a dependable relationship with the United States would strengthen Korea's position vis-à-vis its more powerful neighbors in East Asia. "Korea and America are not natural enemies," he liked to remind his American guests. Listening to him elaborate his vision for better U.S.-DPRK relations, one could almost believe that the United States was guilty of isolating itself from Korea, rather than vice versa. Whoever bears the greater responsibility, families divided by the Korean War shoulder most of the pain of this abnormal situation.

Korean Americans are a golden resource that has been overlooked by both Washington and P'yongyang in their search for better relations. The United States has failed to make divided families an issue in its negotiations with North Korea. While high-level contacts discuss the recovery and repatriation of the remains of U.S. soldiers killed in the Korean War, Korean Americans have not gotten their government's attention about one of the worst humanitarian tragedies of the century. The voices of the MIAs are louder, in fact, than the voices of more than one million Korean Americans, many of whom have not seen or heard from their relatives in North Korea for almost half a century. This oversight is even more unfortunate because reuniting families could do more to produce reconciliation on the Korean peninsula than anything else.

North Korea also has made scant use of this natural bridge to the United States. If given a chance, first-generation Korean Americans, who make up one of the most entrepreneurial minorities in the United States, could help close the technological gap that divides North Korea from the West. So far, however, P'yongyang seems to be far more interested in indoctrinating Korean Americans than in learning from them. North Korea also seems reluctant to permit this highly talented, energetic U.S. minority access to its society for fear that they might spread alien ideologies to its citizens.

Chosen Soren

Members of the Chosen Soren still enjoy the best access to North Korea. At certain times of year, the Koryo Hotel's twin towers are filled and emptied like a pair of lungs by passengers on Chosen Soren charter flights arriving directly from Japan. Because most members of this expatriate society have refused to take Japanese citizenship, they usually travel to North Korea on special passports issued by the organization that are honored in only a handful of countries. The changing age structure of the Koryo's temporary residents, including members of the Chosen Soren, reflects profound changes in P'yongyang's international community that are altering North Korea's relationship to the rest of the world.

As recently as a decade ago, most of P'yongyang's non-Korean visitors were either official delegations from other socialist nations or groups of left-wing sympathizers on pilgrimage to one of the last remaining strongholds of the communist world. In those days, most outsiders doing business in P'yongyang were connected to the Chosen Soren.

The Chosen Soren's business with P'yongyang has fallen on hard times in recent years. More concerned with building socialism than making money, most Chosen Soren joint venture projects were never very competitive in the first place. Many of these investors, in fact, were related to the over 90,000 Korean Japanese who immigrated to North Korea in the sixties. The majority of this generation of businessmen are now retired, and their heirs do not often share their parents' enthusiasm for politically motivated business projects in the DPRK. The pace of their assimilation into Japanese society, moreover, is picking up. Despite Japan's continued discrimination against its resident Korean population, 20 percent of young Korean residents of Japan today choose Japanese spouses.

These demographic trends have aged the Koryo's Chosen Soren visitors, who now travel to P'yongyang more for family reasons than for business. Today eager entrepreneurs who are out to make a buck in what may be Asia's last boomtown are usually of non-Korean descent.

Eastern or Western, old or young, whatever a person's particular reason for being in P'yongyang, almost everyone dines together, making the third-floor dining room at the Koryo one of the most interesting scenes in P'yongyang. It is one of the best-lit places in the capital. The mixture of incandescent and florescent lighting suspended from the mirrored ceiling dazzles the eyes, especially because everywhere else is so dimly lit due to North Korea's energy crisis. Like moths drawn to a candle, foreign residents of the Koryo often linger over meals around the solid rectangular tables placed in orderly columns upon the parquet floor.

Cautious new friendships are usually born in the dining room, where each group is assigned a table for the duration of its visit. Up until several years ago, customers were expected to choose either Korean, Chinese, or Western food from a set menu. Now more and more guests are ordering à la carte. Even a breakfast buffet has recently been introduced.

As North Korea's capital city becomes increasingly accustomed to foreigners, the atmosphere inside the dining room has become relaxed. The relatively slow pace of life in P'yongyang means that diners usually have ample time to become acquainted. The dearth of news about the outside world whets the appetite for conversation, particularly among the few foreigners living in the Koryo for months at a time who have forgotten to bring short-wave radios.

The kind of news that draws Koreans to the Koryo, however, cannot be accessed on BBC or VOA. High officials of the Chosen Soren, some of whom manage P'yongyang's economic interests in Japan and are involved in joint ventures in North Korea, usually travel first-class and stay in government guest houses. These elites prefer to dine in private banquet halls, separate from their more humble compatriots. Important issues of state are discussed elsewhere. But family matters find a home in the Koryo dining room. Here one is likely to see North Koreans requesting the financial assistance of their more prosperous relatives from Japan—the young mother seeking money from the 60-something couple to buy a piano for her musically inclined child, for example, or the somberly dressed couple from the countryside discussing their difficulty in making ends meet with their Chosen Soren peers of retirement age. Asked whether money from Japan could change the lives of North Koreans, a high official from the Chosen Soren smiled and replied, "Money can help, but success usually depends on individual talent, even in this society."

North-South Relations

Both the Democratic People's Republic of Korea and the Republic of Korea are officially committed to reconciliation, but the politics of reunification is still a zero-sum game as far as P'yongyang and Seoul are concerned. Neither half of the peninsula wants to join in a united government on the other Korea's terms. South Korea's fears of the North date back to the communist occupation during the Korean War and involve a healthy respect for North Korea's large, well-disciplined, highly indoctrinated military. North Koreans feel deep regret that their Great Leader died before his dream of a reunified Korea was realized; the persisting division gives them a sense of guilt that helps bind them to his son and successor. Few South Koreans doubt that North Korea's divisions would march south should Kim Jong Il give the command.

North Korea's concerns about a future scripted by the South are more recent. The fate of former officials in Eastern Europe hangs over North Korea's capital like stale tobacco smoke. What chance would they or their children have, P'yongyang's elite wonders out loud, if reunification took place according to Seoul's blueprint?

A plan to dissect North Korea into economic zones controlled by South Korea's giant multinationals has already been widely circulated by Seoul's media. One article, which discussed the number of North Korea's elite who might have to be incarcerated in conjunction with reunification, has even been printed in an ROK government English-language magazine. As one North Korean official stated, "South Korea is greedy for our cheap labor and wants to eat us one bite at a time." It is no wonder that most of North Korea's elites are willing to face an uncertain future with Kim Jong Il given the alternative of second-class citizenship (if not imprisonment) under the capitalist South. Better by far, they insist, to eat reduced rations than to perform manual labor in a new world order dominated by their worst enemy.

The intense hostility and suspicion that divide the peninsula, a legacy of civil war, partition, and almost 50 years' separation, is an even greater obstacle to the reunification of Korea than the armies massed along the 38th parallel. While the cold war has ended almost everywhere else, tensions on the Korean peninsula still threaten to explode at a moment's notice. The ROK and DPRK governments began talking to each other in the early 1970s, but progress toward reconciliation has been slow and painful. Meanwhile, the first generation of divided families lose hope of ever meeting their relatives or returning home again.

Seoul and P'yongyang seemed close in the spring of 1994 when President Jimmy Carter secured agreement from President Kim Il Sung and President Kim Young Sam to hold a summit. That was only weeks before the Great Leader's fatal heart attack. Kim Il Sung's death, unfortunately, initiated a series of events that have made the 120 miles that separate Seoul and P'yongyang seem longer than ever.

Even before the funeral took place, North Korea officially charged South Korea with insulting Kim Il Sung's memory by not offering condolences to P'yongyang and its new leader, Kim Jong Il. Seoul, in fact, doubting that the Dear Leader could long survive his father, had decided to put off the meeting. This decision was supported by polls that showed a vast majority of South Koreans were solidly opposed to mourning the man they blamed for the Korean War. High-level people in South Korea's government took to the media, calling Kim Il Sung a war criminal, while South Korean police battled radicals who were determined to hold traditional mourning rites for the late president as a demonstration of protest against the government.

As even his close associates now admit, in bowing to public opinion in the South, President Kim Young Sam may have missed a golden opportunity to open a new chapter in North-South relations. P'yongyang pounced on Seoul's backtrack on the summit as conclusive evidence of President Kim's "insincerity and unfitness as a dialogue partner," an official position it has yet to soften.

The implied insult to the Great Leader was, moreover, exactly what P'yongyang needed to mobilize public opinion in the North in support for the transition from father to son. This antipathy has become so entrenched that the resumption of productive intergovernmental dialogue may have to wait until the next South Korean elections in 1997.

Given P'yongyang's unwillingness to talk to Seoul, Washington's presence at the negotiation table with the DPRK, however reluctant, has put a strain on relations between the Republic of Korea and the United States. Kim Young Sam's rise to prominence and South Korea's subsequent return to civilian rule in 1994 brought new people to power from the former opposition leader's inner circle, people who felt alienated from the United States during the long years that Seoul was ruled by the military. As a result, even though fewer U.S. flags burn on Korean campuses than in the 1980s, anti-American sentiment has found a voice in Seoul's increasingly democratic process. Today it is former South Korean activists who are most suspicious of the Clinton administration's motives for engaging the North.

In fact, Seoul has little to fear from Washington's dialogue with P'yongyang. Election-year rhetoric brought President Bill Clinton's North Korea policy under attack by Republican candidate Bob Dole. The Democrats' concern not to appear too soft on P'yongyang coupled with the fact that Washington has already obtained much of what it wants from the DPRK (a nuclear freeze and talks over missiles and MIA remains) caution against expecting rapid progress in intergovernmental dialogue, at least until after the U.S. presidential elections in November 1996.

Unfortunately, even North Korea's worsening food crisis has not contributed to better relations between the two Koreas. According to a poll taken in the spring of 1996, South Koreans who favor giving humanitarian assistance to North Korea are outnumbered two-to-one by those who are dead set against it, a fact that made it difficult for South Korea to donate $3 million to the second UN appeal. Without significant shifts in public opinion in North and South Korea, their governments will have little incentive for bold initiatives aimed at reconciliation. This is particularly true for South Korea, where the careers of most high officials who have risked engagement with the North over the years have been destroyed by a fickle public and an increasingly independent media.

Conclusion

Even though he has been dead for almost two years, Kim Il Sung still casts a long shadow across the Korean peninsula. Before passing on, Kim managed to achieve a father-son succession under circumstances that seemed impossible to all but his most faithful supporters. North Korea embraced Kim Il Sung's "solution to the succession question" because (according to the official explanation) the Dear Leader was clearly the best candidate and because only he could guarantee the survival of the revolution.

So far, despite the collapse of communism elsewhere, economic stagnation, confrontation with South Korea and the United States, natural disasters, and widespread hunger, Kim Il Sung's decision seems to have accomplished what he intended. By all outward appearances, Kim Jong Il appears firmly in control, even though he has not officially assumed control of the government. It remains to be seen whether he proves to be a "genius of ten thousand talents," as his father is said to have claimed. Prudence, still, would counsel that the mysterious new leader of this enigmatic nation be given his fair measure of respect.

After Kim Il Sung's death, reunification seems, if anything, more difficult than ever before. U.S. pressure on North Korea has so far failed to restart intergovernmental dialogue on the Korean peninsula, while compassion for North Korea's flood victims has taken a backseat to politics. Although Koreans have traditionally looked to government to take the initiative on major issues confronting society, they may also have to look elsewhere for answers to the most vexing problem they have faced in this century.

One place both Koreas might look for help with reconciliation is to their own private sectors. In this era of increasing international inter-dependency, governments that have loosened constraints on civilians (particularly civilian economic activity) have profited immensely. The sheer volume of interactions required to nurture the simplest joint ven-ture project argues powerfully against micromanagement of the private sector by government bureaucrats.

Despite all the ups and downs that have marked its first half century, Seoul has grown relatively rich, not only because military leaders pro-moted exports but also because South Korea became the first Korean state in history to grant citizens relatively unimpeded access to the outside world. Because these talented and energetic people have proven they can succeed if given a fair chance, the popular but pessi-mistic characterization of Korea as a victim of history is gradually being replaced by a positive self-image.

Private-sector relationships are also the primary reason that the bond between the Republic of Korea and the United States will not be eclipsed by the thaw in the cold war. South Koreans who fear that U.S.-DPRK dialogue may drive a wedge between the United States and South Korea should take a lesson from the Chinese. Even Beijing diplomats who have spent their careers nurturing China's relationship with the DPRK admit that communications with Seoul are far more open and honest than has ever been possible with P'yongyang. This warmth has been achieved primarily because the two governments removed most barriers to private-sector interaction, providing one more example of how South Korea has profited by giving its private citizens a significant role in international affairs.

Its policy toward North Korea, however, remains the single largest exception to South Korea's embrace of modernity. Despite the fact that Korea was partitioned by the victors of 1945 and fought a bloody, devastating, inconclusive civil war, South Korea has built a powerful economy and has laid the foundations for a democratic society. In a single generation, its citizens have carried their language, culture, and work ethic to every continent on the globe, where they make up one of the world's most dynamic expatriate communities. Today the only place off-limits to a South Korean, ironically, is North Korea.

Seoul is still reluctant to permit its citizens the freedom to interact with their North Korean compatriots without close government super-vision. This restriction extends even to South Korea's vibrant religious community, which is increasingly impatient with regulations that prevent its members from responding to invitations to visit the North. June 1996 marked a watershed in the history of interdenominational and interreligious cooperation. For the first time a wide spectrum of religious leaders united their voices in demanding the right to contribute directly to help North Koreans suffering from severe food shortages. Their petition, which insisted that food should not be used as a political weapon, is the most recent indicator that South Korea's nongovernmental community is coming of age.

As events in the mid-1990s have proven, the world cannot afford to ignore either Korea. Whoever ultimately claims credit for ending the bitterness of the division, the future of the peninsula will prove a truth implied in an old nursery rhyme: even though governments may divide a nation, only its citizens can put it back together again.

Language, Politics, and Ideology in the Postwar Koreas

Ross King

Nationalism is a key factor in language reform movements throughout the world. With its emphases on authenticity, uniqueness, and the "link with the glorious past," nationalism is intimately bound with the vernacular. Modern mass nationalism equates authenticity with a particular language and often with a particular script or orthography. Whereas some scholars emphasize the sociohistorical importance of language standardization in the emergence of nation-states, others focus on language planning as a way of fashioning language into both an implement and a focus of national pride. National pride needs language as a resource at both the practical and sentimental levels.[1]

Korea and Korean are no exception. Korean nationalists and linguist-ideologues began to articulate the connection between the Korean nation, Korean language, and Korean script in the 1890s. The Korean language standardization movement was at the center of nationalist resistance under the Japanese occupation (1910–45) until the arrests of Korean linguists in 1942, and the language issue reemerged with liberation from Japan in 1945. However, with the creation of separate republics in 1948, the Korean language debate was doomed to develop in a divided land.

According to a seminal work on language standards and their origins,

> When two or more dialects of roughly equal prestige are simultaneously candidates for emergence, or when a synecdochic dialect [a dialect that

---

1. See Jonathan Steinberg, "The Historian and the *'Questione della Lingua,'*" in *The Social History of Languages*, Cambridge Studies in Oral and Literate Culture 12, ed. Peter Burke and Roy Porter (Cambridge: Cambridge University Press, 1987), and Nanette Twine, *Language and the Modern State: The Reform of Written Japanese* (New York: Routledge, 1991).

has achieved the level of dominance necessary to make it the obvious candidate for "standard language"] must compete with an older standard language (a classical or colonial language), the controversy is traditionally termed a *questione della lingua,* from Italian, the language in which the first and most famous such dispute was openly waged.[2]

The Korean *questione della lingua* surfaced in the late 1890s under the impetus of the Kab'o reforms (1894), a sweeping series of progressive and modernizing reforms enacted by the pro-Japanese cabinet. However, Korean language reform did not begin to gather momentum until the years 1906–8, after Korea had become a Japanese protectorate. The Korean debate centered not on the choice of which variety of Korean to standardize (the Seoul dialect had been the main prestige variety of Korean for several centuries) but on script: how were the Koreans to write Korean—exclusively in the native Korean script, or with the aid of Chinese characters for words of Chinese origin? Linguist-ideologues like Chu Si Gyŏng (1876–1914), the founder of the Korean language movement, began to articulate a nationalist philosophy connecting native Korean language, native Korean script, and independence. Under the impetus of impending Japanese colonial rule, Chu even persuaded the Korean government to establish Korea's first official research and policy institution, the Korea Script Research Institute, which lasted from 1907 to 1909. However, the preoccupation of Korean scholars with narrow questions of script origins and other philological issues kept them from an examination of broader standardization issues, and in any case, their recommendations for a new orthography were ignored by the new, conservative (pro–Chinese script) minister of education in 1909.[3] Unlike many European nations, Korea was not to have a "golden age of vernacularizing lexicographers, grammarians, philologists, and litterateurs."[4]

The stimulus, both direct and indirect, for Korean language standardization was to come from Japanese colonial rule. The Japanese government-general established the first official Korean orthography

---

2. John Earl Joseph, *Eloquence and Power: The Rise of Language Standards and Standard Languages* (London: Frances Pinter, 1987).

3. See Yi Ki Mun, *Kaehwa-gi ǔi Kungmun Yǒn'gu* (Research on Korean Writing During the Enlightenment Period) (Seoul: Iltchogak, 1970).

4. Benedict Anderson, *Imagined Communities: Reflections on the Origin and Spread of Nationalism* (London: Verso Press, 1993), p. 71.

in 1912, initiated work on a dictionary in the same year (published in 1920 as the *Chōsengo Jiten*, a Korean-Japanese dictionary), and revised the official Korean orthography again in 1921 and 1930. Meanwhile, Korean language scholars had continued their efforts at promulgating and refining both the Korean language and the native Korean script, called *han'gŭl*, a neologism coined by Chu Si Gyŏng sometime between 1910 and 1913.[5] These scholars intensified their efforts under the auspices of the Research Society for the Korean Language, formed in 1921 and renamed the Korean Language Society in 1931.

This latter society published in 1933 the *Unified Han'gŭl Orthography*, a radical spelling scheme that rejected traditional phonemic spelling, which is close or identical to actual pronunciation, in favor of a more abstract morphophonemic spelling, which posits one uniform and unchanging shape for each word. For example, using the morphophonemic orthography, the word for "pond" is spelled "못" and is made up of the letters "m" (ㅁ), "o" (ㅗ), and "s" (ㅅ). But notice the pronunciation in the following environments and the two different spelling possibilities:

Pronunciation	Meaning	Phonemic spelling	Morphophonemic spelling
mot	pond	{mot}	{mos}
mose	in the pond	{mo}{se}	{mos}{e}
monman	pond only	{mon}{man}	{mos}{man}

The orthography proposed by the Korean Language Society was also opposed, both literally and figuratively, to the Japanese-sponsored, tradition-based phonemic orthography. Though opposed by some Korean scholars, the 1933 *Unified Orthography* became a rallying point for cultural nationalists and was adopted as the official orthography upon liberation from Japanese rule in 1945.

The Korean Language Society followed up its *Unified Orthography* with the first attempt at defining "standard Korean," the *Collection of Evaluated Standard Korean* of 1936. Whereas the 1933 *Unified Orthography* had simply defined "standard" as the "contemporary Seoul

---

5. See Ko Yŏng Gŭn, *T'ongil sidae ŭi Ŏmun Munje* (Problems of Korean Language and Writing in the Unification Age) (Seoul: Kilpŏt, 1994).

speech of educated middle-class Koreans," the new work gave standard-vocabulary headings followed by lists of nonstandard variants. Those scholars most active in its compilation were Ch'oe Hyŏn Bae, Yi Kung No, Yi Man Gyu, Yi Hŭi Sung, and Yi Yun Jae.

Japanese policy became more and more oppressive in the late 1930s; on the language front, Korean was banned from public use in 1938. Against this background, the Korean Language Society pushed forward with its plans for a massive monolingual dictionary until 1942, when the nearly completed manuscript was confiscated by the Japanese authorities. Many of the scholars were arrested and imprisoned, and two even died in prison.

In closing this potted history of the Korean language movement under the Japanese, it must be stressed that, notwithstanding the efforts of the Korean Language Society's so-called philological incendiaries,[6] the extent and depth of language standardization at this time were not great. The Korean situation under the Japanese was one in which the cultural avant-garde often had to create "a rather shallow illusion of standardization, which, if it serves to increase the dialect's prestige, may largely give way in the 'real' standardization that will follow."[7]

Orthography as Political Battleground in Post-Colonial Korea

Background: The Beginnings of Language Policy in South Korea

The tendency of language debates in Korea to focus on problems of script and orthography intensified after liberation from Japanese rule in 1945. The so-called Liberation Interval from 1945 to 1948—following liberation from Japan, but before the division became fixed by the elections in the South in 1948—and the two years preceding the Korean War were a turbulent period in Korea for language policy. In the South, things got off to a bad start on September 7, 1945, with paragraph 5 of General Douglas MacArthur's first official communiqué, Proclamation No. 1, which declared that "for all purposes during the military control, English will be the official language, and in the event of any ambiguity or diversity of interpretation or definition between any English and Korean or Japanese text, the English text shall pre-

---

6. The term is from Anderson, *Imagined Communities*.

7. Joseph, *Eloquence and Power*, p. 61.

vail." Thus, technically speaking, English became the official language for a time, and this particular policy would feed into later North Korean attempts to build a myth of "American imperialist policy to obliterate the Korean language" in South Korea.

For all practical purposes though, Korean was the official language, and the question of script and writing soon reemerged. The former Korean Language Society had reconstituted itself in August 1945 and took the lead in promoting exclusive *han'gŭl* usage. It was especially active in the field of school textbook production, a subject entrusted to it by the Ministry of Education's National Education Review Committee in November 1945. A December 8, 1945, meeting of this committee voted overwhelmingly to eliminate Chinese characters from textbooks at elementary and secondary levels and to write *han'gŭl* syllables horizontally from left to right rather than vertically from right to left, Chinese- and Japanese-style. A public survey conducted by the U.S. military government in the same month found much support for the elimination of Chinese characters among the public at large.[8]

One of the worst legacies of Japanese rule was a high rate of illiteracy, and U.S. military authorities pursued a policy of *han'gŭl*-only usage coupled with horizontal, left to right writing in order to promote education and literacy in Korean. Some voices in the U.S. administration favored an even more radical horizontalization of Korean writing, whereby one would de-block into its individual constituent parts the *han'gŭl* orthographic syllable and write each individual graph side by side, as with other true alphabets.[9] This particular idea is usually attributed to Chu Si Gyŏng and was even discussed (and rejected) in the deliberations of the Korean Script Research Institute in 1908. This horizontal, side-by-side idea (for example, 한글 for *han'gŭl* would be written ㅎㅏㄴㄱ_ㄹ or ㅎㅏㄴㄱㅜㄹ) continued to attract followers and researchers throughout the Japanese colonial period, and in the heady atmosphere of post-Liberation Korea, interest in it surged in both the North and the South.

This particular reform idea aside, the key points of contention in the South became exclusive *han'gŭl* usage and the elimination of Chinese

---

8. See Lenore Kim Blank, "Language Policies in South Korea Since 1945 and Their Probable Impact on Education," Ed.D. dissertation, University of San Francisco, 1981.

9. In theory, the syllabic constituents can also be taken apart and written side by side vertically, but this suggestion was never entertained by Korean language reformers.

characters. The December recommendations of the National Education Review Committee set off a storm of protest from pro-Chinese quarters, which then prompted more vociferous *han'gŭl*-only cries, most notably from the Korean Language Society. In 1947 Ch'oe Hyŏn Bae wrote a rebuttal to pro–Chinese character conservatives like Cho Yun Je that included a plea for both exclusive *han'gŭl* usage and horizontal, side-by-side writing.

In June 1948 the Ministry of Education launched a "Reclaim Our Language" movement, followed the next month by the publication of its *Rationale for Elimination of Chinese Characters*. In the same month, a constitution was prepared and signed by Syngman Rhee, a longtime proponent of exclusive *han'gŭl* usage, in *han'gŭl* rather than in Chinese characters. Riding what appeared to be a tide of *han'gŭl*-only sentiment, the Korean Language Society on July 24 made a formal proposal to the National Assembly to legislate exclusive *han'gŭl* usage. Resolution No. 6, "The Exclusive Use of *Han'gŭl* as the Official Writing System in the Government," passed by 86 votes to 22 (with 131 members present) on September 30, 1948, but it was amended the next day to include the rider, "For the time being, however, Chinese characters may be used together with *han'gŭl*." Thus, the exclusive *han'gŭl* usage forces, and especially the Korean Language Society, scored a moral victory at least and would continue to brandish the September 30 Resolution No. 6 in defense of exclusive *han'gŭl* usage in subsequent debates.

Meanwhile, the Korean Language Society was catching up on the massive dictionary project that had been interrupted in 1942 by the Japanese authorities. In August 1948 at the time of the proclamation of the Republic of Korea, most of the big names in Korean linguistics and philology were still in Seoul, where the Korean Language Society was headquartered. These included not only the scholars Ch'oe Hyŏn Bae, Kim Yun Gyŏng, Yi Hŭi Sung, and Yi Sung Nyŏng, who would remain in the ROK, but also Yi Kung No, Hong Ki Mun, Yi Man Gyu, Kim Pyŏng Je, Chŏng Yŏl Mo, and Yu Yŏl, who would later be active in the DPRK. Volume 1 of the *Great Dictionary of the Korean Language* had appeared in October 1947, and Volume 2 appeared in May 1949. In July of that year the Korean Language Society formed the Committee for the Promotion of Exclusive *Han'gŭl* Usage and in October changed its name to the Han'gŭl Society, again reflecting the preoccupation with script and writing. It was also in October that the pro–Chinese character forces struck back. In a debate in the National Assembly that lasted from October 26 to November 5, Im Yŏng Sin and other assembly members agitated to reinstate the use of Chinese characters in school textbooks and linked the defection to North Korea of prominent *han'gŭl* scholar and political figure Yi Kung No, co-author of the Korean Language Society textbooks, with his *han'gŭl*-only stance. The attempt by certain conservative South Korean forces to paint *han'gŭl*-only usage "red" did not stick for long, but the Ministry of Education went on the defensive and began investigating the notion of establishing 1,300 Chinese characters for common use in January 1950. In May 1951, after the Korean War was well under way, the ministry officially announced these 1,300 Chinese characters for common use and in September published the *Chart of the 1,000 Most Commonly Used Chinese Characters*. Finally, in June 1952, the Ministry of Education announced the Chinese Characters in Education Act.

These debates from the late 1940s began a pattern of "zigzagging government policies"[10] that would plague South Korea for the next four decades. Policy decisions were in the hands of a weak Ministry of Education unable to impose its will on other branches of the government let alone on the publishing industry and the staunch Chinese character supporters in the newspaper world. The Han'gŭl Society continued its vociferous lobbying efforts but as a private, civilian research organization with no power base and no official link to government policy-making organs, its suggestions were acted upon only when they served the interests of whoever happened to occupy the frequently rotated post of minister of education.

Moreover, Korean philology in the formative decades of South Korea owed more to traditional taxonomic questions of 19th-century school grammar than to 20th-century general linguistic theory as developed in Europe and the United States; this made it even more difficult to achieve consensus on language policy issues. Once the South Korean university system got under way, a conservative pressure group on matters of language and writing came into being within the Department of Korean Language and Literature at Seoul National University (SNU). Led by Yi Hŭi Sung and Yi Sung Nyŏng, both trained in linguistics and philology at Keijō University (SNU's predecessor

---

10. The phrase is from Kim Chin Wu, "Divergence in Language Policies in Korea," in *Papers in Korean Linguistics*, ed. Chin W. Kim (Columbia, S.C.: Hornbeam Press, 1978).

under the Japanese), this group came to articulate a more go-slow, pro-Chinese-character policy than the autodidacts of the Han'gǔl Society. Most of the scholars of this latter group traced their academic lineage back to private nongovernment schools inspired by Chu Si Gyŏng and his pupils under the Japanese regime and were seen as being distinguished more by their fervent patriotism and purism than by their command of linguistic method.

Finally, for many years general linguistics did not exist as an independent academic discipline in South Korea. Rather, linguistics was studied within language and literature departments, chiefly English departments. For nearly four decades the only university linguistics department was the SNU Department of Linguistics, formed in 1946. The decades from 1945 through the 1960s witnessed an importation of Anglo-American linguistic theories, but especially those of American descriptivism and later American structuralism and generative grammar, all of which are at least indifferent if not outright hostile to the notion that language can be planned. The dominant Anglo-American view of language as something organic or living is inimical to the utilitarian view of language as a malleable tool or social institution. This hostility toward prescriptivism, long a hallmark of American structuralism, prompted one European language-planning expert to quip, "The metaphor of language as an organism has influenced the notion of what a language is so strongly that any attempt at influencing its natural development is morally as dubious as cloning."[11] Precisely this sort of view, that language cannot be planned, seems to have taken root in South Korea in the 1940s and 1950s, while a radically different, more utilitarian and functional philosophy of linguistics and its social role was being imported into Korea north of the 38th parallel.

Background: The Beginnings of Language Policy in North Korea

The history of language planning in North Korea is an excellent example of language planning in the service of a nationalist political ideology. As early as May 1946 Kim Il Sung published two speeches, "Culture and the Arts Must Be for the People" and "The Duty of

---

11. Florian Coulmas, "Democracy and the Crisis of Normative Linguistics," in *Language Adaptation*, ed. Florian Coulmas (Cambridge: Cambridge University Press, 1989), p. 178.

Youth in the Construction of Democratic Korea," in which he urged that government workers avoid difficult technical words and that they go to the masses to seek out the forms actually spoken and written. In terms of orthography, the North and South did not differ much for the first two or three years after Liberation. The Korean Language Society had published a revised version of the *Unified Orthography* in 1946, and this served in the North through 1947. Thus, Kim Yong Jin's *Explanation of the Plan for a Unified Orthography*, published in July 1947 in P'yongyang, followed the 1946 Korean Language Society revisions, as did Kim Chong O's *Han'gŭl Reader* of the same month.

The greatest language problem in the first years of the North Korean state was illiteracy: at the end of World War II, 2.3 million North Koreans, almost one-fourth of the population, were illiterate.[12] Adult schools and *han'gŭl* schools were formed in January 1946, and it is claimed that as a result of two major Shock Campaigns to Eradicate Illiteracy, the first conducted from December 1947 to August 1948 and the second from December 1948 to March 1949, illiteracy had all but disappeared by the end of 1949.

On the academic front, on February 3, 1947, the Interim People's Committee, through its Decision No. 175, laid out the general directions for future language policy:

> Today, as we stand on the road of construction of an independent, self-reliant, democratic state, the unification and development of Korean language and literature based on scientific ideals and continuous research are the basis for refining the cultural construction of the Korean people and are a matter of urgent demand.[13]

Kim Il Sung oversaw the transfer in early 1947 of the Research Society for Korean Language and Literature, formed in July 1946, to Kim Il Sung University, where linguist-revolutionary Kim Tu Bong was president. This research body, through its journal, *Korean Language Research,* began the task of refining and standardizing the Korean language. In December 1947 Kim Tu Bong, a major figure in the

---

12. Data from Kim Chin Wu, "Divergence in Language Policies in Korea," p. 252.

13. Cited in Ko Yŏng Gŭn, "Pukhan ŭi muntcha kaehyŏk e kwanhan Yŏn'gu" (Research on Script Reform in North Korea), *Chu Si Gyŏng Hakpo* (Chu Si Gyŏng Journal) Vol. 12 (1993), pp. 24–69.

North Korean communist movement, made a presentation to the Central Committee of the North Korean Workers' Party on his ideas for a new Korean orthography.

Lest it seem strange that a leading North Korean communist, indeed, a main rival to Kim Il Sung for power, should be expounding on orthographic reform, it should be noted that Kim Tu Bong was the author of a highly regarded Korean grammar in 1916, *Chosŏn Malbon* [Korean Grammar]. A direct disciple of Chu Si Gyŏng, Kim Tu Bong was eventually forced by the Japanese to flee to Shanghai, where he published a revised and expanded version of his grammar in 1923. One of the main points of his second grammar was his advocation of radical reform of the Korean script on two counts: a more thorough implementation of the morphophonemic principle and completely horizontal, side-by-side *han'gŭl* writing. It was this book that had kicked off the wave of interest in horizontal, side-by-side writing during the Japanese colonial period. Kim Tu Bong had remained in contact with the Korean Language Society scholars throughout his exile in Shanghai; in fact, a payment by the society to Kim for services contributed in the matter of the dictionary project was used by the Japanese as evidence to make its series of arrests of Korean linguists in 1942. Thus Kim Tu Bong retained his linguistic interests throughout his political activities in exile, and once in a position of power in newly liberated North Korea, he moved quickly to put his linguistic theories into practice.

Lectures about and discussions of the new Korean orthography continued at Kim Il Sung University in January and February 1948, and the orthography was presented to the Research Society for Korean Language and Literature on January 15, 1948. According to Ko Yŏng Gŭn, the new Korean orthography had as its ultimate goals the abolition of Chinese characters, the reform of spelling in the direction of morphophonemic principles, and preparation for complete horizontalization of the writing system.[14] In October 1948 the Research Society for Korean Language and Literature was placed under the Ministry of Education, and the publication in the same month of the *Russian-Korean Dictionary,* the first of many, was a sign of paramount Soviet influence. The Research Society for Korean Language and Literature began publication of its journal, *Korean Language Research,* in March 1949. A language purification movement was an-

---

14. Ko Yŏng Gŭn, "Pukhan ŭi muntcha kaehyŏk e kwanhan Yŏn'gu."

nounced, and abolishment of Chinese characters and exclusive *han'gŭl* usage were proclaimed in September 1949, along with the enactment of compulsory elementary education. Questions of writing and orthography were at the forefront at the Grand Research Symposium in Honor of the 505th Anniversary of the Creation of the Korean Script in January 1949 and at the Research Symposium to Commemorate the 34th Anniversary of the Death of Chu Si Gyŏng in July. Finally, December 1949 witnessed the publication of the first North Korean grammar, the *Chosŏnŏ Munpŏp,* and April 1950 marked the official publication of the *New Korean Orthography.* With the outbreak of the Korean War in June 1950, the North Korean linguistic journal *Korean Language Research* ceased publication, and language policy activity ground to a halt.

South Korea, 1953–55: The Simplified Han'gŭl Spelling Controversy

The language question in South Korea resurfaced in the form of a debate, prompted by President Syngman Rhee himself, over the new Korean orthography developed by Korean linguists during the Japanese occupation. This debate, known as the simplified *han'gŭl* spelling controversy, began on April 27, 1953, with the infamous Prime Minister's Directive No. 8, Abolishment of the Current Orthography and Use of the Old-Style Spelling. It reads:

> It is a well-known fact that our *han'gŭl* was originally created with convenience of use in mind. However, in light of the fact that the orthography currently in use has more than a few complicated and inconvenient features, the President has ordered on more than one occasion that this be simplified; at the 32nd meeting of the Council of State of April 11, Tan'gun 4286, it was decided that all government documents, all textbooks authorized by the government, and any printed matter typed on a typewriter should use the simplified orthography. While it is considered that [the publication of] textbooks and typewritten materials will be somewhat delayed owing to considerations of preparation, it is deemed possible for all government documents to use the simplified orthography effective immediately; thus, it is instructed that this be enacted, henceforth, in accordance with this directive.[15]

---

15. The translation is mine.

The directive encountered immediate criticism and resistance from academia, the public, and the press, forcing the minister of education to resign. Eager to find academic support for his views, in July 1953 President Syngman Rhee had a 50-member National Language Deliberative Committee established within the Ministry of Education. The 25-member Han'gŭl Subcommittee met 11 times between October 19 and December 25 before making its final recommendations on the question of simplifying Korean orthography: Keep the current morphophonemic (abstract) orthography and adopt horizontal, side-by-side *han'gŭl* spelling.

Ignoring these recommendations, Rhee published a special *Presidential Discussion* on March 27, 1954, in which he ordered that the current morphophonemic orthography be simplified within three months. This *Discussion* revealed a number of Rhee's views on writing. First, he advocated a return to the phonemic spelling of the turn-of-the-century Korean translation of the New Testament. Unlike China, with its difficult characters and high illiteracy, Rhee argued, Korea had an excellent script; if only the stubborn, regressive Korean-language scholars would abandon the unnecessarily complex orthography, Korea might enjoy one of the highest literacy rates in the world. Moreover, harking back to Korea's only pure Korean script newspaper, the *Independent*, Rhee lamented the fact that there was not a single *han'gŭl*-only newspaper in Korea and asserted that a simplified spelling system would "make it easier for foreigners to learn our language." Finally, Rhee claimed the simplified spelling would simplify typing (as it would require fewer keys) and code-based communications, and he expressed his hope that the elegant simplicity of his proposed spelling would convince newspapers to abandon the use of Chinese characters.

On July 3, 1954, the new minister of education, Yi Sŏn Gun, promulgated the *Plan for a Simplified Han'gŭl Spelling*. In its details, this spelling followed the 1921 revised Korean orthography of the Japanese government-general almost exactly. Only ten syllable-final consonants were allowed (/k/, /n/, /l/, /m/, /p/, /s/, /ng/, /lk/, /lm/, /lp/) as opposed to the 26 of the *Unified Orthography*. A syllable-final consonant is any consonant or consonant cluster written after a vowel in a Korean orthographic syllable (remember that Korean is written in syllable blocks). Depending on the level of abstractness of the spelling system, different numbers of syllable-final consonants are allowed in the orthography:

the more abstract the system is, the more syllable-final consonants are allowed. The overriding spelling principle of the *Plan for a Simplified Han'gŭl Spelling* was phonemic rather than morphophonemic, and certain etymological spellings were rejected (for example, 가치 for *kach'i,* "together; like," was preferred to 같이, where 같– is the base for "be like, resemble"). Finally, the simplified spelling revised certain standard words in the direction of colloquial usage (갑 for 값 , "price," and 부억 for 부엌 "kitchen").

The rationale published with the simplified spelling cited a Ministry of Education statistical study claiming that the ten new syllable-final consonants accounted for 93.8 percent of all occurrences in running text, thus justifying the jettisoning of the less frequent, more abstract syllable-final consonants of the *Unified Spelling.* The simplified spelling was more convenient for writing, allowed a reduction of 397 syllables in typesetting work, and eliminated several keys on *han'gŭl* typewriters. The choice of orthographic "s" (ㅅ) for underlying /s/, /t/, /ch/, /ch'/, /t'/, and /ss/ "is consistent with our people's traditional aesthetic sensibilities," and overall the spelling was more suited to "children and adult illiterates."

In a further defense of the simplified spelling, six days later, on July 9, 1954, the Ministry of Education cited the work of famous European scholars of Altaic (Mongolic, Manchu-Tungusic, and Turkic) languages as justification of its ten syllable-final consonants. But the European Altaicists were simply stating a number of typological facts about Altaic languages in general and then noting the similarities between these languages and Korean. The defenders of the simplified orthography were making the (perverse) argument that, "because other Altaic languages do not typically allow consonant clusters, Korean, too, should not allow its orthography to reflect certain types of syllable-final consonant(s)" and were simultaneously trying to invoke the prestige associated with Western scholarship. In its defense of simplified spelling, the ministry also cited the *Hunmin Chŏngŭm Haerye* (the *Explanations and Examples* to the *Hunmin Chŏngum,* the work that promulgated the Korean script in 1446) and Ch'oe Se Jin's *Hunmong Chahoe* (a famous early Chinese-Korean dictionary of 1527). This document criticized the current morphophonemic spelling that fixed nouns and verb stems in one shape as too abstract, and it cited the Finnish-Swedish Altaicist G. J. Ramstedt's Korean grammar. The views of Ferdinand de Saussure and Leonard Bloomfield were marshaled against etymological spellings. Like the good structuralists they were, de Saussure and Bloomfield felt that writing should be phonemic. Thus, they opposed the retention of spelling archaisms (such as etymological spellings) that reflected an earlier stage of the language no longer accessible to speakers. Finally, the ministry's document again cited the Korean people's traditional "loving usage" of the orthographic syllable-final consonant /s/ as a rationale for the abolition of the syllable-final consonants /t/, /t'/, /ch/, /ch'/, and /ss/. In other words, the defenders of the simplified orthography were invoking tradition and claiming that because (the largely phonemic, as opposed to abstract) Korean orthography since the 1440s had routinely written "s" for underlying /t/, /t'/, /ch/, /ch'/, and /ss/, Koreans had a close affinity for "s", and should continue to write it in these cases.

Both the *Plan for a Simplified* Han'gŭl *Spelling* and the accompanying rationale were greeted with scorn and derision by Han'gŭl Society scholars and the public alike as soon as they appeared. President Rhee published another stubborn *Discussion* on July 13 in which he reiterated his intention to abolish the current orthography and push through his simplified spelling. For Rhee, the *Unified Spelling* presented "many obstacles to the development of civilization in Korea," and he maintained that "the majority of the masses all consider my position to be correct."

It was at approximately this juncture in July 1954 that the most vehement criticisms of the simplified spelling appeared in the press. Mid-July also coincided with a visit to Seoul by Yale professor Samuel E. Martin whose monograph *Korean Morphophonemics*, destined to become a classic in the field, would appear in the same year. Martin published an open letter to the minister of education in the English-language daily, the *Korea Times,* and this letter appeared in Korean translation in the *Han'guk Ilbo* (one of Korea's major daily newspapers) on July 10. In his letter, Martin praised the Han'gŭl Society and its *Unified Spelling*, sharply criticized the simplified spelling as a retrograde step (he was about to publish a dictionary in the other orthography), and warned that if the reform went through Korea would become the laughingstock of the world for knuckling under to the whims of a linguistically uninformed politician in technical questions of language policy. Moreover, Martin pointed out that the financial support promised by the Rockefeller Foundation for the remaining volumes of the *Great Dictionary of the Korean Language* had been placed in jeopardy by the actions of the Ministry of Education, and that indeed his own dictionary project, currently under way at Yale University, was being compromised by the spelling controversy.

The tug-of-war over the simplified spelling dragged on for another year until September 1955, when Syngman Rhee, in his final *Discussion* on the issue, rescinded his simplification order and called the matter closed. The affair ended in victory for the Han'gŭl Society and its *Unified Spelling*, but it is likely that the resolute opposition to the simplified spelling was due more to an aversion to the high-handed, dictatorial style of its would-be perpetrator, Syngman Rhee, than to any firm belief in the inherent superiority of morphophonemic as opposed to phonemic spelling.[16] Thus, although the 1933 *Unified Spelling* was indeed in need of revision in many places, South Korea would have to wait until the 1970s for the dust from the 1950s *han'gŭl* controversy to settle and for a new regime to set the wheels of reform back in motion.

North Korea, 1949–58: The Six New Graphs Controversy

Korean orthography became a political battleground in South Korea in the 1950s, and political concerns, in the form of opposition to Syngman Rhee, ultimately helped postpone orthographic reform there. A similar story was played out in North Korea, beginning with Kim Tu Bong's advocacy of his new Korean spelling in 1947. Kim's ideas were announced as the new Korean orthography on January 15, 1948, though they were not officially published until April 1950, and found full expression in the *Korean Grammar* of 1949.

The preface of the *New Korean Orthography* reads:

> The *New Korean Orthography* is based on the fundamental missions of language and writing. On the one hand, it takes as its point of departure an examination and critique of the South Korean Korean Language Society's *Plan for a Unified* Han'gŭl *Spelling*. On the other hand, it takes as its point of departure the forward-looking perspective of the inevitable abolition of Chinese characters and writing reform (complete horizontal writing), both of which must be carried out in the near future for the sake of the development of Korean language and literature.[17]

---

16. See Kim Min Su, *Kugŏ Chŏngch'aek-non* (Korean Language Policy) (Seoul: Tower Press, 1973/1984), p. 240.

17. Cited in Ko Yŏng Gŭn, "Pukhan ŭi muntcha kaehyŏk e kwanhan Yŏn'gu," p. 27. The translation is mine.

The new spelling introduced a number of innovations. For example, the order and number of *han'gŭl* letters were changed. The most radical innovation was the introduction of six new letters. These were designed to represent the morphophonemic alterations arising in six different classes of irregular verb in Korean. In other words, they were meant to take to a new extreme the abstract morphophonemic principle. The new spelling thus regularized certain irregular verb conjugations: for example, the 15th-century sign for /z/ (defunct since the 16th century) was to be resurrected for the alternation "t ~ r" in verbs like "to listen": *tŭtta tŭrŏ yo* would be written *tŭzta tŭzŏ yo*. Likewise the 15th-century sign for the glottal stop was to be resurrected.

However, the only North Korean publications to actually use the new Korean orthography were the linguistics journal *Korean Language Research* (and that only in articles about the new spelling) and the 1949 *Korean Grammar*, the only work written with the six new graphs. After the Korean War, the revised *Korean Orthography* of 1954 did not include mention of the prior new Korean orthography, although it did retain certain minor features.

It would appear that the new Korean orthography was on shaky ground from the first. With the weakening of Kim Tu Bong's political position in late 1957 and his purge in March 1958, the stage was set for a complete repudiation of his orthographic ideas, and in 1958 the pages of the new linguistics journals *Korean Language and Literature* (1956–60) and *Language and Writing* (1958–62) carried several attacks on the six new letters and on Kim Tu Bong. Even old friends like Yi Kung No, who had made presentations praising the new Korean orthography in October 1949, were forced to turn on Kim Tu Bong. In any case, the new Korean orthography episode from 1948 to 1958 in North Korea was another good example of the Korean script and reform of Korean orthography serving as the battleground for politics. But for Kim Tu Bong's political demise, the six new letters and horizontalized writing might well have become official policy in the DPRK. As we shall see below, the side-by-side, horizontal writing idea survived the Kim Tu Bong debacle to be fought over another day in the North.

The Beginnings of North-South Divergence

While the new Korean orthography controversy went on behind the scenes, other language-planning efforts were pushed in the North: in

1952 the *Labor News*, North Korea's major newspaper, published a series of articles called "Concerning a Few Problems in the Purification of the Korean Language." At a meeting of the Central Committee of the party in 1955, Kim Il Sung again urged cadres to use simple words that the masses could understand, and in 1956 the new academic journal *Korean Language and Literature* appeared, again concerned mostly with the problems of Chinese character loans and language purification.

Starting in 1958 yet another linguistic journal, but of a more popular nature, appeared—*Language and Writing. Language and Writing* was published from 1958 through 1962 and seems to have been a sounding board for the various conflicting opinions on language planning at the time. The very first issue carried articles on orthographic reform that show that even with the purge of Kim Tu Bong in March 1958 and the rejection of his six new letters, orthographic reform was still a vital issue. In one article, Yi Man Gyu advocated writing *han'gŭl* horizontally side-by-side, arguing that this would be easier on the eye and would increase reading speeds. He then went on to criticize *han'gŭl* for its unshapely, squarish graphs: *han'gŭl* was unsuited for cursive writing and mechanized type, and Yi suggested further research into the reform of individual graph shapes. The second issue of *Language and Writing* carried a five-page article with writing systems proposed by the journal's readers—six systems in all. The next issue, number 3, carried public castigation of Kim Tu Bong and his new letters; the party considered as counter to its unificatory goals Kim Tu Bong's 1957 suggestion that his six new graphs be implemented immediately and unilaterally throughout the North.

Language and Writing was only a quarterly in 1958, but it expanded to a monthly starting in 1959. In addition to the early concerns with *han'gŭl* orthography, the journal carried articles on topics ranging from Esperanto to the Korean classics. Most articles, though, concerned the development of standardized speech in North Korea: regular columns entitled Language Purification, Dialect and Standard Language, and Words to Know drilled home new coinages. The journals are rich in extensive word lists comparing dialect with standard and Sino-Korean expressions with newly formed Korean replacements. Frequent features on uninvited "foreignisms"—the July 1962 issue scorned the use of *ppai ppai* (bye-bye), for example—and the macaronic language in the southern half of the peninsula stressed the need to safeguard the purity and Korean essence of the language. Other articles advised readers on the placement of the *sai p'yo* (an orthographic device used to alert readers to certain unexpected features of pronunciation), on standard pronunciation, or on spelling problems with the syllable-final consonants, and some solicited readers' opinions on proposed coinages, spellings, and Sino-Korean substitutions.

Overall, the tone of the two major North Korean linguistics journals of the late 1950s to mid-1960s was one of passionate, at times zealous, but still experimental and undirected attempts at concerted, even radical, language reform. A linguistic revolution was in the making, but it had not yet been fully centralized and subordinated to the demands and vision of the North Korean state.

Language Policy in North Korea Since the 1960s

After the ups and downs of language policy in the 1950s and the shelving of Kim Tu Bong's plans for radical orthographic reform, North Korean language policymakers since the 1960s have concentrated on creating a DPRK variety of standard Korean, promoting the variety of Korean spoken around P'yongyang to the status of standard. As part and parcel of this newer, more stable, and long-range language policy, North Korea has constructed an elaborate ideology and mythology around the Korean language. In terms of nationalism's need for language as a resource at both the instrumental and sentimental levels, whereas North Korea's first stabs at language planning in the 1950s dwelt more on practical considerations of script and orthography, policies since the 1960s have given equal if not more weight to sentimental issues. Thus North Korea has constructed its language policies according to the need to change and mold the Korean language to conform to the demands of North Korean communist ideology and nationalism.

Starting approximately in 1961 the scope of the journal *Language and Writing* seems to have broadened. The earlier stress on technical problems of lexicon and standard gave way to a broad emphasis on the proper use of Korean in all phases of communist life: suggestions on telephone manners and language in the household as well as articles outlining language-teaching policies in the schools supplemented the regular columns on language development after 1960. The August 1962 issue of *Language and Writing* carried the first article to mention Kim Il Sung's philosophy of *juche* (self-reliance), but only three months after this first and most explicit linkage of Kim Il Sung's nascent political philosophy and the country's equally young language policy, *Language and Writing* ceased to be published.

The next significant dates in the history of North Korean language planning were January 3, 1964, and May 14, 1966, when Kim Il Sung published his *Conversations with Linguists*.[18] These two *Conversations* were to determine language policy for the next two decades and beyond. In his 1964 *Conversation,* Kim Il Sung first addressed the issue of orthographic reform:

> If North and South Koreans come to write different characters, they will not understand [each other] when they write letters, and they will no longer be able to understand each others' newspapers, journals, and other printed materials. We communists absolutely cannot permit such an orthographic reform that would divide our own people.

Indeed, argued Kim Il Sung, if the writing system changed, the entire nation would become illiterate overnight. However, he did not completely reject the notion of *han'gŭl* reform and recommended that research be continued: he too admitted that the squarish *han'gŭl* was not perfect.

Kim Il Sung's 1964 *Conversation* was also important as a nationalist statement about the Korean language. The following lines are quoted frequently in the quarterly language-planning journal *Cultured Language Learning,* which appeared in 1968 in the place of *Language and Writing*: "Our language is rich in expression and can express both complicated thoughts and subtle emotions: it can move people and bring them both to tears and laughter. Because our language is capable of expressing clearly the rules of etiquette, it is also useful in people's communist moral upbringing." For Kim Il Sung, the Korean language was a tool or a weapon in the communist struggle. The major problem he envisioned was the process of cleansing the language of foreign, especially Sino-Korean, elements: "We have a good word like *tambay* [tobacco], so why should we use a word like [Sino-Korean] *yŏkch'o*? We should also use *toldari* [stone bridge] for [Sino-Korean] *sŏkkyo*." In cases where Sino-Korean/Korean doublets or competing forms exist,

---

18. The original Korean versions of these texts are reproduced as appendices in *Pukhan ŭi Ŏhak Hyŏngmyŏng* (North Korea's Linguistic Revolution), ed. Pukhan Ŏnŏ Yŏn'guhoe (Seoul: Tosŏ Ch'ulp'an Paegŭi, 1989). All translations are mine.

said Kim, the native forms should be promoted as much as possible.

Interestingly enough, Kim Il Sung conceded the necessity to teach Chinese characters in the schools if not to use them in daily life. As for other foreignisms, although Kim Il Sung conceded that it is acceptable to retain a word as basic as *ttŭrakttorŭ* (from the Russian for "tractor"), he urged research into the construction of a new technical terminology and called for cooperation with experts in the respective technological fields. He ended his 1964 *Conversation* by calling for the linguistic mobilization of North Korea and a social movement to spread the habit of "using Korean correctly."

In his 1966 *Conversation with Linguists*, Kim Il Sung dwelt on the question of standard language and defined in detail the role that linguists would have to play in the development of Korean. Citing frightening cases of language interference all around—leftover Japanisms, rampant Sino-Korean tendencies in workers' speech, corrupted speech habits of Koreans living near the Chinese border, pernicious influences from repatriated Koreans from Japan, and the fact that the only Korean elements visible in the South Korean newspapers were an occasional *ŭl* or *rŭl* (object markers) sandwiched between Chinese characters—Kim concluded that "we the communists must save the national character of our language and develop it further."

Kim stressed the utility of Korean regional dialects in enriching the language and expressed his interest in a new native Korean naming campaign that would prefer pure Korean elements over Sino-Korean ones for both place names and personal names.

Then Kim returned to the concept of "standard language":

> [W]e must replace the word "standard language" [*p'yojunŏ*] with a different term: if we use the word "standard," it is possible to interpret it incorrectly as meaning the Seoul standard language: thus we need not use it. Rather than taking P'yongyang speech . . . as standard and calling it *p'yojunŏ*, we who are building socialism should call it by another name. *Munhwa* [cultured language] is not all that great a term either, but this is the substitute that has emerged.

Thus, the new standard language was to take P'yongyang speech as its model. Recognizing that the older citizens were set in their linguistic habits, Kim called for new glossaries and word lists, but he emphasized above all the importance of education for the new cultured language.

After noting again the need to teach students at least to recognize certain Chinese characters, Kim Il Sung once more lamented the inconveniences of *han'gŭl*: it was too squarish, unsuited to mechanized printing, and difficult to type. However, Kim rejected any attempt at romanization of the script and alluded to a new linearized side-by-side 24-character alphabet:

> If we do it with Latin characters, we will not be able to express all our sounds. . . . Having seen the examples written "side-by-side" in Chu Si Gyŏng's posthumous writings, I see that it is not bad. It looks like we should improve on this and refine it. . . . However, I am not saying we should reform the script right away. Our people are one nation: therefore, we need not reform the writing until the entire country is united.

The above excerpts from Kim Il Sung's 1964 and 1966 *Conversations with Linguists* have formed the basis of all North Korean language policy since 1966. Not surprisingly, the *Conversations* were followed by supporting editorials, articles, a new dictionary, and the introductory issues of *Cultured Language Learning*. This new journal replaced all other linguistics journals and became the main discussion forum for linguists among themselves and with the masses.[19]

Language and Political Ideology in North Korea

The relationship between communist ideology and language policy had always been close in North Korea, but it received new attention and acquired historical justification after the late 1970s. Like its predecessors, *Cultured Language Learning* has consistently carried articles and editorials on the importance of the Korean language in building Korean communism. However, starting with the fourth issue of 1979, these ideological columns appeared in a new subsection entitled "Forward with the Linguistic Revolution!" Although this did not signify any change in policy, it reflected a new emphasis on the ideological side of developing P'yongyang speech as the new standard.

Articles typically begin with a hortatory quote from Kim Il Sung stressing the importance of the Korean language as a powerful weapon in the development of the nation's economy, culture, science, and tech-

---

19. Werner Sasse, "The 'Cultured Language': Implementation of a Policy in North Korea," *Korean Linguistics* 2 (1980), pp. 647–676.

nology. An article in the first issue of 1980 called for a campaign (*kkamppaniya* [from Russian: they have not "refined" this word yet]) to refine further the language along *juche* lines, and this campaign discourse has remained a feature of the language-planning journals.

From time to time articles have returned to the language aspect of the reunification issue. An article in the third issue of 1980 entitled "Our Profound Desire to Develop Our Language in a Unified Manner" hammered home the single people–single language–single writing system theme with quotations from Kim Il Sung, and a new series of articles begun in the third issue of 1981 treated the sociohistorical development of the Korean language. The second article in this series bore the title "The Korean Language Has Been Our Sole National Language Since Ancient Times." A related development in North Korean language planners' efforts to construct a "link with the glorious past" has been a series of articles on language during the Three Kingdoms (Koguryŏ, Silla, and Paekche) period (57 B.C.–668 A.D.), with a special emphasis on materials from Koguryŏ (37 B.C.–668 A.D.). An article in the fourth issue of 1981 claimed that, contrary to the claims of the "government-patronized scholars" of the South, the Korean peninsula already possessed a unified language during the Three Kingdoms period. Another article in the next issue went so far as to suggest that the early Koreans possessed a common form of writing even before the Three Kingdoms period and *idu*, a prealphabetic Korean transcription system based on Chinese and used in administrative contexts. This mysterious writing was called *sinji* or *sinsi*.

Most significant of all was an article in the third issue of 1982 entitled "After the Three Kingdoms Period, the Koguryŏ Language Played a Leading Role in the Development of Our Language." This article argued that it was under the powerful Korean dynasty of Koguryŏ that the Korean people and its language were at their strongest: Koguryŏ's speech, and not that of Silla as the "bourgeois corrupt scholars" of the South would have it, gave way to Koryŏ speech and then to modern Korean. Likewise, the North Korean scholars continuously lambast South Korean scholars for their blind belief in the Ural-Altaic heritage of the Korean language: for North Korean scholars, the Korean language is unique and thus cannot be related to other tongues.

The North Koreans also invoke recent history in their efforts at building up Korean as a nationalist symbol. The third issue of 1981 reminded readers of the harsh language policy under the Japanese occupation; the Japanese referred to their own language as the national language, flooded the Korean language with Japanese words, and eventually forbade the use of Korean. But since the Japanese are no longer on the scene, the North Koreans have invented a new myth of a similarly destructive U.S. policy vis-à-vis Korean. The fourth issue of 1980 quoted Kim Il Sung as urging the people to "extend the struggle against the policy of national-language linguicide of American imperialism."

The North Looks South: The Myth of a
U.S. Policy to Obliterate Korean

North Korea has attempted to elaborate a myth of primordial northern primacy in the prehistory of the language. The stress on the Koguryŏ language as the root of ancient Korean has been part of a larger North Korean myth that arose in reaction to the South Korean myth of an Altaic heritage for Korean. This latter myth was attributed by the North to a U.S. reactionary conspiracy to persuade South Koreans that their language was somehow derived, second-rate, and not autochthonous and hence fit for outside control.

The first major statement on this particular North Korean myth was a 164-page 1975 monograph entitled *The Reactionary Nature of American Imperialism's Policy to Eradicate the Korean Language*.[20] One of the first points made in the book is that the U.S. military government declared English the official language of Korean government. The book then contends that this particular policy has remained in place ever since and virtually every language-policy-related move made by the South Korean puppet regime was in fact just one more step in a conspiracy to push Korean aside and turn it into a gibberish mixture of American English, Chinese character words, and Japanese, thereby destroying a crucial element of the Korean national identity. American English had invaded the Korean language in the South; not only were official government documents in English, but so were street signs and store signs, advertisements, and names of institutions. The September 30, 1948, South Korean government resolution on the

---

20. Academy of Social Sciences, *Mije ŭi Chosŏnmal Malsal Chŏngch'aek ŭi Pandong-sŏng* (Resisting the American Policy of Korean Language Eradication) (P'yongyang: Sahoe Kwahak Ch'ulp'ansa, 1975).

exclusive use of *han'gŭl* was portrayed as a sly ruse perpetrated by the reactionary pro-U.S. regime to sneak in Chinese characters through the back door (recall the amendment to the resolution made the next day), thus further diluting the purity of the Korean language and increasing illiteracy in the South. What the South Koreans were portraying as a battle for exclusive *han'gŭl* usage was a cynical camouflage for exclusive Chinese character usage. As for the *han'gŭl* simplification controversy, this was a plot to jeopardize the financial support promised by the Rockefeller Foundation for the Han'gŭl Society's dictionary project; Syngman Rhee's attempt to reinstate the "old" spelling was the U.S. authorities operating behind the scenes to put in place the old missionary orthography, which was "easier for the Yankees to read." Thus, U.S. policy through the 1950s was purportedly to "subvert the social functioning of the Korean language in South Korean society."

The same monograph devoted several sections to criticism of the development of supposedly reactionary linguistic theory in South Korea. One unnamed South Korean scholar was castigated for his paper "Korean Christianity and the *Han'gŭl* Movement" for describing the U.S. missionaries as a positive influence in the establishment of exclusive *han'gŭl* usage. The alleged goal of U.S. "reactionary bourgeois linguistic theory" was to instill an inferiority complex vis-à-vis English in the minds of South Korean linguists. The classic structuralist notion of language as a system of signs was ridiculed in favor of a definition anchored in socialist thought: "the fundamental essence of language lies in the fact that it is a powerful weapon serving in the construction of revolution."

Special derision was saved for the Altaic theory, which painted the Korean language and culture as imports rather than acknowledging that these had existed on Korean soil, unchanged, since time immemorial:

> The un-scientificness of this theory lies in the fact that, instead of studying the Korean language on the basis of extensive research in allied fields, it blindly follows and toadies to the claims and opinions of Western and American scholars. . . . Because the Koreans are no longer [native to Korea] but a people transferred in from another locale, [they are] incapable of possessing [their] own indigenous traditions.[21]

---

21. *Mije ŭi Chosŏnmal Malsal Chŏngch'aek ŭi Pandong-sŏng*, pp. 62–63.

Likewise, the South Korean insistence that the Koguryŏ language differed from that of Silla and that this latter language preceded Middle Korean was portrayed as a plot to rationalize and perpetuate the division of Korea. Claims like these were repeated and elaborated frequently in the pages of *Cultured Language Learning* through the 1980s. Though there was usually a kernel of truth in what the North Koreans wrote, many of their claims were preposterous. Most pieces on the macaronic Korean of South Korea began with the following quotation from Kim Il Sung:

> Our Korean language, a valuable national resource of the masses and locus of our national pride, is suffering a dire crisis in South Korea. Through the policy of extermination of the Korean language of the American imperialists, our language is gradually losing its purity and turning into a gibberish mixture.

Thus, the tendency in South Korean not only to import a vast number of American English loanwords but also to make up nonsense English words was derided. Likewise, the use by some South Koreans of the Japanese hedges "*eto*" and "*maa*" was singled out for ridicule. An illustrative piece from 1985 cited the following example from a South Korean newspaper, with the foreign words in bold:

> **Misŭ** K'im ŭn **Orient'ŭ Ellekt'ŭrik**sa e kŭnmu, t'oegŭn kil e **K'osŭmosŭ** paekhwajŏm esŏ **shop'ing, P'ari** yangjangjŏm esŏ k'oorongt'aeksŭ ro wŏnp'isŭ rŭl match'uŏtta. Chyŏmŏn peik'ŭri esŏ korŭtk'e rŭl mŏkko **p'at'ŭnŏ** wa **K'ŭrisŭt'al Hot'el** esŏ yŏllin **K'akt'eil P'at'i** e ch'amgahago.

> [**Miss** Kim works at the **Orient Electric** Company; on the way home from work, she did some **shopping** at the **Cosmos** Department Store, and had a **colontack**[22] **one-piece** fitted at the **Paris** Western-style clothes store. She ate a **croquette** at the **German bakery,** and then attended a **cocktail party** with her **partner** at the **Crystal Hotel.**]

One unusual article in *Cultured Language Learning* called for North-South cooperation on linguistic issues. Another piece in the next issue claimed that the Chun Doo Hwan military dictatorship was un-

---

22. Korean is notorious for concocting new words based on English models that sound English (or foreign) but do not actually exist.

dermining Korean phonetic habits by promoting an English-like aspirated pronunciation of Korean /p/, /t/, and /k/, which are normally unaspirated or only mildly aspirated in proper names like Kimp'o Airport (K'imp'o), Pusan (P'usan), and Taegu (T'aegu).

The South Looks North

While South Korea has not developed any systematic portrait of language in the North, there are nonetheless certain stereotypes. North Korean neologisms (for example, the word ŏrumbosungi for "ice cream," which is aisuk'urim in Seoul) are periodically ridiculed on Seoul radio and television. The general idea is to make fun of the bungling North Korean attempts at coining new expressions.

South Korean linguists seem to have followed North Korean linguistic developments with a morbid fascination since the 1970s, when the first North-South talks revealed a startling degree of divergence in the language of the two sides and prompted the first South Korean research into language in the North. South Korean research since then has been marked by a finger-pointing tone and much indignation over accusations such as those described in the section above. Thus, Hong Yŏn Suk concluded in her study of North Korean language policy that "North Korea misuses the national language merely as a tool for Party policy. The rationale for the literacy campaigns was simply to render Party policy intelligible to the entire population."[23] Sim Jae Gi, professor of Korean language and literature at Seoul National University, was incensed at a 1986 piece alleging that South Korean children ask their mothers for money as follows:

Madŏ	ogane	tao
English: "mother"	Japanese: "money" (okane)	Korean: "please give"[24]

This North Korean example implied that the South Korean language was one-third English (in as basic a word as "mother"), one-third

---

23. Hong Yŏn Suk, Nambukhan Ŏnŏ Kaenyŏm ŭi Ijilhwa Yŏn'gu (Research on Divergence in Language Concepts Between North and South Korea) (Seoul: Research Institute of National Unification, 1976), pp. 62–63.

24. Sim Jae Gi, "Munhwaŏ wa Mal-tadŭmki" (The Cultured Language and Language Purification), Kugŏ Saenghwal 15 (1988), pp. 2–20.

Japanese, and one-third Korean. Lee Hyun Bok, another linguist at Seoul National University, wrote that Korea now had two different standard languages and that "such an unwelcome and really antinational move was unilaterally initiated by the North Korean side." Professor Lee was concerned to demonstrate the factors that had "caused P'yongyang speech to diverge so much from the Seoul standard," as if Seoul speech had been standing still since 1933. He concluded that

> Left alone to take its own natural course of development, the Korean language in the South has hardly changed except in some minor points. . . . The South-North linguistic gap has been made and widened by the radical and deliberate deviation of P['yongyang] S[tandard] from the traditional norm. . . . Unless a serious attempt is made by the two sides, especially by the North, to bridge the gap, the South-North divergence is bound to continue in future, leading eventually to an irreparable language barrier.[25]

Thus, the attitude among South Korean linguists seems to be one of betrayal—the North Koreans caught them when they weren't looking.

Stylistics in North Korea Since 1978

In 1980 it was predicted that stylistics would become an important topic in North Korean language planning for the decade,[26] and this prediction was borne out. Discussions of style were held about both spoken and written language. Concerning style in the spoken language, many articles in *Cultured Language Learning* urged North Koreans to use the honorifics properly and to develop a polite and modest delivery. Short vignettes in the journal presented everyday conversations on the telephone, in the park, at the bus stop, in school, and the like. An article in the fourth issue of 1981 urged schoolteachers to use the high formal style when addressing pupils: the teachers were a valuable model in the development of so-called refined speech in the children.

Some articles contained guidance on the proper protocol in greetings and titles, such as one entitled "How Do We Address Our Conversation Partner?" and others treated intonation and speed. The second

---

25. Lee Hyun Bok, "Differences in Language Use Between North and South Korea," *International Journal of the Sociology of Language* 82 (1990), pp. 71–86.

26. Sasse, "The 'Cultured Language.'"

issue of 1982 contained an article on the latter that recommended the
following speech velocities: 100 syllables per minute (spm) in normal
speech, 150–170 spm when reading poetry, 240–250 spm when reading a newspaper out loud, and 260–270 spm when reporting an event,
and finally, when quoting the Great Leader, "you should enunciate by
dropping speed and deepening your voice more than you would in
other situations."

Another interesting aspect of the encouragement of polite, refined
speech could be seen in an article in the second issue of 1981 entitled
"Women's Polite and Simple Speech." This article provided two pages
of examples of demure, polite, and feminine turns of phrase for the
consumption of Korea's mothers. As the lead-in quotation from Kim Il
Sung read,

> Of course, it is important for women to struggle for the progress of their
> liberation and their rights. . . . But beyond thinking of just their rights,
> liberation, and equality, they must not forget the inherent beautiful nat-
> ural gifts that they have possessed since ancient times. . . . Ladies must
> be ladylike. Polite and simple speech-style and carriage lifts peoples'
> spirits, and they are able to receive confidence, popularity, and respect.

Thus, women should be careful to use only the politest forms, even
when talking to people of lower status: rather than say, "Bring me the
book" (*Ch'aek ŭl kajyŏ wa*), they should say, "Would you please go
and get the book for me?" (*Ch'aek ŭl chom kajyŏda chugenni?*) or
"Won't you please get the book for me?" (*Ch'aek ŭl chom kajyŏda
churyŏm?*).

Recommendations on style in writing focused on repetition, the
proper use of mimetic words and proverbs, and simile and metaphor.
Articles with titles like "Synonyms and Word Choice" and "Describing Nature" provided guidance on written style; word lists gave
abundant examples of synonyms, antonyms, and mimetics. Repetition was supposed to increase the persuasive power of one's writing: *chŏryak hago chŏryak hago, tto chŏryak haja!* (Let's save,
save, and save!) and *chŏnjin, chŏnjin, t'ujaeng tto chŏnjin!* (Forward, forward, forward with the struggle!). Mimetics and other de-
scriptive words abounded; for example, the back cover of the second
issue of 1980 listed nearly 150 words—nouns, verbs, and adverbs—
having to do with "walking."

Orthographic Reform Since the Late 1970s

The issue of orthographic reform turned up again in two issues of *Cultured Language Learning* from the end of the 1970s: "On the Problem of the Number of Graphs in Orthographic Reform" in the third issue of 1979 and "On the Problem of the Shape of Graphs in Orthographic Reform" in the first issue of 1980. Both articles treated their subject in considerably greater technical detail than the usual heavily politicized articles. The 1979 article quoted Kim Il Sung's 1964 and 1966 remarks on orthographic reform but went on to point out the inconveniences of some of the graphically complex vowel signs.

The 1979 article also noted the inconsistency in writing the reinforced consonants, which are single phonemes, with two graphs and raised the criticism of *han'gŭl*'s squarish shape and unsuitability for printing. The inconsistency stems from the fact that in an ideally phonemic writing system, each unitary phoneme is represented by a unitary graph. Since the reinforced consonants in Korean are separate phonemes, it would be more consistent to write them with separate, independent graphs instead of doubled preexisting graphs. The article also noted that a revised horizontal, side-by-side system of 24 characters was in use in telegraph communications: "This is because the telegraph machines used today to send telegrams have only a limited number of keys. Especially those telegraph machines in general use throughout the world today have no more than 20 to 30 keys." Thus, the anonymous authors of the article recommended a new orthography with fewer than 30 graphs and seemed to favor a more strictly phonetic system, writing that "if a phonetic writing system is to express sounds in the most logical fashion, it should strive to express each sound with one symbol."

The 1980 article on graph shapes in orthographic reform quoted Kim Il Sung as saying, "As far as possible, we should write 'side-by-side' so as to facilitate printing and to render words easier to understand." The article also pointed out a number of considerations to be kept in mind while reforming the graph shapes. All this suggests that radical script reform was under serious consideration as a policy option in the late 1970s and early 1980s.

North Korean Developments Since 1986

The year 1986 was a milestone in Korean language planning because it heralded the 20th anniversary of Kim Il Sung's 1966 *Conversation with Linguists.* The third issue of *Cultured Language Learning* from that year carried a report on a "scientific discussion meeting" in honor of the occasion. Perhaps more significantly, the journal *Korean Language and Literature,* defunct since 1960, resumed publication in April 1986. The publication of *Cultured Language Learning* continued apace, but the reappearance in 1986 of the specialized and academic *Korean Language and Literature* signaled an easing of the 20-year-old concentrated effort to create a new standard language.

Whereas earlier a number of linguistic topics either were left unexplored, being considered irrelevant to the immediate goals of the cultured language movement, or were simply subordinated to the general campaign to turn the Korean language into a weapon of communist revolution, in the last decade the spectrum of linguistic research in North Korea seems to have widened considerably. The third issue of *Cultured Language Learning* in 1994 contained the articles "Some Problems in Korean Dialectology Research," "An Understanding of 'Environmental' Linguistics" (the first mention I have seen in North Korean literature of Noam Chomsky), and "A Study of the Creation and Use of the Jurchen Script."

Nonetheless, issues of the journal since 1986 have continued to hammer away at the same old themes. A typical issue is divided into six major subsections: a few lead editorials related to the writings of Kim Il Sung on language, and more recently, to the writings of Kim Jong Il on language and literature, language in film, and the like; "Let's Write More Topical Works"; "The Literary Arts and Language Form"; "Cultured Language Education in School"; "Language and Our Life"; and "Knowledge of Our Language." Other regular features include "Ask Anything at All" (write-ups of questions sent in to the National Language Evaluation Committee), "New Books," "Proverbs," "Telephone Talk," "Vocabulary Notebook" (newly refined words), "Common Sense," "Letters to the Editor," and so on. Two issues from 1994 contained lead essays by Kim Jong Il on the *juche*-based development of the Korean language, several discussions of Kim Il Sung's style in his memoirs, analyses of some of Kim Jong Il's neologisms as well as of his written style, pieces on mimetics in 18th-century traditional novels, the use of ellipsis in literary prose, the receding of P'yongyang dialect in the wake of the spread of the cultured language, some new agricultural terms, and place-names related to Tan'gun.

A most curious point, and perhaps also an appropriate one on which to finish this section, is that the second issue of 1994 contained two articles on script: "The *Hunmin Chŏngŭm*—Our Most Excellent Indigenous National Script" and "The *Sinji* Writing Is Our Nation's Original Script," the latter by no less a scholar than Yu Yŏl of the original Korean Language Society. Yu Yŏl asserted that in connection with the discovery by North Korean archaeologists of the tomb of Tan'gun, whose bones were claimed to be carbon-dated to 5011 years before 1994, North Korean linguists also uncovered the ancient Korean script in use during the kingdom of ancient Chosŏn. The author explains that the *sin* of *sinji* or *sinsi* meant "big" and that the *ji* meant "person"; hence "*sinji* script" means the "great person's script" or "king's script" and indicates the writing system in use during Tan'gun's time. Yu Yŏl reproduced the only extant 16 graphs of the *sinji* script and alleged that the graphs were so distinct and systematic as to be distinguished from the scripts of all of Korea's neighbors:

> We can see that this is a script of an extremely refined, high order. Of course, since we have only 16 graphs, this cannot be seen as a text showing all of the *sinji* script systematically. Thus, it is still impossible to say concretely how many graphs this script had, what sounds they represented, and so forth.

Nonetheless, Yu Yŏl asserted that the script must have been a phonetic one and a syllabary at that.

Conclusion

Perhaps because of the nature of the Korean language, writing and orthography have become the centers of political controversy on more than one occasion since the invention of the Korean script in the 15th century. The significant gap in Korean between abstract underlying phonological form and the concrete surface substance of these forms in pronunciation led from the very inception of the Korean script to confrontations between those who would write according to phonemic principles and those who adhered to morphophonemic principles.

In the 20th century the Japanese colonial government and ROK president Syngman Rhee opted for the surface solution against vociferous opposition from the scholars of the Korean Language Society, who championed the 1933 *Unified Spelling* and its more abstract solutions.

In North Korea, radical reform in the guise of an ultra-morphophonemic solution which would have spelled irregular verbs right out of existence and pushed through another of Chu Si Gyŏng's ideas—horizontal, side-by-side writing—went to the brink, but it was reined in with the purge of Kim Tu Bong in 1958.

Since the end of the 1950s *han'gŭl* controversy in South Korea, and due perhaps in part to language views inherited from the importation of Anglo-American linguistics after the Korean War, language policy in the ROK has been an inconsistent and half-hearted effort. Since the abortive new Korean orthography and the purge of Kim Tu Bong, language policy in North Korea has become an important part of the DPRK's socialist revolution. North Korea has indeed worked systematically to mold the Korean language into a pure, nationalist weapon of communism.

A comparison of the official institutions responsible for language policy in South and North Korea is instructive. South Korea only created its National Language Research Office in 1984, which was recently promoted to National Language Research Institute and placed under the Ministry of Culture and Sports. In North Korea the National Language Evaluation Committee with its 18 terminological subcommittees is attached directly to the cabinet and boasts a staff and budget far more robust than those of its ROK counterpart. Even the names of these two institutions are indicative of the language views behind them: in English, the ROK's institution calls itself the National *Academy* [emphasis added] of the Korean Language, a term that belies what has been called a "fundamental belief that language is in decadence"; academies are "cosmetic rather than remedial cultural accretions." One prominent linguist juxtaposes these academies to language-planning boards like that of the DPRK, with their "strong post-scientific sense of progress and positivism."[27]

A curious mixture of language, orthography, and political ideologies has defined the Korean *questione della lingua* in the 20th century.

> Every time that the language question appears, in one way or another, it signifies that a series of other problems are beginning to impose themselves: the formation and enlargement of the ruling class [followed by] the need to stabilise the most intimate and secure links between that

27. Joseph, *Eloquence and Power*, p. 112.

ruling group and the popular national masses, that is, to reorganise cultural hegemony.[28]

The stark contrast between North and South Korean language policies and the ideologies behind them also mirrors the observation that in standardization situations, "the controllers will either be disposed toward upper-class usage or will be strong democratic ideologues."[29] Clearly South Korea exemplifies the former and North Korea the latter case. A linguist with a slightly different angle on the North-South contrast posits that "it is the duty of every State to measure the cost of, and more generally, to evaluate, in accord with the energies it intends to invest in its defense, the importance it places in its *linguistic sovereignty* [emphasis in original]."[30] It would appear that the ROK has placed far less value on and invested much less energy in its linguistic sovereignty than the DPRK.

The history of the Korean *questione della lingua* since Liberation and the Korean War should also prompt us to ask if Korea has ever really had a unified standard national language. South Korean linguists like Lee Hyun Bok,[31] who by confusing the concepts of "standard national language" and "prestige variety" would have us believe that Seoul speech "has been taken as standard Korean for over 500 years," miss the point. The point is that "standard national languages, to be learned in schools and written, let alone spoken, by more than a smallish elite, are constructs of varying, but often brief, age."[32] They are ideologies,[33] cultural artifacts,[34] and a form of symbolic domination.[35]

Another scholar writes that "language standardization is one of the more dominant instruments for inducing common social expectations

28. Cited in Joseph, *Eloquence and Power*, p. 206.

29. Joseph, *Eloquence and Power*, p. 118.

30. See Claude Hagège, "Voies et destins de l'action humaine sur les langues," in *Language Reform: History and Future*, Vol. 6, ed. Istvan Fodor and Claude Hagège (Hamburg: Buske Verlag, 1983), pp. 1–8.

31. Lee Hyun Bok, "Differences in Language Use Between North and South Korea," p. 72.

32. Eric Hobsbawm, "Introduction: Inventing Traditions," in *The Invention of Tradition*, ed. Eric Hobsbawm and Terence Ranger (Cambridge: Cambridge University Press, 1983), p. 14.

33. See James Milroy and Lesley Milroy, *Authority in Language: Investigating Language Prescription and Standardization* (New York: Routledge, 1985).

34. See Einar Haugen, "The Scandinavian Languages as Cultural Artifacts," in *Language Problems of Developing Nations*, ed. Joshua Fishman et al. (New York: John Wiley & Sons, 1968), pp. 267–284.

35. See P. Bourdieu, *Ce que parler veut dire* (Paris: Fayard, 1982), p. 34ff.

among a citizenry" and goes on to note that "the more conservative a nation becomes, the more it uses language as a constraint against social, political, religious, and ethnic minorities in order to deny them full access to the mainstream culture. This process . . . relates to the needs and concerns of the power elite of a nation."[36] Language standardization is achieved through language planning, and "it is high time that we recognize that language planning is undertaken by those who are in a position of power to undertake such policies and is therefore designed to serve and protect their interests."[37]

The extent of divergence observable between the emerging national standard Korean languages of the ROK and the DPRK is far greater than one would normally expect after the passage of a mere four decades.[38] Korea is in a classic pluricentric-language situation. A pluricentric language is a language with more than one center; that is, it is used as the standard language, but with differing norms, in more than one country (as Spanish and German are). This circumstance is due to a combination of the limited extent and depth of standardization prior to national division and to the differing societal attitudes and ideologies regarding language and language planning that have developed in the ROK and the DPRK since the 1950s. It is a commonplace now to caution against comparisons of the two Koreas to former East and West Germany, and language is no exception. The German language in 1945 had been the object of concentrated standardization for well over one and a half centuries. In Korea, concerted standardization efforts did not get under way until the late 1930s, after which they were stymied first by Japanese colonial oppression, then by national division and the Korean War. For all practical purposes, language stan-

---

36. Robert St. Clair, "From Social History to Language Attitudes," in *Attitudes Towards Language Variation: Social and Applied Contexts*, ed. Ellen Bouchard Ryan and Howard Giles (London: Edward Arnold, 1982), pp. 164–174.

37. G. Williams, "Review of J. Fishman (ed.), 1980: Variance and Invariance in Language Form and Context (*International Journal of the Sociology of Language*, 26)," *Journal of Multilingual and Multicultural Development* 2 (1981), pp. 219–225. Cited in Joseph, *Eloquence and Power*, p. 221.

38. See Kim Chin Wu, "Divergence in Language Policies in Korea"; Kim Chin Wu, "Korean as a Pluricentric Language," in *Pluricentric Languages: Differing Norms in Different Nations*, ed. Michael Clyne (New York: Mouton de Gruyter, 1992), pp. 239–260; and Kim Chin Wu, "Underlying Causes of Linguistic Divergence in Korea," in *Yŏnsan To Su-hŭi Sŏnsaeng Hwa'gap Kinyŏm Nonch'ong* (Commemorative Theses in Honor of the 60th Birthday of Professor To Su Hŭi) (1994), pp. 965–975.

dardization has proceeded since the late 1950s in two separate states, each isolated from linguistic developments in the other. Linguistic unification in Korea will not be easy.

Few other nations, save perhaps Turkey and one or two others, have approached language policy and planning in a broader, more systematic, and (apparently) more successful fashion than North Korea. North Korean language policy has from its inception been intimately connected with political and ideological issues. It is interesting that a controversial issue like script reform—an issue closely related to the problem of Korean cultural unity and political reunification—should have reappeared 20 years after the debacle of Kim Tu Bong and his six new letters in 1958. It is probably safe to say that any serious attempt at introducing new, more efficient graphs will be a sign that the North Korean regime has given up the notion of unification, peaceful or not, and has resigned itself to building a new people and nation, replete with a new language and alphabet.

In the meantime, before Korean unification does come, South Korean linguists and language planners will have to swallow their indignation, stop their finger pointing, and think long and hard about issues like linguistic sovereignty and language planning. The promotion of the National Language Research Office to academy status is a step in the right direction, but South Koreans would do well to note the example of Sweden, where society feels and believes that "language is somehow a national resource which should be tended and taken care of, and improved if possible"; it is "possible to plan and execute change in language"; it is "appropriate to have national institutions concerned with language planning"; and "it is appropriate for someone who has a language problem to go to a national institution and ask for technical help."[39] As of 1993 the ROK National Academy of the Korean Language was still struggling for a reasonable budget for its small-scale operation within the Ministry of Culture and Sports allocations and had little or no expertise in, or research activity concerning, the language-planning experiences of other nations. Indeed, most of the ROK literature on language policy from the past two decades is marked by an almost total lack of knowledge of the vast literature on language policy and

---

39. Charles Ferguson, "National Attitudes Toward Language Planning," in *Language in Public Life*, Georgetown University Round Table on Languages and Linguistics 1979, ed. James E. Alatis and G. Richard Tucker (Washington, D.C.: Georgetown University Press, 1979), pp. 51–60.

planning in the world's major languages. This is to be contrasted with the situation of the North Koreans, who in the late 1940s and 1950s were paying close attention to the language planning experiences of the USSR, the PRC, and the Mongolian People's Republic.

Whatever one may think about language planning in general and about North Korea's so-called successes in language planning over the past four decades in particular, there is no question that Korean unification will present a language-planning problem of serious magnitude. It is also safe to assume that, in one form or another, the *questione della lingua* will surface again in a unified Korea.

Chronology

Compiled from issues of *The U.S.-Korea Review* published by The Korea Society.

July 1993

26   DPRK leader Kim Il Sung's younger brother, Kim Yong Ju, makes his first official appearance since May 1975 at the dedication of a monument in P'yongyang "to the victory in the fatherland war." The younger Kim, once seen as a potential successor to Kim Il Sung, is described as a former vice-minister of the State Administration Council and is ranked between Chon Pyon Ho and Han Song Yong, numbers 10 and 12, respectively, in party hierarchy.

31   After months of investigation into the ROK's Yulgok arms-procurement project (a military equipment program named after the 16th-century official Yi I, also known as Yulgok), two former defense ministers, Lee Jong Koo and Lee Sang Hoon, are indicted on graft charges. Former Air Force chief of staff Han Chu Sok is indicted on a similar charge. Six defense-contractor executives are fined for having bribed Lee Sang Hoon and Han Joo Sok.

August 1993

3–10   North Korea allows three inspectors from the International Atomic Energy Agency (IAEA) into the country for the first time since May. The IAEA charges in a statement that "the overall degree of access granted is

August 1993 *(continued)*

still insufficient for the agency to discharge its responsibilities."

4   In a report issued on Prime Minister Kiichi Miyazawa's last day in office, Tokyo for the first time acknowledges that the Japanese military forced Asian and European women, called "comfort women," to work in army brothels during World War II and offers its first apology for those atrocities. In his first speech to parliament, the new prime minister Morihiro Hosokawa announces, "I would like to take this opportunity to express our profound remorse and apologies for the fact that Japan's actions, including acts of aggression and colonial rule, caused unbearable suffering and sorrow for so many people."

7   The ROK launches its third submarine, the *Choe Mun Son*, which is also the second to be built by the Korean yard at Mokp'o. At the launch President Kim proclaims, "We are one of the most peace-loving peoples in the world. But we were humiliated several times since we lacked the power to defend ourselves. Such a humiliation must not be repeated."

9   ROK president Kim Young Sam orders the dismantling of the former Japanese colonial government building in downtown Seoul, currently home to the National Museum, to complete the full restoration of Kyongbok Palace, the royal sanctuary of the Choson dynasty. "It is desirable for the nation to dismantle the former Japanese colonial government building as soon as possible in order to recover the respect and self-esteem of the Korean people," declares President Kim.

12   In a long-awaited anti-corruption move made in a nationally televised address, ROK president Kim Young Sam issues a Presidential Emergency Order effective immediately banning the use of incorrect or false names on bank and brokerage accounts. The ban is intended to

bring about economic justice. "Without real-name financial accounts, a sound democracy cannot flower,"
notes Kim. Users of wrong names, whether false or
borrowed, have two months to change false names on
accounts to their real names, after which fines will be
levied. The Korean composite stock price index falls
32.37 points, or 4.5 percent, in shortened trading on
"Black Friday," the largest one-day drop in the market's
37-year history.

17   The Board of Audit and Inspection sends letters to former ROK presidents Chun Doo Hwan and Roh Tae
Woo, asking Chun about his role in the construction of
the Peace Dam and Roh about his part in the Yulgok
arms-procurement project. Chun and Roh refuse to answer the board's questions, making open statements on
the issues instead.

18   Striking workers at Hyundai Heavy Industries Company accept a tentative pay agreement, ending a seven-
week strike. On July 21 workers from Hyundai Motor
Company, on strike since June 16, narrowly voted to
accept a package agreement with Hyundai management.

19   The Maxtor Corporation in San Jose, California, which
designs and makes high-performance Winchester data-
storage products, announces that Hyundai Electronics
Industries Company will invest $150 million in Maxtor
and will receive about 19.4 million shares, or about 40
percent of its common stock. Under a signed letter of
intent for partnership, Hyundai may not acquire more
than 45 percent of Maxtor.

The ROK officially asks Russia for restitution and bilateral negotiations for compensation for the 1983 down-
ing of Korean Air Lines (KAL) 007, which killed 259
people. In Moscow the Russian commission investigating the crash concludes that the tragedy resulted from

August 1993 *(continued)*

"a series of blunders and mistakes" by KAL pilots and that the former Soviet Union "bears no guilt for this incident."

20   An Anglo-French consortium GEC Alsthom, defeating a German bid, is awarded priority in negotiating a contract to supply trains for a 250-mile high-speed rail line to link Seoul with Pusan. The line, with a contract estimated at $13.2 billion, is scheduled to begin service in 2001.

24   In Seoul North Korean defector Im Young Sun, 30, describes conditions of widespread hardship and growing political dissent within the DPRK. Im, who identifies himself as a first lieutenant in the North Korean army, tells of an alleged nuclear accident that occurred as North Korea tried to move a reactor at Yongbyon to an undisclosed site to hide it from an international inspection taking place. He also reports pervasive food shortages. Im claims that ten army generals were executed in late 1992 for plotting against Kim Il Sung and his son Kim Jong Il. "Quite a few people are dissatisfied with Kim Il Sung," says Im. "We can't do anything because if we try, we are destroyed, we are killed." None of Im's reports can be confirmed.

31   A five-member delegation from the IAEA led by Deputy Director General Brund Pellard arrives in P'yongyang for five days of discussions with North Korea on nuclear inspections.

September 1993

27   From Vienna the IAEA announces that North Korea has canceled new talks on nuclear inspections. "Regrettably, the readiness of North Korea to implement the safeguards agreement appears to have diminished rather than grown," says IAEA head Hans Blix.

November 1993

1   In Seoul district court, Chung Ju Young, the 78-year-old CEO of Hyundai, is convicted of embezzlement and presidential election law violations and is sentenced to three years in prison. Chung is found to have illegally diverted $63.6 million from the Hyundai Group to finance his 1992 presidential bid on his United People's Party ticket.

After IAEA director general Hans Blix tells the UN General Assembly that the DPRK's noncompliance with international safeguards "has been widening," the assembly adopts a nine-point resolution urging North Korea to comply with IAEA demands for a full inspection of its nuclear facilities. The resolution, jointly submitted by 51 nations, is adopted by a vote of 140 to 1. North Korea votes against the resolution; 9 nations abstain, including China, Cuba, Iraq, and Vietnam.

4–5   The United States and the ROK hold the 25th annual Security Consultative Meeting and the 15th Military Committee Meeting in Seoul. The United States and the ROK agree to postpone the decision to suspend the annual Team Spirit military training exercise and to put off the second phase of the pullout of U.S. forces from the ROK. The ROK agrees to a $260 million share of the expense of maintaining U.S. forces in Korea, a $40 million increase from 1993. The United States and the ROK agree that peacetime operational control of the Korean Armed Forces, currently under the authority of the commander of the Korea-U.S. Combined Forces Command (CFC), is to be transferred to South Korea by December 1, 1994. The two sides discuss the transfer of wartime control over the U.S. Seventh Fleet to the CFC to increase U.S. strategic support in the event of war on the Korean peninsula.

6–8   Japanese prime minister Morihiro Hosokawa arrives in Kyongju, South Korea, and apologizes to Koreans for their suffering under Japanese colonial rule. "From the

November 1993 *(continued)*

depths of my heart, I deeply repent and apologize for the unbearable sufferings the people of the Korean peninsula underwent during Japan's colonial rule," says Hosokawa. "I was deeply impressed by the prime minister's frank attitude, which past Japanese prime ministers have not had," commented President Kim. "We must open a new era."

8   The ROK announces plans to open and "internationalize" its economy by easing or lifting various restrictions on foreigners. Under the new reform plan, the ROK will reduce the number of industries that are off-limits to foreign investors from 224 to 92 by 1998. Among other changes, the corporate tax rate on foreign firms will be cut from 25 percent to 15 percent, and foreign companies and joint ventures with foreign participation will be allowed to purchase land for factories and housing without seeking prior government approval beginning in March 1994.

9   The DPRK presents a proposal to create a three-phase plan to develop a 621-square-kilometer Free Economic and Trade Zone linking Rajin, Sonbong, and the Tumen River. The proposal, presented at the workshop of the UN Development Program-sponsored Tumen River Area Development Program in Seoul, is reported to span 17 years at a cost of $1.52 billion. The forum is attended by representatives from South and North Korea, China, Russia, and Mongolia.

15   The ROK and the United States hold a joint ten-day military training exercise involving the majority of ROK and U.S. troops stationed in Korea, the 28th annual training exercise. The counter-espionage exercise "Hwarang Drill" is held simultaneously.

19   Former ROK defense minister Lee Chong Ku is sentenced to three years in prison and fined 180 million won for accepting bribes in connection with the Yulgok

military buildup program. Earlier, former defense minister Lee Sang Hoon receives a suspended sentence and a 30-million-won fine for accepting bribes related to Yulgok.

20–23 President Kim Young Sam visits Washington for a summit meeting with President Bill Clinton. President Kim receives an honorary doctorate from The American University and the Averell Harriman Democracy Award from the National Democratic Institute and is feted at the White House.

30 At P'anmunjom, North Korea turns over the remains of 33 UN soldiers killed in the Korean War.

December 1993

2 In Vienna IAEA director general Hans Blix tells the IAEA board of governors meeting that the DPRK's refusal to allow nuclear-related inspections means that the IAEA "cannot provide any meaningful assurance" that the DPRK is not producing new plutonium, falling just short of declaring that the continuity of safeguards has been broken by the DPRK.

In response to CIA director R. James Woolsey's comments on "Larry King Live" on November 30 that armed conflict cannot be ruled out on the Korean peninsula and that the United States must be prepared to deal with such a conflict, North Korea responds, "This is an exasperating statement that could be uttered by none other than a trigger-happy element intending to push the situation on the Korean peninsula to the brink of war."

3 In New York the DPRK presents Tom Hubbard, deputy secretary of state for East Asia and Pacific Affairs, with an offer to open some of its nuclear sites to interna-

December 1993 *(continued)*

tional inspection, but it restricts international inspectors at the two most critical installations. The DPRK's proposal calls for linking the arrival of international inspectors to two announcements: the United States and the ROK would jointly announce the cancellation of Team Spirit, and the United States and the DPRK would set a date for a new round of high-level deliberations at which broader economic and political relations would be discussed. "Obviously, we're not entirely satisfied with the response of the North Koreans to the proposal we put forward," says President Clinton. "There must be unrestricted access to all declared sites," declares IAEA spokesman David Kyd. "Restrictions on the two facilities are not negotiable."

7   At P'anmunjom, North Korea turns over the remains of 31 UN soldiers killed in the Korean War.

9   The DPRK convenes the Sixth Session of the Ninth Supreme People's Assembly (SPA). The younger brother of DPRK leader Kim Il Sung, Kim Yong Ju, 71, is appointed to the Politburo and is named as one of the nation's three vice presidents.

      The DPRK Foreign Ministry says that its offer to the United States to open a limited number of sites to nuclear inspection was the largest concession it could make. The DPRK also says, however, that once the two countries can agree on a package solution it will agree to full inspections of the sites it had denied to the IAEA. "We have encouraged the United States to show some flexibility," says an official from the ROK's Foreign Ministry.

13   At the GATT negotiations in Geneva, the ROK agrees to open its rice markets with a ten-year grace period for tariffication and minimum market access of at least 1–4 percent of its rice consumption during the grace period.

14   At P'anmunjom North Korea turns over the remains of 33 UN soldiers, bringing to 114 the number of remains returned by the DPRK to the UN command this year.

16   President Kim Young Sam, responding to public backlash over the opening of the ROK's rice market, replaces Prime Minister Hwang In Sung with Lee Hoe Chang, the popular former Supreme Court justice and head of the Bureau of Audit and Inspection who played a major role in President Kim's anti-corruption campaign.

January 1994

5   In Washington the United States and the DPRK reach an agreement in principle on the inspection of the DPRK's seven declared nuclear sites.

9   According to the Korean Maritime and Port Administration, ferry service between the ROK and the PRC, connecting Inchon with Dalian and Pusan with Shanghai, will commence in April at the earliest.

11   The ROK's ten largest *chaebol* exported $47.32 billion in 1993, or 57.4 percent of total exports, reports the Ministry of Trade, Industry, and Energy. Samsung, Hyundai, Lucky-Goldstar, and Daewoo account for 40.2 percent of the ROK's total exports of $82.44 billion. Samsung was the nation's largest exporter, accounting for 12.7 percent of total exports, up from 11.2 percent in 1992.

14   Japanese police raid companies in the Tokyo area suspected of shipping to North Korea electronic equipment that could be used in missile development in violation of export controls. Russia is reported to sell 40 decommissioned submarines to the DPRK through a Japanese intermediary. The Toen Trading Co. says that it sold the subs destined for the port of Rajin on North Korea's east coast to the DPRK on the condition that they be used for scrap metal.

January 1994 *(continued)*

22   In Vienna the DPRK again rejects IAEA calls for nuclear inspections, ruling out routine or ad hoc inspections of its facilities under the Nuclear Nonproliferation Treaty. Noting its special position outside the regime treaty, the DPRK calls the detailed IAEA inspection demands absurd.

25   The ruling Democratic Liberal Party and the opposition Democratic Party of the ROK agree to hold the next parliamentary elections in April 1996 and the next presidential election in December 1997.

27   The Reverend Billy Graham arrives in the DPRK (his second visit) for a six-day stay. Reverend Graham conveys a verbal message from President Clinton to North Korean president Kim Il Sung. Leaving the DPRK, Reverend Graham carries a message from Kim Il Sung for President Clinton.

Following a request from Gen. Gary E. Luck, commander of United States forces in Korea, the United States is reported to be looking favorably at the deployment of a battalion of Patriot missiles to support ROK defenses against possible North Korean aggression. The request from General Luck is reported to have been made last year to the Joint Chiefs of Staff in an outline of flexible deterrence options. Responding to the proposed Patriot deployment and the recent visit to Seoul by CIA director R. James Woolsey, the DPRK says that "the military and intelligence measures taken by the United States are premeditated provocative measures which will bring the situation on the Korean peninsula to an extremely reckless phase of war."

February 1994

1   The ROK's Ministry of Trade, Industry, and Energy announces that merchandise trade between North and South increased 2.6 percent to $177.9 million on a customs

clearance basis for 1993. North Korean exports grew 4.9 percent to $170.8 million, while imports of South Korean goods fell 3.3 percent to $7.1 million. From 1989 to 1993, North Korean shipments totaled $470.3 million, while South Korean exports totaled $24.5 million.

The U.S. State Department releases its annual report on human rights. For the ROK, the report concludes "the overall human rights situation improved significantly . . . a result of the fundamental shift in attitude and policy of the Kim administration." The report is critical of human rights conditions in the DPRK, moving the Korean Central News Agency to call the report "a brazen interference in the internal affairs of our country and an intolerable insult to the socialist system of our style centering on the popular masses."

By voice vote, the U.S. Senate approves a "Sense of the Senate" amendment introduced by Sen. John McCain (R-Ariz.) urging the administration to continue support for U.S.-ROK military exercises; ensure sufficient military forces, including Patriot anti-missile defense systems, to defend South Korea; seek consensus on economic sanctions isolating North Korea; and ensure that resolving the issue of arms proliferation in the DPRK is an urgent national security priority.

9   After a meeting of the ROK National Security Council, ROK president Kim Young Sam says that the government "will not abandon its efforts to resolve the North Korean nuclear problem through dialogue, even if it is referred to the Security Council. Even if dialogue fails, the government has to prepare for everything so that the people can trust their government and have confidence in the government with regard to their safety and survival." President Kim faults exaggerated reports from the United States that he says can aggravate tensions on both sides of the peninsula.

February 1994 *(continued)*

21   The IAEA says in Washington that the DPRK is "linking the date of the receipt of the IAEA inspection with the dates of . . . action measures . . . related to currently expected contacts" between the United States and the DPRK. "We have indicated publicly, and they certainly know, that we're willing to discuss the date for the third round [of high-level U.S.-DPRK] talks when inspections have commenced," says State Department spokesman Mike McCurry.

26   The IAEA announces in Vienna that its safeguard inspectors have received entry visas from the DPRK and that the team (six inspectors and a technician) will arrive in P'yongyang on March 1 to begin inspection of the DPRK's seven declared nuclear facilities.

March 1994

3   As IAEA inspectors arrive in P'yongyang to begin inspections at the DPRK's Yongbyon nuclear facility, the United States announces its agreement to meet with the DPRK on March 21 in Geneva to begin a third round of negotiations. The ROK government announces the suspension of the Team Spirit military exercise with the United States for 1994, with the United States in agreement. Representatives from the ROK and DPRK resume discussion in the joint security area at P'anmunjom on the exchange of special envoys who will address inter-Korean issues, including the nuclear issue. North-South talks break down after the North demands that the planned Patriot missile deployment be scrapped.

9   In London *Jane's Sentinel* reports that the DPRK is developing two new ballistic missiles. In Washington, CIA director R. James Woolsey confirms intelligence reports on the DPRK's new long-range missiles, the Taepo-dong-1 and the Taepo-dong-2, named after the sites where they are under development. The missiles have ranges of 1,000 and 2,000 miles, respectively.

According to Woolsey, North Korea is "a key part of this sort of devil's brew of three or four countries together with Iran, Iraq, and Libya that are engaged directly and indirectly in terrorism as well as in proliferation of weapons of mass destruction."

16 In Vienna IAEA inspectors returning from North Korea report that the DPRK had severed a seal installed last year on the entrance to a "hot cell" for handling radioactive material. In addition the inspectors are not allowed to search for telltale radioactive particles in ventilation and filtration equipment near the hot cell. On March 21 the board of governors of the IAEA says that it is not in the position to verify that there has been no diversion of nuclear materials at the facility, and it adopts a resolution referring the North Korean nuclear issue to the UN Security Council by a vote of 25 in favor, 1 against (Libya), with 5 abstentions (China, India, Indonesia, Brazil, and Lebanon). North Korea says it will regard international sanctions against it over the nuclear issue as a declaration of war.

17 In Seoul North Korea is reported to have designated the northwestern coast from Sinuiju to Nampo as its second Free Economic and Trade Zone, joining the Rajin-Sonbong zone on the northeast coast.

24 In Moscow Russian deputy foreign minister Vitaly Churkin proposes that a multilateral conference be held to resolve growing tensions with North Korea. The conference would include Russia, the United States, Japan, China, and North and South Korea.

24–30 ROK president Kim Young Sam visits Japan, where he meets with Prime Minister Morihiro Hosokawa, addresses the Japanese Diet, and receives an honorary degree from Waseda University. During his visit Kim renews his hope for a visit to the ROK by Emperor Akihito and Empress Michiko. President Kim proposes

March 1994 *(continued)*

that the ROK, Japan, and China undertake joint endeavors including the development of Asian medicines, standardization of Chinese characters, and formation of a Northeast Asian environmental consultative organization. Returning to Seoul after meetings in Beijing with President Jiang Zemin and Premier Li Peng, President Kim declares the "just-concluded visits have given the ROK an opportunity to open an Asian-Pacific era with Japan and China . . . [and] have opened a new horizon in ROK-Japanese cooperation and ROK-Sino cooperation."

30   The ROK Ministry of Finance announces that as of next month U.S. investors will be able to trade Korean stocks in the United States by investing in depository receipts. The ministry allows 250 blue-chip companies of the 699 listed on the Korea Stock Exchange to issue to Americans the dollar-denominated depository receipts, taking the already-circulating issues as security.

31   After days of negotiation over wording, UN Security Council president Jean-Bernard Merimée issues a statement calling on the DPRK to allow the IAEA to complete its inspection activities begun on February 15, 1994.

April 1994

2   The Bank of Korea announces that the ROK's gross national product grew an inflation-adjusted 5.65 percent to 263,860.9 trillion won ($328.7 billion) in 1993. Per capita GNP rose to $7,466 from $7,007.

15   Kim Il Sung's 82nd birthday is celebrated in North Korea. CNN, the *Washington Times*, and NHK are allowed to report from the DPRK.

18   In Paris the Anglo-French consortium GEC Alsthom, the maker of the French bullet trains, announces that after months of wrangling over details it has won a $2.1

billion contract to supply the ROK with 46 high-speed trains to link Seoul and Pusan. The ROK estimates the entire project, due for completion by the end of 2001, will cost $13.2 billion.

20   U.S. secretary of defense William J. Perry and ROK defense minister Rhee Byong Tae agree to delay the Team Spirit military exercises until November, publicly on grounds that the exercise would destroy crops belonging to farmers whose land is traversed by tanks and personnel during the maneuvers, but also so as not to provoke the DPRK while trying to persuade it to allow full nuclear inspections.

28   The DPRK announces its intention not to participate in the meetings of the Military Armistice Commission, to disband the Neutral Nations Supervisory Commission, and to seek negotiations with the United States to replace the 1953 Armistice Agreement with a peace treaty. The United States replies that "as for North Korea's proposal that the United States and North Korea negotiate a new peace arrangement, we note that in February 1992, North and South Korea agreed that the question of peace and security on the peninsula should be resolved primarily through inter-Korean dialogue. We strongly support that approach."

30   The ROK's Supreme Court, upholding a lower court's ruling, sentences a U.S. soldier, Pvt. Kenneth Markle, to 15 years in prison for the 1992 murder of a South Korean woman.

At Mokp'o, Daewoo Shipbuilding and Heavy Machinery delivers the *Inchon*, the ROK's first submarine, to the ROK navy.

May 1994

6   In Vienna the IAEA, responding to the DPRK's decision to allow IAEA inspectors to witness the replace-

May 1994 *(continued)*

ment of spent uranium rods at the 5-megawatt reactor at the Yongbyon nuclear facility as well as to its persistent refusal to allow the inspectors to sample the fuel and measure its radioactivity, says, "We received a letter from North Korea a short while ago, but it does not constitute the basis for sending an inspection team to the DPRK. Therefore the IAEA will not send an inspection team to North Korea."

14   North Korea announces that it has begun to replace fuel rods at the Yongbyon experimental nuclear reactor without IAEA inspectors present to determine whether plutonium has been extracted from the spent fuel.

28   IAEA inspectors leave North Korea after the DPRK rejects proposals for monitoring the refueling of its 5-megawatt reactor. "It is utterly nonsensical to tell us to suspend the refueling of the reactor," says a North Korean analyst. Three of the five UN inspectors in the DPRK leave the country as negotiations collapse.

30   The UN Security Council holds an emergency meeting and council president Ibrahim Gambari issues a statement regarding "the IAEA's assessment that if the discharge operation at the 5-megawatt reactor continues at the same rate, the IAEA's opportunity to select, segregate, and secure fuel rods for later measurements in accordance with IAEA standards will be lost within days."

June 1994

2   In Vienna IAEA director general Hans Blix informs the UN Security Council that the IAEA can no longer determine whether North Korea has diverted nuclear material, because the DPRK has removed all but 1,800 of the 8,000 fuel rods, including 300 critical rods comprising the core element, in the 5-megawatt power plant in Yongbyon. The IAEA reports that it has concluded that

the discharge of spent fuel from a 5-megawatt experimental nuclear power reactor has made it impossible to select fuel rods for later measurements that would reveal any diversion of fuel in past years. "We have no basis for holding a third round of high-level talks with North Korea, and we will seek further action in the UN Security Council," says U.S. assistant secretary of state for political-military affairs Robert L. Gallucci.

10   The Bank of Korea, in "The Estimated Gross National Product of North Korea in 1993," reports that North Korea's GNP fell from $21.1 billion in 1992 to $20.5 in 1993, with an estimated economic growth rate in 1993 of negative 4.3 percent from 1992. Per capita GNP is said to have fallen from $943 in 1992 to $904 in 1993.

"It is clear we have reached something of a watershed in our relationship with North Korea," says IAEA director general Hans Blix in Vienna as the IAEA votes to suspend some $250,000 in technical assistance to the DPRK. In response North Korea announces that effective June 13 it is withdrawing its membership in the IAEA, in accordance with paragraph D of article 18 of the IAEA statute, saying that it would no longer allow IAEA inspections and would not be bound to any rules or resolutions of the IAEA. North Korea's foreign minister Kim Young Nam faxes the DPRK's intentions to U.S. secretary of state Warren Christopher.

13   North Korea withdraws from the IAEA.

14   Nearly three years after inviting bids, the Korea High-Speed Rail Construction Authority concludes a $2.1 billion contract with GEC Alsthom to build a high-speed railway linking Seoul and Pusan. The system is scheduled for completion by September 2001.

15   Former U.S. president Jimmy Carter enters the DPRK via P'anmunjom, accompanied by his wife, Rosalyn,

June 1994 *(continued)*

three advisors, and six secret service agents, for a three-day visit. Carter says on July 9, "My wife, Rosalyn, and I will be visiting North Korea and South Korea next week. We will be going as private citizens, representing the Carter Center. The initiative for this trip has been from Korea, not Washington, and I have no official status relating to the U.S. government."

16   The U.S. Senate approves by a 93 to 3 vote a nonbinding resolution offered by senators Bob Dole and John McCain urging President Clinton to "immediately take all necessary and prudent actions to enhance the preparedness of U.S. and South Korean troops to deter and, if necessary, repel an attack from North Korea."

18   After meetings with North Korean president Kim Il Sung, Jimmy Carter returns to Seoul carrying a proposal from Kim Il Sung for a North-South summit. South Korean president Kim Young Sam says he accepts "any time, any place, and with no conditions." In addition to freezing nuclear activity and allowing IAEA inspectors to remain in the DPRK with monitoring equipment, Kim Il Sung proposed the following to former president Carter: an official declaration by the United States not to use nuclear weapons against North Korea and a commitment to eliminate all nuclear weapons from the peninsula; a reduction of DPRK and ROK military forces to 100,000 each; a cancellation of demands for U.S. troop withdrawal from the ROK; a suggested withdrawal of all troops from both sides of the DMZ; permission for DPRK-U.S. teams to visit the burial sites of at least 3,000 Americans killed during the Korean War, locate remains, and return them to families; and an affirmation of his desire to receive U.S. aid in converting a graphite-moderated nuclear reactor to a light-water reactor.

28   A four-point agreement is signed at P'anmunjom by the ROK deputy prime minister and unification minister

Lee Hong Koo and the DPRK's Supreme People's Assembly Reunification Party chairman Kim Yong Sun calling for the first summit between the Koreas, the first round of the summit to be held in P'yongyang from July 25 to 27.

July 1994

4   The South Korean *Maeil Kyungje Shinmun*, quoting UNDP sources, reports that DPRK president Kim Il Sung has named his younger brother and DPRK vice president, Kim Yong Ju, to head the development program in the Rajin-Sonbong Free Economic and Trade Zone.

8   North Korea's "Great Leader" Kim Il Sung dies at the age of 82, having been in power for 46 years. The Korean Central News Agency reports that Kim received medical treatment for arteriosclerosis of the cardiovascular system and on July 7 "suffered from a serious myocardial infarction owing to heavy mental strain, which was followed by a heart attack." The DPRK organizes a 273-member funeral committee, chaired by Dear Leader Kim Jong Il. The ROK declines to send a condolence message.

11   Hyundai founder and honorary chairman Chung Ju Young, 79, is sentenced to three years in prison for having illegally funneled more than $52 million in Hyundai company funds into his 1992 presidential campaign. Chung's sentence is immediately suspended by the court, which cites his advanced age and his contributions to the country's development.

The ROK's Economic Planning Board discloses that North Korea has recently allowed the U.S. branch of McKenzie and Co., an international business management consulting firm, to open an office in P'yongyang "to make an economic diagnosis with a view to solving the limitations of its economic structure."

July 1994 *(continued)*

DPRK Reunification Committee chairman Kim Yong Sun informs ROK Unification minister Lee Hong Koo that "due to the mishap on our side as was made public through an important announcement [the death of Kim Il Sung on July 8], we cannot but postpone the planned talks between the highest authorities of the two sides." The North-South summit is postponed indefinitely.

15   The U.S. Senate passes an amendment as part of the 1995 foreign aid bill by a vote of 95 to 0 barring aid to North Korea until the Clinton administration certifies that the DPRK has halted its nuclear weapons program, has no nuclear weapons, and has exported no weapons-grade plutonium. No U.S. aid to North Korea exists at present.

19   The funeral of North Korean president Kim Il Sung is held in P'yongyang, rescheduled from July 17. An estimated 2 million North Koreans are present at the three-and-a-half hour procession. South Korea prohibits any of its citizens from accepting the North's invitation to attend Kim's funeral.

21   In New York, U.S. and North Korean officials agree to resume the third round of high-level negotiations in Geneva on August 5.

31   Japanese prime minister Tomiichi Murayama, expressing "profound remorse," announces a Japanese initiative to spend $1 billion over the next ten years on a Peace, Friendship, and Exchange Initiative, to include funding for vocational training centers for Asian women, historical research on the war, and increased exchange with its Asian neighbors. The proposal includes no government compensation for surviving comfort women, nor does it address the demands for repatriation and compensation for ethnic Koreans on Sakhalin.

September 1994

2   The State Department confirms that former president Jimmy Carter has received an invitation from Kim Jong Il to act as an intermediary in the ongoing U.S.-DPRK nuclear-inspection negotiations. On September 20 former president Carter meets with DPRK ambassador to the UN Park Gil Yon at the Carter Center in Atlanta. Carter meets with ROK ambassador to the United States Han Seung Soo on September 21 and with opposition leader Kim Dae Jung on September 22.

8   The journal of the ROK's Korea Development Bank, *Industrial Economy*, estimates that it would cost South Korea 1,200 trillion won ($1.5 trillion) for national unification over the next decade should the North Korean regime abruptly collapse. The publication also predicts a cost of 1,800 trillion won should reunification come in the year 2000 through a gradual improvement of Seoul-P'yongyang relations.

9   U.S. ambassador-at-large Robert L. Gallucci announces that the United States and the DPRK will meet on September 10 in P'yongyang and Berlin. "In Berlin, a team led by Gary Samore from the U.S. side (Kim Jong U, vice chairman of the State External Economy Commission, leads the North Korean delegation) will discuss three issue areas that came up under the settlement. The light-water reactor project is one, the disposition of the spent fuel in the storage pond is two, and modalities for meeting the interim energy requirements of the DPRK with conventional energy will also be discussed in Berlin. In P'yongyang, a team led by Lynn Turk from the Department of State's East Asia Bureau will discuss with the DPRK the modalities of establishment of liaison offices. . . . They are not intended to make policy, they are intended to exchange views and to get at facts so that we'll be better prepared to move forward if we can make progress in the talks that take place in Geneva."

September 1994 *(continued)*

10   On arrival in P'yongyang by plane from Beijing on September 10, Lynn Turk and his delegation become the first U.S. diplomatic mission to visit North Korea since the end of the Korean War.

13   At P'anmunjom the DPRK delivers the remains of 14 U.S. soldiers who died during the Korean War to representatives of the UN Command. Since 1990 the remains of 208 U.S. soldiers have been delivered to the U.S. side on ten separate occasions.

16   Pohang Iron and Steel Co. (POSCO) and Korea Electric Power Corp. (KEPCO) are set in October to become the first South Korean companies to be listed on the New York Stock Exchange in the form of American Depository Receipts. Nine other firms that have qualified for the New York Stock Exchange are expected to join in 1995.

20   Jimmy Carter meets with DPRK ambassador to the UN Park Gil Yon at the Carter Center in Atlanta.

21   Jimmy Carter meets with ROK ambassador to the United States Han Seung Soo at the Carter Center in Atlanta.

22   Jimmy Carter meets with Kim Dae Jung at the Carter Center in Atlanta.

23   High-level U.S.-DPRK negotiations resume in Geneva. At the 38th annual meeting of the IAEA in Geneva, the general meeting adopts a resolution on the North Korean nuclear weapons program by a vote of 76 for, 1 against (Libya), with 10 nations abstaining (including China, India, and Pakistan).

26   North Korean political, religious, academic, and cultural organizations send official letters to counterparts in South Korea extending invitations to travel to North

Korea in early October to attend the ceremony for the completion of the tomb of Tan'gun, the legendary founder of the Korean nation.

October 1994

4   In P'yongyang a spokesman for the Tan'gun Tomb Reconstruction Committee says that "the dedication ceremony is delayed, because we have to wait for South Koreans invited to attend the meeting."

16   DPRK leader Kim Jong Il appears in public for the first time in nearly three months as the official 100-day period officially set to mourn the death of Kim Il Sung ends.

21   After returning earlier in the week from consultations in P'yongyang and Washington and with a letter of assurance to the DPRK from President Clinton, the U.S. and the DPRK negotiators announce in Geneva an agreed framework on an overall resolution of the nuclear issue on the Korean peninsula.

Thirty-two people die in Seoul as the Songsu Bridge, a major commuter bridge, collapses. Seoul mayor Lee Won Jong is dismissed on the day of the collapse; his successor, Woo Myung Kyu, resigns on November 1 after 11 days in office, saying he feels morally responsible. Rep. Choe Byung Yul of the DLP is named mayor.

28   Dong Ah Construction Co. chairman Choi Won Suk officially offers to rebuild the Songsu Bridge and donate it to the city of Seoul.

November 1994

1   General Electric's Power Systems, based in Schenectady, New York, announces that it has signed a contract worth nearly $500 million with Korea Electric Power

November 1994 *(continued)*

Corp. (KEPCO) to provide four STAG 207FA combined-cycle generating units for the 2,000-megawatt expansion of KEPCO's Seo Inchon power plant, one of the world's largest combined-cycle power plants.

7   "I will take step-by-step measures aimed at promoting South-North economic cooperation . . . including permission for our businessmen to visit the North," says ROK president Kim Young Sam. "We have reached the point when we should seriously reexamine this topic and start pushing for a policy of economic cooperation with North Korea." The DPRK's Korean Central News Agency responds, "The proposal of the traitor [Kim Young Sam] was . . . camouflage for concealing the dark designs of the puppets for national division and total confrontation." A spokesman for the ROK Unification Board says, "If you look at the text carefully, North Korea has not really rejected our offer. . . . It talks of the National Security Law and other issues we have heard many times before. But it does not say anything about not allowing companies to send missions North."

12   Halla Engineering & Heavy Industries Ltd. signs a $1 billion contract with McDonnell Douglas Corp. to supply wings for MD-95s, a 100-seat aircraft MDC plans to develop.

In accord with the October 21 agreed framework, U.S. and North Korean nuclear experts open talks in P'yongyang on the safe storage of spent nuclear fuel. The U.S. delegation is led by Norman Wulf, assistant director of the Arms Control and Disarmament Agency.

14–18   According to the DPRK-U.S. agreed framework of October 21, 1994, experts of the DPRK and the United States hold "useful and constructive discussions in P'yongyang from November 14 to 18, 1994, on the safe storage and final disposal of spent fuel removed from the 5-megawatt experimental atomic power plant. During the discussions, there [are] extensive exchanges of information, including a visit to the 5-megawatt experimental reactor power plant and the spent-fuel storage basin at the Yongbyon Center for Atomic Energy Research. A plan for treatment of the water in the spent-fuel storage basin [is] discussed. The experts on both sides agree to meet again to discuss outstanding technical and operational matters in December 1994."

28   The IAEA reports in Vienna that its inspectors in North Korea confirm a halt of the North Korean nuclear program in accordance with the October 21 agreed framework with the United States. "The IAEA visited the nuclear facilities in Yongbyon and Taejon and confirmed that these facilities were not in operation and that construction work has stopped."

30   The United States and the ROK sign an agreement turning over peacetime operational control of South Korean military forces to the ROK as of December 1, 1994. Under the agreement, signed by U.S. ambassador to the ROK James T. Laney and ROK foreign minister Han Seung Joo, the ROK chairman of the Joint Chiefs of Staff now has peacetime operational authority over the ROK armed forces and will not have to notify the ROK-U.S. Combined Forces Command of troop mobilization. "The transfer of operational control means that the U.S. military continues its transition from a leading to a supporting role in the defense of the Republic of Korea," said Col. Michael Sullivan of the Combined Forces Command.

December 1994

2   According to a State Department press release, "delegations of the United States and the DPRK met in Beijing from November 30 to December 2 to hold talks on the

December 1994 *(continued)*

supply of light-water reactor power plants to replace the DPRK's graphite-moderated reactors and related facilities. Both sides reaffirmed their intention to cooperate to secure the conclusion of an agreement for the provision of a light-water reactor project to the DPRK within the time frame and in accordance with the terms of the U.S.-DPRK agreed framework of October 21, 1994. The talks addressed complex matters and were serious and useful. The two sides agreed to meet again for further talks in January 1995."

5   Opposition politicians end a month-long boycott of South Korea's parliament. The opposition Democratic Party, whose leader, Lee Ki Taek, resigned from parliament on November 25, had been protesting a decision by state prosecutors not to seek indictments for the sake of national unity against former presidents Chun Doo Hwan, Roh Tae Woo, and others for the December 12, 1979, "coup d'état-like" incident which brought Chun to power.

6   U.S.-DPRK talks begin in Washington on opening diplomatic offices in each other's capitals. The five-member North Korean delegation is led by Pak Sok Gyun, a deputy director in the Foreign Ministry specializing in U.S. affairs; the U.S. side in the discussions is led by Lynn Turk, coordinator for U.S.-DPRK affairs at the State Department.

7   The ROK's Trade Ministry approves Samsung's request to produce automobiles using Nissan technology, despite strong opposition from other South Korean car makers, whose autoworkers strike briefly to protest the decision. Samsung plans to produce 65,000 sedans with two-liter engines in 1998 and says it will spend $5.4 billion to attain an annual capacity of 500,000 cars by 2002.

The ROK's Honam Oil Refinery Co., Ltd., a division of the Lucky-Goldstar Group, announces that it has won a contract for the supply of 50,000 metric tons of Bunker C oil to North Korea in bidding organized by the U.S. Department of Defense.

10   The ROK's National Unification Board approves applications from six South Korean companies to visit North Korea. "The government decided that the submitted applications met the requirements prescribed by the pertinent laws and were also in keeping with the objectives of the Measures to Energize South-North Cooperation," said the National Unification Board. The companies include Lucky-Goldstar, Samsung, Hyundai, Ssangyong, Yongshin Trading, and Taedong Chemical. Ssangyong Group vice chairman Lee Chou Bom, with a 12-man team, flies into P'yongyang from Beijing on December 13.

11   U.S. senators Frank H. Murkowski (R-Alaska) and Paul Simon (D-Ill.) arrive in P'yongyang from Beijing on a U.S. Air Force plane, the first U.S. military plane to fly into North Korea since the end of the Korean War in 1953. "We got 90 minutes with the foreign minister and all sorts of briefings from all sorts of officials," said Senator Murkowski at a press conference in Seoul. "But whenever we asked to see Kim Jong Il we were told he is still in mourning for his father." Asked about the U.S.-DPRK agreed framework, Murkowski says, "As far as any efforts to scuttle that agreement, I don't anticipate any. The agreement will be examined thoroughly."

16   Delegations from the United States, Japan, and South Korea, led by Robert L. Gallucci, Tetsuya Endo, and Choe Dong Jin, respectively, meet in San Francisco to discuss implementation of the U.S.-DPRK agreed framework and establish a multilateral consortium, tentatively named the Korean Energy Development Organization (KEDO), to be headquartered in New York. "The Republic of Korea will play a central role in the

December 1994 *(continued)*

financing and construction in the DPRK of two light-water reactors of the Korean standard model. Japan also confirmed its intention to play an appropriate role in managing and funding the light-water reactor project to be carried out by KEDO," according to a joint statement. "The United States would also participate, noting that it had already taken the initial steps for the provision of heavy fuel oil and was preparing to facilitate the safe storage and disposition of spent fuel."

The South Korean National Assembly approves the Uruguay Round agreement. Of 211 parliament members present, 152 vote to support the bill, and 58 vote against, with one abstention. ROK minister of trade, industry, and energy Kim Chul Su is one of the three candidates in the running for the top position of the new World Trade Organization.

17   After straying into North Korean airspace, an unarmed, two-seat U.S. Army OH-58C helicopter is downed in North Korea. Chief Warrant Officer David Hilemon is killed in the incident. Chief Warrant Officer Bobby Hall is held by the North Koreans for questioning over what they term an "espionage mission." President Bill Clinton says "This tragic loss of life was unnecessary." U.S. representative Bill Richardson (D-N. Mex.), in North Korea on a previously scheduled trip, arranges for the return of Hilemon's remains on December 22. U.S. general Gary E. Luck, commander of UN forces in Korea, conveys his regrets over the incident in a letter to North Korean leader Kim Jong Il. In response to a North Korean request, U.S. deputy assistant secretary of state Thomas Hubbard flies by military plane to Seoul and crosses the DMZ on his way to P'yongyang to continue negotiations for the release of Bobby Hall.

30   According to a U.S.-DPRK agreed statement of understanding issued in P'anmunjom, "in connection with the incident in which a U.S. military helicopter intruded

into DPRK airspace on December 17, 1994, U.S. deputy assistant secretary of state Thomas Hubbard visited P'yongyang from December 28 to 30, 1994, as a special presidential envoy representing the U.S. administration and held discussions with DPRK officials concerned. At the end of these discussions, both sides have reached the following understanding: 1) The U.S. side has acknowledged the legally unjustified intrusion into DPRK airspace by a U.S. military helicopter. The U.S. side has expressed its sincere regret over this action and has assured the DPRK it will take steps to prevent any recurrence of such incidents in the future; 2) Both sides have agreed to maintain military contact in the appropriate forum to identify and take measures for preventing occurrences that threaten peace and security on the Korean peninsula." U.S. chief warrant Bobby Hall is returned by North Korea after being held for 13 days.

31   ROK president Kim Young Sam is named by Corretta Scott King as the 1994 winner of the Martin Luther King Jr. Nonviolent Peace Prize. "President Kim's life and work provide an inspiring example of uncompromising dedication to the principles of nonviolence in pursuit of human rights and democracy," writes Mrs. King in a letter to President Kim. "We present this award with the faith that it will also build new bridges of understanding between African Americans and Koreans," says Mrs. King in Seoul. "It is sad to recall that there are periods when the relationship between African Americans and Korean Americans, who often live in close daily contact with each other, deteriorate," says President Kim. "However, I believe we are successfully overcoming such problems."

January 1995

1   According to a letter sent by DPRK leader Kim Jong Il to the North Korean people, "we are seeing out the year 1994 in bitter tears and ringing in the new year. Let all

January 1995 *(continued)*

of us energetically work with one mind to make our country, our motherland, more prosperous, as soldiers and disciples of the Great Leader, Comrade Kim Il Sung."

6   ROK president Kim Young Sam, in his New Year policy statement, calls for globalization to be the nation's policy goal for 1995.

9   According to a DPRK Foreign Ministry spokesman, "under the framework agreement between the DPRK and the United States, the two countries are to lower the barriers to trade and investment, including the lifting of restrictions on telecommunications services and financial transactions within three months of the date of the agreement as part of the full normalization of political and economic relations. In order to implement the framework agreement, the Administration Council of the DPRK has decided to lift from mid-January the restriction on the import of U.S. commodities and the ban on entry of U.S. trading ships into DPRK ports."

10   The United States, the ROK, and Japan hold two days of working meetings to discuss a draft agreement on the establishment of the Korea Energy Development Organization, the international consortium charged with building light-water reactors for North Korea. The three nations meet again for talks in Tokyo from January 19 to 20.

12   The ROK National Unification Board authorizes four more South Korean companies to travel to North Korea to explore business ventures. The companies are the Hanhwa Group, the Tongyang Group, the Sinwon Group, and the Daewoo Group.

DPRK ambassador and permanent representative to the UN Park Gil Yon is granted permission to travel to Atlanta for discussions with CNN, Coca-Cola, and the Carter Center.

16   The ROK National Unification Board announces that inter-Korean trade in 1994 totaled over $227.9 million, the highest level since the beginning of North-South trade in 1988. The overall trade volume increased 14.6 percent from 1993, with $202.95 million worth of goods imported by the South from the North and $24.95 million exported by the South to the North.

20   In a letter of invitation dated December 28, 1994, the DPRK invites Roger Clinton, younger brother of U.S. president Bill Clinton, to the DPRK to perform in P'yongyang in April. "It will deepen the understanding between the peoples of the Democratic People's Republic of Korea and the United States if Mr. Roger Clinton visits our country in April 1995 to perform at the P'yongyang International Sports and Culture Festival."

      In a "modest change," President Clinton signs an executive order lifting a few of the long-standing barriers to U.S. trade with North Korea. "Further relaxation of economic sanctions against North Korea will depend on further verified progress on the nuclear issue as well as progress in other areas of concern," says the U.S. State Department.

21   According to a U.S.-DPRK statement, "experts from the DPRK and United States had a second meeting in P'yongyang from January 18 to 20, 1995, to discuss the safe storage and ultimate disposition of the spent fuel discharged from the 5-megawatt experimental reactor power plant. The discussions were useful, constructive, and resulted in significant progress. Some of the DPRK and U.S. experts are visiting the spent-fuel storage basin at the Yongbyon Center for Atomic Energy Research to analyze the chemical composition of the water in that basin."

24   The DPRK proposes "a great national meeting of the Korean people" to be held on August 15, 1995, to commemorate the 50th anniversary of liberation from Jap-

January 1995 *(continued)*

anese colonial rule. "If the nation jointly celebrates the 50th anniversary of liberation in a grand style, it will provide a good opportunity for the North and the South to dispel misunderstanding and distrust," says the DPRK's *Rodong Shinmun*. The ROK's vice unification minister responds that the North's suggestion "will not substantially improve South-North relations" and calls for dialogue between authorized parties. The DPRK invites ROK opposition Democratic Party leader Lee Ki Taek to North Korea. The ROK's National Unification Board replies that "inter-Korean dialogue cannot be achieved merely through visits to the North by certain individuals, political parties, and social organizations. The government's basic stance on South-North dialogue is that the door is always wide open for dialogue between responsible authorities of the two sides."

February 1995

1   According to a U.S.-DPRK statement made in Berlin, "delegations from the DPRK and United States met in Berlin from January 28 to February 1, 1995, to hold a second round of talks on the supply of light-water reactor power plants to replace the DPRK's graphite-moderated reactors and related facilities. . . . The two sides agreed that some progress had been made and recognized that major issues which must be agreed upon for the conclusion of the supply agreement include the type of reactor, scope of light-water reactor supply, financial terms, contractual arrangements, nuclear safety and liability, and necessary assurances in connection with the light-water reactor project. . . . Further talks on the light-water reactor project will be held as soon as possible in March 1995." During the negotiations North Korea is reported to ask the United States to provide $500 million to $1 billion worth of economic and technical assistance and is said not to agree with a draft U.S. contract

on the supply of light-water reactors that would clearly identify South Korea as the supplier.

8   A decree from the Central People's Committee of the DPRK officially designates February 16, the birthday of the Dear Leader Kim Jong Il, as the "greatest holiday of the nation." Kim Jong Il turns 53 on February 16, 1995.

22   Koo Cha Kyung, 71, chairman of the Lucky-Goldstar (LG) Group, the ROK's fourth largest *chaebol*, announces that he will turn over the group chairmanship to his son Koo Bon Moo, 50. The transfer makes the LG group the first of the ROK's *chaebol* to have third-generation family leadership.

25   Reuters reports that "as the Geneva agreement has entered its initial stages of implementation, both the governments of South Korea and the United States expect North Korea to fulfill the agreement faithfully. . . . With such expectations, the two sides have agreed not to hold the Team Spirit exercise slated for March of this year."

The United States announces that it has sold $112 million in military missiles to South Korea for potential use against enemy ships and radar. The package includes 136 AGM-88B high-speed anti-radiation missiles (HARM) made by Texas Instruments Inc. at a cost of $64 million.

March 1995

4   According to the World Bank, "Korea signed . . . with the World Bank its last loan agreement: this date marks a turning point for the country in its rapid transformation from poverty to prosperity. South Korea becomes the first former beneficiary of the World Bank's most concessionary credit terms to become a full-fledged lender to less fortunate nations.

6   South Korean opposition members occupy the houses of Hwang Nak Joo, speaker of the National Assembly, and Lee Han Dong, vice speaker, and prevent them

March 1995 *(continued)*

from leaving in an attempt to prevent their ruling party from passing an electoral revision law. After riot police threaten to storm the homes, Hwang and Lee are released after having been detained for one week.

9   The United States, Japan, and South Korea formalize the establishment of the Korean Energy Development Organization (KEDO) in New York.

17   The first direct export of U.S. grain to the DPRK, resulting from the easing of trade restrictions, is shipped from Seattle. The cash purchase of 54,000 tons of corn by the North Koreans is made from the Bartlett Grain Co. of St. Louis, Missouri.

20   KEDO names Stephen W. Bosworth, former U.S. ambassador to the Philippines and Tunisia and current president of the U.S.-Japan Foundation, as its executive director. Deputy executive directors are Choi Young Jin, director of international economic affairs in the South Korean Foreign Ministry, and Itaru Umezu, head of the Japanese Foreign Ministry's Multilateral Cooperation Department.

25   The third round of U.S.-DPRK discussions on the provision of light-water nuclear reactors to North Korea begins in Berlin. As with previous rounds, Gary Samore leads the U.S. delegates and Kim Jong U leads the North Korean delegation.

28   An 11-member Japanese delegation led by former prime minister and foreign minister Michio Watanabe arrives in North Korea to discuss the renewal of DPRK-Japan bilateral negotiations toward normalization. The delegation includes lawmakers from the ruling Liberal Democrat Party and its partners in Japan's ruling coalition, the Socialists, and the Sakigake party.

30   A new political party, the United Liberal Democrats, is formally inaugurated, with former Democratic Liberal Party chairman Kim Chong Pil as president.

April 1995

3   American Chamber of Commerce in Korea president James Riddle says in a press conference that the chamber is planning a survey and not a sales or investment mission to North Korea. "We are not going with our pockets full of money," says Riddle, stressing that the chamber would hope to meet with only industrial leaders in the DPRK to discuss telecommunications, power generation, transportation, and other infrastructure ventures.

20   The ROK says that Russia has agreed to provide tanks, including T-80 battle tanks, helicopters, and other military and industrial hardware worth more than $450 million over the next three and a half years in partial repayment for ROK loans totaling $1.5 billion. Under the terms Russia will repay $225 million in the form of steel, aluminum, and other industrial goods, $209 million in military hardware, and $23 million in helicopters.

21   U.S.-DPRK talks in Berlin reach an impasse on the six-month target date for agreeing on the construction of two new light-water reactors in North Korea. At issue is the North's refusal to accept South Korean-type models. North Korea refuses a U.S. proposal to upgrade the negotiations to higher-level talks. North Korea agrees without preconditions to a renewal of talks with the United States at a higher diplomatic level.

28–30   North Korea holds the P'yongyang International Sports and Cultural Festival for Peace from April 28 to 30. The festival is cohosted by Japanese wrestler-turned-politician Antonio Inoki, leader of the New Japan Pro-Wrestling Co.

May 1995

3   An Amnesty International delegation departs North Korea after a week-long visit to discuss legal reforms

May 1995 *(continued)*

and prisoner cases, the second time Amnesty International has been allowed to visit the DPRK. In a statement Amnesty International said that it "welcomes the information received on legal reforms and the opportunity it was given to discuss extensively aspects of the DPRK legal system. It also welcomes new information received on individual cases. However, it remains concerned about a number of these cases and is seeking further information. Amnesty International is also urging the DPRK to accede without delay to the Convention against Torture and Other Cruel, Inhuman, or Degrading Treatment or Punishment. Throughout the discussions with Amnesty International, DPRK officials said they were concerned about misinformation being circulated on the human rights situation in the country. Amnesty International pointed out that openness, international accountability, and regular access to the country by independent observers, including international human rights organizations and the International Committee of the Red Cross, were among the best safeguards against any misinformation."

11   In Los Angeles Samsung Corp. donates $500,000 to the U.S. College Board to help cover administrative costs associated with adding Korean to its list of foreign language achievement tests.

15   ROK president Kim Young Sam appoints Park Young Sik as the new minister of education, replacing Kim Sook Hee. Since 1994, Park, the former president of Yonsei University (1988–92), has led the Public Officers Ethics Committee. Kim also names Rep. Lee Sung Ho of the ruling Democratic Liberal Party to replace Suh Sang Mok as the minister of health and welfare. Kim names Jin Nyum, former minister of energy and resources, as the new minister of labor, replacing Lee Hyun Koo, who was arrested on charges of receiving 275 million won in kickbacks.

20 Talks on the North Korean nuclear issue resume between the United States and North Korea in Kuala Lumpur following the breakdown of technical talks in Berlin in April. Deputy Assistant Secretary of State for East Asian and Pacific Affairs Thomas Hubbard leads the U.S. delegation; Vice Foreign Minister Kim Gye Gwan leads the North Korean delegation.

23 The Olympic Council of Asia awards the 2002 Asian Games to the South Korean city of Pusan over the Taiwanese city of Kaohsiung.

The Hyundai Corp. announces it will invest $1.3 billion to build a semiconductor manufacturing plant in Eugene, Oregon, the first chip plant investment in the United States by a Korean company. Construction of the plant will begin in August and is scheduled to be completed in early 1997. When operational, the plant will produce 30,000 8-inch 64-megabyte wafers per month and will be the largest single factory of its kind in the world.

26 A visiting delegation from the DPRK reportedly asks Japan for emergency rice supplies. "North Korea is facing grain shortages due to bad weather," says Lee Song Rok, chairman of the DPRK's Foreign Trade Promotion Committee. Japan reaches a preliminary agreement with North Korea to deliver 300,000 metric tons of rice, which Japanese officials say the DPRK will pay for under a long-term interest-free loan.

31 North Korea seizes the South Korean fishing boat *No. 86 Woosung*, which had strayed into DPRK waters trying to take a shortcut to its home port of Inchon.

June 1995

7 U.S. representative Bill Richardson (D-N. Mex.) arrives in Beijing after four days of intense high-level meetings in North Korea. Representative Richardson says he told North Korean leaders that resolving the nuclear issue

June 1995 *(continued)*

was Washington's top priority and also urged North Korea to work with the United States to find and exhume the remains of 8,200 U.S. soldiers still missing in action from the Korean War.

10   *China Daily* reports that Mineral Technologies Inc., a New York-based mineral developer, says that it has reached an agreement with the North Korean company Korean Magnesia Clinker Export and Import involving tens of thousands of tons of magnesia, a raw material used in products employed by the steel industry to coat blast furnaces, worth several million dollars annually. The deal, coming after a five-member North Korean trade mission's visit to New York, would mark the DPRK's first exports to the United States since the Korean War. The PRC and the DPRK are the world's primary sources of natural magnesia.

13   The U.S. and the DPRK issue a joint press statement upon the conclusion of negotiations in Kuala Lumpur over the provision of light-water nuclear reactors to North Korea.

McDonnell Douglas announces in Paris that Korean Air has placed a firm order to purchase three MD-80 intermediate-range twin jets. The airplanes are slated for delivery in January, February, and March and are the MD-83 versions of the twin jet. Korean Air is scheduled to accept delivery of two MD-82s in July from previous orders. The five aircraft increase Korean Air's fleet of McDonnell Douglas twin jets to 14.

Pratt & Whitney announces that Korean Air selects the PW4000 engine family to power its new Airbus A330 and Boeing 777 aircraft. The value of the order to Pratt & Whitney, including firm, option, and spare engines, is approximately $850 million.

15   The Japanese government announces the establishment of the Asian Peace and Friendship Foundation for

Women to support medical and social welfare projects for former comfort women. The fund is expected to pay surviving comfort women a modest sum, cover their general medical expenses, and underwrite other projects to raise the status of women in Asia.

19   U.S. technicians arrive in North Korea to begin the process of rendering harmless the 7,200 nuclear fuel rods in the cooling plant at the Yongbyon nuclear site. The delegation is led by Norm Wulf of the Arms Control and Disarmament Agency and includes technical personnel from the Department of Energy, the Center Corp. of San Diego, and the Nuclear Assurance Corp. of Atlanta.

20   In secret talks between the ROK and the DPRK in Beijing—the first official contact in 15 months—the two reach a reported $270 million agreement in which the DPRK receives 150,000 tons of rice from the ROK. The DPRK is said to have sought 300,000 tons of rice. The DPRK will repay the ROK for the rice with zinc and other raw materials over a period of more than ten years. The agreement is signed by the DPRK's vice chairman of the Asian Pacific Committee, Chun Gum Chol, and the ROK's deputy finance minister Lee Sok Chae. ROK deputy prime minister and national unification minister Rha Woong Bae announces that the rice aid agreement is expected to pave the way for the release of the crew of No. 86 Woosung, still being held by North Korea. "The ship, laden with our hope and love, sails toward new horizons in inter-Korean relations," says ROK prime minister Lee Hong Koo as the Sea Apex leaves the South Korean port of Tonghae with the first 2,000 tons of rice. The ROK suspends further shipments of rice and orders back two freighters en route to the DPRK after the Sea Apex is forced to fly a North Korean flag as it enters the North Korean port of Chinjae. The DPRK's Samcholli General Corp. sends a

June 1995 *(continued)*

letter apologizing for the incident, and an official apology is faxed by DPRK negotiator Chun Gum Chol in his capacity as an advisor to the Committee for the Promotion of External Economic Cooperation, expressing regret "for the mistakes of working-level officials." "After reviewing the North Korean response cautiously ... the government has decided to accept it positively," says the ROK, which resumes rice aid shipments.

27   Local elections are held in the ROK. Korean citizens have the opportunity to elect provincial governors, metropolitan mayors, the chief executives of smaller cities, counties, and autonomous districts, and local community councils. Since 1961 these positions had been appointed by the national government. In the elections the ruling Democratic Liberal Party (DLP) loses 10 of 15 contests for control over major cities and provinces. Cho Soon of the main opposition Democratic Party (DP) is elected mayor of Seoul, collecting 40.8 percent of the 4.98 million ballots cast and defeating independent representative Park Chang Jong and DLP candidate Chung Won Shik. Cho, an economist who has been deputy prime minister and governor of the Bank of Korea, has only recently joined the DP and has been critical of the government's policies toward dealing with traffic, pollution, and other problems. The DP, backed by Kim Dae Jung, wins all three posts in the southwest Cholla region. Kim Chong Pil's United Liberal Democrat Party, formed in March, wins three provinces and a city. The DLP wins elections in Pusan, Inchon, and three provinces.

29   The Sampoong Department Store, a five-story luxury-goods retail center in the Kangnam section of Seoul, collapses, leaving 142 dead with 288 remaining unaccounted for. Ultimately, the death toll will climb to over 650. More than 900 are injured in the collapse, which authorities blame on shoddy construction. The Seoul prosecutor's office arrests store owner Lee Joon, his

son, and two others on charges of criminal negligence in connection with the collapse. "The collapsed Sampoong Department Store has destroyed South Korea's dignity and pride," says Speaker Hwang Nak Joo before a special meeting of the ROK's National Assembly.

July 1995

6   The South Korean government grants approval to the Daewoo Corp. to visit the DPRK to set up an industrial joint venture. Daewoo has said it will invest $5.2 million in plants to make shirts, blouses, jackets, and bags in the port of Nampo. The Daewoo delegation to the DPRK will for the first time include technicians who could start hands-on work. Six of the 13 Daewoo officials will be allowed to stay in the DPRK for 60 days, the rest for one year.

8   The DPRK marks the first anniversary of the death of Kim Il Sung.

17   In Glenview, Illinois, LG Electronics Co. (LGE), a subsidiary of the LG Group, announces that it has agreed with Zenith Electronics Corp. to acquire the U.S.-owned television maker for $351 million. LGE will take a controlling stake in Zenith with 57 percent of its outstanding common stock, the biggest investment a Korean company has ever made to take over a controlling stake in a foreign company. LGE previously owned 1.45 million shares, or less than 5 percent of Zenith common stock. The deal is signed at Zenith headquarters in Glenview by LGE president John Koo and Zenith president and chief executive officer Al Moschner. Zenith was the last major U.S.-owned television manufacturer.

18   Japanese prime minister Tomiichi Murayama offers Japan's "profound apologies" to women forced to serve as sex slaves for Japanese soldiers during World War II.

July 1995 *(continued)*

"What we did was inexcusable," says Murayama. "I offer my profound apologies to all those who as wartime comfort women suffered emotional and physical wounds that can never be healed."

After a 14-month investigation, the Seoul District Prosecutor's Office announces that it has "no authority to indict" former presidents Roh Tae Woo and Chun Doo Hwan and 56 others for their alleged roles in the brutal suppression of civilian protesters in Kwangju in 1980, rejecting three complaints filed against them by 379 individuals. The prosecutor's office ruled that the suppression of the civilian protesters by martial law troops "was not subject to a probe of investigative authorities and judicial judgment," as it was "a highly political action."

Veteran opposition leader Kim Dae Jung announces his return to politics and his intention to form a new political party, to be called the National Congress for New Politics.

19   In a nationwide television broadcast, ROK president Kim Young Sam declares the site of the collapsed Sampoong Department Store a Special Disaster Area. The official death toll from the June 29 collapse of the department store has risen to 459, with 176 still unaccounted for.

22   The Korean Energy Development Organization (KEDO) begins formal operations in New York.

27   The Korean War Veterans Memorial is dedicated in Washington on the National Mall. The memorial consists of a polished granite wall featuring faces etched in stone, a UN walkway with the names of the 22 nations that participated in the United Nation's effort in Korea, 19 poncho-clad statues, and a pool of remembrance around the inscription "Freedom Is Not Free." The in-

scription at the memorial's apex reads, "Our nation honors her sons and daughters who answered the call to defend a country they never knew and a people they never met." The memorial is dedicated to the 54,246 Americans killed in action, the 8,177 still listed as missing in action, the 103,284 wounded, and the 7,140 individuals taken as prisoners of war. In Washington for a state visit, President Kim Young Sam addresses the U.S. Congress, receives an honorary doctorate from Georgetown University, and participates in official ceremonies marking the dedication of the Korean War Veterans Memorial.

31   A two-day inter-Korea symposium on national reunification takes place in Beijing, the first meeting coorganized by the North and South since 1945. The symposium is jointly organized by the ROK's Seoul National University and the DPRK's Social and Political Studies Institute. A total of 26 South and North Korean scholars participate in the symposium.

Representatives from 32 nations and the European Union attend the inaugural general conference of KEDO in New York. At the conference KEDO forms three advisory committees tasked respectively with the construction of the light-water reactors, the disposal of spent fuel rods, and the supply of heavy oil to North Korea. KEDO is led by executive director Stephen Bosworth, with Choi Young Jin and Itara Umezu as deputy directors.

Pak Yong Gil, widow of the late Reverend Moon Ik Hwan, is arrested on her return to South Korea via P'anmunjom after traveling to North Korea without prior approval from the ROK government. Pak, 71, who secretly entered North Korea on June 28 and met with North Korean leader Kim Jong Il, is arrested by the Agency for National Security Planning on charges of violating the South Korean National Security Law.

July 1995 *(continued)*

The South Korean ship *Samsun Venus* leaves from Pohang for the North Korean port of Ch'ongjin with a cargo of 5,000 tons of rice. On August 2 the South Korean government is notified by Singapore's Dayi Shipping, a shipping agent designated by North Korea, that Lee Yang Chol, chief mate of *Samsun Venus*, was found taking photos of Ch'ongjin port from his cabin with a compact camera. Lee's action is termed "premeditated espionage and a provocation" by North Korea, which holds the ship and its crew. After the alleged spying incident, North Korea calls off the third round of DPRK-ROK rice talks scheduled for August 10 in Beijing. ROK vice minister of finance and economy Lee Sok Chae sends a telegram to the DPRK's Chon Kum Chol, advisor to the North's Committee for the Promotion of External Economic Cooperation, to "express regret over the fact that Lee Yang Chol, first mate of the ship, took a photograph of Ch'ongjin port in violation of the North Korean law," and he promises that such a mistake will not be repeated and that the remaining rice will be delivered to the North. In June, Lee and Chon had signed an agreement in Beijing providing for Seoul to deliver 150,000 tons of rice to North Korea.

August 1995

11   The South Korean government announces a special amnesty for 3,169 prisoners and ex-convicts on the occasion of the 50th anniversary of national liberation from Japanese colonial rule. Included in the amnesty are 855 public security-related offenders and 2,134 criminals, particularly businesspeople convicted of bribing government officials or on other charges. The amnesty includes Kim Sun Myung, 70, who joined the DPRK army when the Korean War broke out. Kim is freed after serving 43 years and 10 months of a death sentence which had earlier been commuted to life imprisonment. Kim, prisoner No. 3597, had refused to

denounce the DPRK and had been the world's longest-serving known political prisoner.

13   On August 13 at 10:00 A.M., the North Koreans allow *Samsun Venus* and its 21-member crew to leave Ch'ongjin port. The *Dooyang Brave*, with a cargo of 10,000 tons of rice, leaves the South Korean port of Yosu for the North Korean port of Nampo.

15   In nationwide ceremonies under the theme The 50th Anniversary of Liberation, Looking Forward to Unification and the Future, Korea marks the 50th anniversary of liberation from Japanese colonial rule. In a symbolic display, the spire on top of the central dome of the former headquarters of the Japanese governor general's office, the symbol of Japan's colonial rule and now the National Museum building in central Seoul, is removed and lowered to the ground to mark the beginning of the dismantling of the massive granite structure.

17   AT&T announces in New York that it has been awarded a $540 million contract by Korea Mobile Telecom (KMT) to supply wireless infrastructure equipment for KMT's nationwide network. Under the multiyear agreement, AT&T will supply and install its AUTOPLEX wireless communications infrastructure equipment.

A South Korean tanker, the Chinese-registered *Wei Shan Hu*, carrying 20,000 tons of oil, departs from the port of Ulsan for the North Korean port of Sonbong. Yunkong Ltd. has been awarded a contract from KEDO to ship 40,000 tons of Bunker C oil to the North. The remaining 20,000 tons are scheduled to be shipped within the month.

22   A KEDO-dispatched survey team arrives in the DPRK to conduct surveys on proposed sites for two light-water reactors.

August 1995 *(continued)*

25   In Washington the United States and South Korea reach an agreement to amend the 1988 Record of Understanding Concerning Market Access for Cigarettes. The 1988 agreement ensured market access in Korea for foreign cigarettes, limited the type and rates of cigarette taxes, and provided guidelines for advertising of cigarettes. The ROK had requested consultations to amend the agreement because it wanted to increase cigarette taxes and sharply limit advertising in an effort to protect public health. The agreement reached provides for Korea to introduce measures to reduce smoking through changes in tax and advertising policies.

September 1995

5   According to a press release from the Office of the Resident Representative and UN Resident Coordinator in P'yongyang, "floods affect large parts of the DPRK. Following three episodes of heavy rainfall over the periods of July 7–15, July 26–August 12, and August 17–20, the DPRK government reports that 75 percent of the country has been affected by floods. To date, 60 to 70 persons are missing and feared drowned in the floods, which have caused severe damage to housing, and to agricultural and industrial production as well as to the infrastructure of the country. The government estimates the total cost of the floods at $15 billion U.S."

27   South Korea's highest court ends a centuries-old ban on marriages between people who have the same surname. The court rules that such marriages are now legal, providing that the couples first get married abroad. The ruling is said to increase the pool of potential mates by some 25 percent.

28   The United States and Korea reach a memorandum of understanding of trade in automobiles, increasing market access for U.S.-made passenger vehicles in Korea. The agreement contains provisions on Korea's auto tax

system, standards, certification procedures, advertising, auto financing, consumer perceptions, and future consultations. "While much more needs to be accomplished to fully open the Korean auto market, this agreement is a significant step forward in creating a more competitive environment for U.S. autos, particularly the mid-size vehicles U.S. companies produce," said U.S. trade representative Mickey Kantor. "Although I have not designated Korea's auto practices as Priority Foreign Country Practices under Super 301, we will monitor closely the quantitative and qualitative criteria in the agreement and will examine whether a WTO case would be appropriate." South Korea is the world's third-largest auto exporter and fifth-largest manufacturer.

29   In Dearborn, Michigan, Ford Motor Co. and Kia Motors Corp. agree to a joint-venture partnership in a new company, Ford Motor Co. of Korea, to be 90 percent owned by Ford and 10 percent owned by Kia. The venture will make Ford the first North America-based automotive firm to open a distribution unit in Korea, according to Ford, which will move to import Ford cars, minivans, and sport utility vehicles into Korea. The unit is projected to be fully operational and independent Ford dealers will be in place in Korea by April 1996.

October 1995

5   Japanese prime minister Tomiichi Murayama asserts in Parliament that the 1910 Japan-Korea treaty annexing Korea was signed in a legal and valid way. Murayama's remarks are expanded upon by Koken Nosaka, the chief cabinet secretary and the government's chief spokesman, who says that Japan's annexation of Korea was completed by legal procedures rather than under compulsion. "The Korean government has always said that the 1910 annexation treaty between Korea and Japan

October 1995 *(continued)*

was signed under coercion and was against the will of the Korean people," responds the South Korean government.

16   The second round of talks between the Korean Energy Development Organization (KEDO) and the DPRK begins in New York. The first round of talks was held in Kuala Lumpur, Malaysia, from September 11 to 16. The talks are aimed at concluding a light-water reactor supply agreement. The delegations are led by KEDO executive director Stephen Bosworth and Ambassador Ho Jong from the DPRK side.

25   One week after killing a North Korean infiltrator, South Korean police announce the capture of a second North Korean, Kim Do Shik, 33, after a shoot-out some 100 miles south of the DMZ. After four days of hunting for another North Korean infiltrator who survived the gunfight, Park Kwang Nam, 31, is killed in a mountainous area in Puyo.

An opposition member of the South Korean National Assembly, Kang Soo Rim of the Democratic Party, alleges that the General Dynamics Corp. paid former president Roh Tae Woo at least $100 million in 1991 in a successful bid to have the ROK purchase the company's F-16 fighters. "We absolutely deny these allegations," a General Dynamics spokesperson says to the *Washington Post*. "It's maddening and frustrating that they have resurfaced."

26   The ROK reports the defection of O Yong Nam, a North Korean military officer said to be a relative of North Korea's late defense minister O Jin U. O, who is questioned by the ROK's Agency for National Security Planning, is the second DPRK military officer reported to defect this year. On October 12 the ROK announced the defection of a DPRK army colonel, the highest-ranking officer to seek asylum since the Korean War, who arrived in Seoul via a third country.

27   The U.S. State Department announces that it will provide an additional $200,000 in humanitarian aid to North Korea to help it recover from the effects of severe floods during July and August. The aid will be sent to the DPRK by the Agency for International Development through the UN Children's Fund.

November 1995

3   Following the 27th U.S.-ROK Security Consultative Meeting in Seoul, South Korea agrees to increase its contribution to the cost of maintaining U.S. troops on the Korean peninsula. After two days of meetings with South Korean defense minister Lee Yang Ho, U.S. secretary of defense William Perry announces that the ROK will increase its share by 10 percent a year for three years. The ROK currently pays $300 million annually of the estimated $1 billion cost of maintaining the 37,000 U.S. troops in Korea. Under the new accord the ROK will contribute an additional $30 million next year and by 1998 will contribute a total of $399 million. Secretary Perry says that the United States is willing to revise the legal document governing the rights and obligations of U.S. troops in accordance with South Korean demands, provided that it preserves "just treatment" for Americans.

The corporate heads of 23 South Korean companies, meeting at the Federation of Korean Industries (FKI), adopt a resolution to never again make secret political donations. FKI chairman Chey Jong Hyun, head of the Sunkyong Group and in-law of former president Roh, issues an apology to the South Korean people for "the past's undesirable connections between politicians and businessmen." The chairman of Hanbo Group and the former chairman of the collapsed Hanyang Group are the first of many Korean corporate chairmen to be questioned by prosecutors on former president Roh's political slush fund.

November 1995 *(continued)*

8   The United Nations General Assembly elects Chile, Egypt, Guinea-Bissau, Poland, and South Korea to serve two-year terms on the UN Security Council. The new council members replace Argentina, the Czech Republic, Nigeria, Oman, and Rwanda, whose two-year terms on the council expire at the end of this year. The five permanent members of the Security Council, with the power of veto, are the United States, Russia, Britain, China, and France.

December 1995

1   The Korean Overseas Information Service (KOIS) launches Korea Window, a World Wide Web server site on the Internet. The site, in English, will include some 10,000 pages of written material, 5,000 pictures, and 400 audio and video files. The main menu of Korea Window includes Exploring Korea, News on Korea, Korean Heritage, Events, Forum, and Webs in Korea. The address for Korea Window is http://www.kois.go.kr.

3   Former South Korean president Chun Doo Hwan is arrested in his hometown of Hapchon, South Kyongsang province, and taken to Anyang Prison after refusing to answer questions regarding his role in the 1979 army mutiny and brutal May 1980 suppression of the pro-democracy Kwangju uprising. "The prosecution's reinvestigation is not to uncover the truth, but rather to meet political needs arising from the current political situation," says Chun in a statement prior to his arrest. "I have already given all the answers that I could to the prosecution and the hearings conducted by the 13th National Assembly. The prosecution has already completed its investigation of the incidents." In jail, Chun begins a hunger strike which lasts for 27 days.

5   Former South Korean president Roh Tae Woo is indicted on charges of accepting bribes in return for gov-

ernment favors amounting to some $368 million from 35 businesses while in office from 1988 to 1993. Roh has been held in the Seoul Detention House since his arrest on November 16. Several of South Korea's leading businessmen, including seven *chaebol* chairmen, are indicted for having given bribes to Roh. The seven business chairmen indicted, without physical detention orders, are Samsung's Lee Kun Hee, Daewoo's Kim Woo Chung, Dong Ah's Choi Won Suk, Jinro's Chang Jin Ho, Daelim's Lee Joon Yong, Dongbu's Kim Joon Ki, and Daeho's Lee Kun.

11   South Korean state prosecutors probing business kickbacks to ex-president Roh Tae Woo question Kim Yong Ho, vice president of the Seoul branch of the U.S. firm Lockheed Martin, over a 52-hour period. Prosecutors are examining a $5 billion contract made during the Roh administration, under the Yulgok military buildup in 1991, to buy 120 F-16s from General Dynamics, reversing an earlier plan to buy F-18s from McDonnell Douglas. General Dynamics was mostly acquired in 1992 by Lockheed Corp., which merged with Martin Marietta early in 1995 to form Lockheed Martin. Kim, the former head of General Dynamics in Seoul, denied any involvement in unethical activity, and General Dynamics reiterated the company's position that "all of its business in Korea has been appropriate and legal" and that the allegations of bribery are "without merit or substance." Questioned at the same time is Kim Chong Hwi, 60, Roh's top national security advisor. Former top military officers, including two defense ministers, Lee Jong Koo and Lee Sang Hoon, and Air Force chief Han Chu Sok, have already been questioned by prosecutors.

12   In his first public statement since the jailing of the two ex-presidents, President Kim Young Sam declares, "We will have to firmly guard the democracy which we have won at the cost of our blood, sweat, and tears by

December 1995 *(continued)*

bravely liquidating the vestiges of militarism and exorcising the ghost of the coup d'état." In a reversal of his earlier position to let history be the judge of prior action, Kim states that "righting the wrongs of history is, indeed, a revolution to restore our honor and regain self-esteem. . . . Through the former president's corruption case, I have been able to confirm that the roots of this grave betrayal of the trust and expectations of the people lie in the December 12 and May 17 and 18 incidents. We can no longer overlook, in the name of reconciliation, their acts and attitude which have disgraced the people and our history."

15   The Korean Energy Development Organization (KEDO) and North Korea sign an accord on the scope of supply of two light-water nuclear reactors to the DPRK.

18   The biggest trial in South Korea's history begins as former president Roh Tae Woo, 63, and 14 others, including 7 top *chaebol* chairmen and 5 former aides, face charges relating to the slush-fund scandal. The former president admits to taking money from 35 business groups but denies that the cash was in return for favors.

The International Committee of the Red Cross redoubles aid appeals for North Korea, stating that 130,000 people are on the brink of famine after not receiving food rations for five months. To date, the global response to the original appeals for aid has been extremely limited.

19   On the last day of its 100-day regular session, the South Korean National Assembly passes a controversial bill, drafted by the ruling New Korea Party in response to the November 24 instructions of President Kim Young Sam, paving the way for the prosecution of former presidents Chun Doo Hwan and Roh Tae Woo. Under the special law, the 15-year statutory limitations on Chun

and Roh were suspended until February 24, 1993, when Roh's term in office expired. As a result, indictments can be sought against Roh and Chun until February 24, 2008.

21   Former presidents Chun and Roh are indicted on charges relating to their roles in the December 12, 1979, military mutiny. Six charges are leveled against Chun, including leading the mutiny, attempted murder of superior officers, murder of a guard, and illegal movement of troops. Roh is also charged on six counts, including participation in the plotting of a military insurrection, attempted murder of a superior officer, murder of a guard, illegal movement of troops, and disengagement from a designated post under martial law.

27   The owner and founder of Seoul's Sampoong Department Store, Lee Joon, 73, is convicted of criminal negligence and jailed for 10 years. Deemed South Korea's worst peacetime disaster, the store collapsed on June 29, killing more than 650 people.

28   United Nations food agencies report that 2.1 million children risk starvation in flood-damaged North Korea and estimate that North Korea will fall 1.2 million tons short of its total grain requirement of 6 million tons for 1996.

29   The Hyundai Group announces a major personnel shake-up, naming a new chairman and moving many founding-generation managers out of active involvement. Chung Mong Koo, 57, chairman of Hyundai Precision & Industry Co. and second son of Hyundai founder Chung Ju Young, is named as successor to current Hyundai chairman Chung Se Yung, who becomes honorary chairman. Chung Mong Kyu, 33, the only son of Chung Se Yung and current vice president of the Hyundai Motor Co., is named as chairman of Hyundai

December 1995 *(continued)*

Motor Co. Park Byung Jae, vice president of Hyundai Motor, is selected as the auto company's president, and Chung Mong Hyuk, vice president of Hyundai Oil Refinery, is moved to president of the oil company. The personnel changes, affecting some 404 executives, are said by Hyundai to mark a generational change in the group's management, with the emergence of young managers in many key posts.

January 1996

3   Hyundai chairman Chung Mong Koo announces he will appoint directors from outside the company to help polish its image.

The DPRK accepts an invitation to compete at the 1996 Summer Olympics in Atlanta, ensuring a 100 percent turnout rate for the Centennial Games. North Korea's confirmation was the last of a record number of 197 nations agreeing to participate.

12   South Korean prosecutors indict former president Chun Doo Hwan, who has been under arrest since December 3, on charges that he used pressure, such as the threat of taxes, to elicit $275 million in bribes. The investigation leading to the indictment reports that Chun amassed a political slush fund of some $1.2 billion, exceeding the $630 million slush fund of his successor Roh Tae Woo. Also indicted are five former senior officials of the Chun administration: Ahn Hyun Tae, Chun's former security chief; Song Yong Wook, former director of the National Taxation Office; Ahn My Hyuk, former chief of the National Security Agency; Il Sa Kong, former minister of finance and a prominent economist; and Lee Won Jo, former president of the Bank Supervisory Bureau.

14   The first shipload of equipment for use in the construction of two light-water reactors in the DPRK leaves the

South Korean port of Pusan bound for the North Korean port of Rajin for transport to Shinpo on the northeast coast of North Korea. Large drilling machines, mud pumps, and other equipment for a geological survey are loaded on the Chinese-flagged ship *Yanlong IV*.

16   After two days of negotiations between Seoul and Washington, both sides agree to grant South Korea greater jurisdiction over U.S. soldiers charged with crimes in an effort to ease anti-U.S. sentiment. They agreed in principle that U.S. suspects in certain crimes will be turned over to local authorities after being indicted, replacing the current system which allows the U.S. military to maintain custody of its service people involved in all crimes until all appeals have been completed.

17   It is announced that Kim Woo Chung, Daewoo Group chairman, will be tried from January 26 on charges of offering bribes for arms deals during Roh Tae Woo's administration. Kim Chong Hwi, Roh's former chief aide for security and foreign affairs, will also stand trial on charges of accepting a total of $164,000 in bribes in 1992 from domestic and foreign companies in connection with South Korea's huge arms-procurement program.

18   The ROK government announces that trade between Taiwan and South Korea surged 48 percent to $6.35 billion in the first 11 months of 1995, recovering from a slump following their 1992 severance of diplomatic ties.

Three retired South Korean army generals, close aides to former president Chun, are arrested on charges of involvement in the Kwangju massacre. Over one month later, 3 more former generals are arrested in conjunction with the military crackdown, bringing the total number of arrests to 14.

January 1996 *(continued)*

22   Lee Hoe Chang, a popular former prime minister known as South Korea's "Mr. Clean," joins the ruling New Korea Party to provide support for President Kim's anti-corruption crusade.

23   South Korean prosecutors formally charge Roh Tae Woo and Chun Doo Hwan with treason surrounding the 1980 army massacre of pro-democracy activists. Both former presidents already face mutiny charges in conjunction with the 1979 coup that brought them to power and corruption charges for amassing slush funds during their rule.

Kim Dae Jung, veteran opposition leader, accuses President Kim of seeking punishment for Roh and Chun as "a cynical election ploy."

30   North Korea gives the IAEA approval to inspect all of its unfrozen nuclear facilities now that KEDO, represented by the United States, Japan, and South Korea, has agreed to build two 1,000-megawatt light-water reactors in the North by 2003.

February 1996

2   The U.S. Department of State announces it will contribute $2 million to help alleviate famine in North Korea. The money will be provided to the United Nations World Food Programme (WFP) through the U.S. Agency for International Development. This decision comes one week after South Korean and Japanese government officials advise Washington of their plans not to provide further assistance, claiming North Korean citizens are not in "dire straits." The Korean Central News Agency responds by claiming the United States' "humanitarian steps ... will remove distrust between the DPRK and the United States and create an atmosphere favorable for a smooth implementation of the DPRK-U.S. framework agreement."

9   South Korean prosecutors demand a five-year jail term and a fine of 230 million won for Kim Chong Hwi, Roh Tae Woo's former chief secretary, for accepting bribes linked to a state arms procurement program. He was indicted in December for accepting 50 million won from Daewoo Group, 100 million from Hanjin Group, and 80 million won from a U.S. arms dealer in connection with aircraft imports.

South Korea rejects Japan's demand to stop building a wharf on a disputed island (known as Tokdo in Korea and Takeshima in Japan) located in the Sea of Japan, or the East Sea to Koreans. Seoul authorities claim, "Tokdo is our territory both historically and under international law," and the Japanese state the island "is historically, and in the view of international law, an integral part of Japan." In December South Korea ratified the United Nations Convention on the Law of the Sea, which allows it to impose a 200-mile exclusive economic zone off its shores, and Japan is expected to do the same. The disputed island lies within 200 miles of both shores. On February 15 South Korea conducts high-profile military exercises near the islet.

14   The U.S. and the ROK announce their plans to cancel Team Spirit exercises for the third consecutive year in an effort to "encourage North Korea to forgo its suspected nuclear weapons program."

15   A 25-year-old North Korean man, attempting to seek asylum from a harsh court sentence in the DPRK, kills three Korean guards and then turns the gun on himself in the Russian embassy compound in P'yongyang.

16   Kim Jong Il celebrates his 54th birthday. He does not attend the series of gala celebrations held in his honor.

19   Kim Jong Il goes to a mass meeting marking his birthday; it is his first public appearance in a month.

February 1996 *(continued)*

21   South Korean media report that North Korea "is recall-
        ing children of high-ranking officials living or working
        abroad" in an effort to stop the string of defections that
        total more than 80 people over the past two years.

22   The U.S. again rejects North Korea's proposal for a
        temporary U.S.-DPRK peace accord with Washington
        to replace the 1953 Korean War armistice. A State De-
        partment spokesman says, "We would never think of
        entering into any agreement with North Korea that did
        not include our ally, the Republic of Korea."

26   Former president Chun Doo Hwan, on the opening day
        of his corruption trial, denies taking bribes and vows to
        protect the identities of those who benefited from his
        slush fund. He claims his fortune came from political
        donations.

        A South Korean government agency announces that
        North Korea's two-way trade shrank from $2.11 bil-
        lion in 1994 to $2.06 billion in 1995. These esti-
        mated figures are gathered from North Korea's
        trading partners since the North does not publish
        trade figures.

March 1996

20   South Korea's Central Bank reports that the ROK's
        gross domestic product grew 9 percent in 1995 from a
        year ago, the highest growth rate since 1991. Exports
        of goods and services increased 24.1 percent in 1995,
        and merchandise exports rose 25.3 percent, due pri-
        marily to increased shipments abroad of South Korean
        automobiles, semiconductors, and machinery. Per ca-
        pita GNP was $10,076 in 1995, ranking the ROK 32nd
        in the world.

21   A 6,538-ton cargo ship carrying food aid to North
        Korea sinks in stormy seas in the Taiwan Strait.

April 1996

4   Commenting on the Armistice Agreement, North Korea's Korean Central News Agency announces, "Firstly, the Korean People's Army shall give up its duty, under the Armistice Agreement, concerning the maintenance and control of the military demarcation line and the DMZ. Secondly, the Korean People's Army shall, as a follow-up step to the first measure, have its personnel and vehicles bear no distinctive insignia and marking when they enter the joint security area of P'anmunjom and the DMZ."

5–7   On three consecutive evenings starting on April 5, North Korea sends several hundred troops into prohibited areas of the 151-mile-long DMZ. "What have they done? They've come into the security area near P'anmunjom in numbers in excess of those permitted by the Armistice Agreement," says U.S. State Department spokesperson Glyn Davies. "They've brought in armaments that aren't permitted, and they're not wearing the kind of insignia that's required by the armistice agreement. Those three things . . . add up to a kind of serious walking away from the Armistice Agreement." ROK president Kim Young Sam places troops on their highest level of readiness in 15 years. "We see this as primarily a political rather than a military move," says Pentagon spokesman Kenneth Bacon.

11   South Korea holds its National Assembly elections. In a better-than-expected showing, President Kim's New Korea Party (NKP) loses its parliamentary majority but retains 139 of the 299 seats. "Our party was not able to achieve our original target, but . . . we won almost half of the seats, especially in the capital, and this is politically significant," says the ruling NKP in a statement. Kim Young Sam's NKP wins 27 of the 47 seats in Seoul, the first time a ruling party has won more than half the seats in the capital. Faring worse than expected,

April 1996 *(continued)*

Kim Dae Jung's National Congress for New Politics (NCNP) wins a total of 79 seats, up from the 55 it held in the prior session. "The government of Kim Young Sam mobilized all television to magnify and exaggerate reports on the DMZ issue," says the NCNP in a statement. "We believe the poor results were firstly due to our lack of ability and effort. But a bigger reason is outside forces such as television, prosecutors, and police which downplayed the opposition." Kim Chong Pil's United Liberal Democrats wins a total of 50 seats, the Democratic Party, led by Kim Won Ki and Chang Eul Byung, wins 50 seats, and independent candidates garner a total of 16 seats. Voter turnout is a record-low 63 percent according to the Central Election Management Commission.

16   In a summit meeting on South Korea's Cheju Island, President Clinton joins with President Kim to unveil a joint U.S.-ROK proposal to hold a four-party meeting (with the DPRK and China) for the promotion of peace on the Korean peninsula. This is the fifth time the two presidents have met since President Kim took office in February 1993. "I don't see this proposal as being new or innovative," says Russian ambassador to Seoul Georgi Kunadse. "Russia still has national and security interests directly related to the Korean peninsula and we will be pursuing these interests. . . . South Korea has been remarkably incapable of bringing North Korea to the negotiating table and I really wonder if this time it will be any different." North Korea's Foreign Ministry responds in a statement that

As for the matter of preserving peace on the Korean peninsula, it should be discussed and decided upon by the DPRK and the United States, signatories to the Armistice Agreement. We have no clear notion of why the U.S. side, which knows this fact better than anyone else, abruptly proposed "quadrilateral talks." Now that the Korean peninsula is in a situation strikingly similar to the state of war, it is urgently required that the outdated Armistice Agreement should be replaced by a peace agreement. . . . We have long since proposed it as a major issue to conclude a peace agreement between the DPRK and the United States. We are not yet certain whether the "proposal for quadrilateral talks" is aimed at concluding a genuine peace agreement between the signatories to the Korean Armistice Agreement. As is known to all, the North and the South of Korea have already agreed upon nonaggression, reconciliation, and cooperation, and a document on the agreement has been published all over the world. The point of issue is that the document has not been carried into practice. It is entirely because the North-South dialogue has been suspended due to the South Korean authorities. We are not certain, either, whether the "proposal for quadrilateral talks" is related to this issue. We are now examining the proposal of the U.S. side to see whether it seeks another purpose and whether it is feasible.

20   Officials from the United States and North Korea begin two days of bilateral missile talks in Berlin centered on U.S. concerns about P'yongyang's production and sales of long-range ballistic missiles to the Middle East, including Syria and Libya. The United States seeks to encourage North Korea to join an international agreement to restrict export of such weapons. The U.S. delegation is led by the State Department's political and military affairs deputy assistant secretary of state for nonproliferation, Robert Einhorn; the DPRK's delegation is headed by Lee Hyung Chul. "The talks were useful and made a good beginning," says a U.S. negotiator. "We intend to continue our dialogue but the method of doing that will be determined later."

Glossary

Agency for National Security Planning (ANSP). ROK foreign and domestic intelligence agency. Until 1981 it was called the (Korean) Central Intelligence Agency.

Agreement on Reconciliation, Nonaggression, and Exchanges and Cooperation Between the South and the North. A series of agreements signed by the prime ministers of North and South Korea at the height of progress in the 1990–92 high-level negotiations to ease tensions on the Korean peninsula. In the agreements the two sides resolved to settle disputes peacefully, set up communications, and exchange information. It was signed on December 13, 1991, and was followed at the end of the month by a six-point "denuclearization" declaration in which both sides agreed not to produce or possess nuclear weapons.

Armistice Agreement. The agreement to end the Korean War, signed at P'anmunjom on July 27, 1953, by the United Nations Command (representing UN, U.S., and South Korean forces) on the one side and the supreme commander of the Korean People's Army and the commander of the Chinese People's Volunteers on the other. The purpose of the agreement was to stop the fighting and prevent outbreaks of hostilities "until a peaceful settlement is achieved"; however, no permanent peace treaty replacing this supposedly temporary truce has yet been negotiated.

Basic Agreement. See Agreement on Reconciliation.

Blue House. Colloquial English term for the South Korean presidential establishment, derived from the blue-tile roof of the presidential residence, Chongwadae.

Chaebol. Korean term for business conglomerates such as Hyundai, LG (formerly Lucky-Goldstar), Samsung, Daewoo, and Sunkyong.

Cholla. Refers to North and South Cholla provinces in southwestern Korea. Also referred to as the Honam region. Home area of Kim Dae Jung. Kwangju is its main city.

Chosen Soren. Association of North Koreans living in Japan. Also known as Chochongnyon or Chongnyon.

Chun Doo Hwan. President of the Fifth Republic of Korea, 1980–88. During Chun's term, the so-called Fifth Republic irregularities—for example, Chun's relatives' illegal economic activities—overshadowed his achievement in leading the nation to ˉeconomic recovery. On December 31, 1989, Chun testified before the National Assembly on the Fifth Republic irregularities and the Kwangju Incident of 1980. At the end of 1990, Chun completed a two-year period of contemplation at a remote temple in Kangwon province and returned to Seoul, where he now lives in virtual seclusion. Indicted at the end of 1995 and on trial beginning in early 1996 for his involvement, with Roh Tae Woo, in the December 12, 1979, military putsch (see 12/12 Incident) and the orders to use ROK military troops against the citizens of Kwangju (see Kwangju Incident). Chun was found guilty and sentenced to death. That sentence is being appealed.

Ch'ungch'ong. Refers to North and South Ch'ungch'ong provinces in west-central Korea. Home area of Kim Chong Pil. Main city is Taejon.

Chung Ju Young. Founder and honorary chairman of the Hyundai business group, he played a significant role in the Roh Tae Woo government's *Nordpolitik*, notably in creating commercial links to the former Soviet Union and attempting to take South Korean investment into North Korea. In 1991, after facing a tax investigation, he decided to enter politics and founded the Unification National Party (UNP). In the December 1992 election he placed third, with about 16 percent of the popular vote.

Combined Forces Command (CFC). The military command structure created jointly by the United States and South Korea in 1978 to replace the United Nations Command structure dating from the Korean War. The mission of the CFC is to coordinate the use of U.S. and ROK military units in the defense of South Korea. Until 1994, the commander in chief (CINC) of the forces was the U.S. general who was concurrently the CINC of the United Nations Command, U.S. Forces Korea, and the Eighth U.S. Army. On December 1, 1994, peacetime control of the ROK forces was handed over to the South Korean government, but control will revert to the United States in time of war.

Demilitarized Zone (DMZ). An area of two kilometers on both sides of the Military Demarcation Line, 155 miles long, that forms the border between South and North Korea. The DMZ was set aside by the Armistice Agreement of July 27, 1953, as a buffer zone to prevent an outbreak of hostilities.

Democratic Justice Party (DJP). Established in 1981 by President Chun Doo Hwan. Roh Tae Woo became its chairman in 1985. On January 22, 1990, under President Roh, the DJP merged with two of the three opposition parties to form the Democratic Liberal Party. Renamed the New Korea Party in early 1996, it is headed by Kim Young Sam.

Democratic Liberal Party (DLP). Formed by the merger of the DJP and two opposition parties, the Reunification Democratic Party, headed by Kim Young Sam, and the New Democratic Republican Party, led by Kim Chong Pil, on January 22, 1990, it commanded more than a two-thirds majority in the ROK National Assembly until the assembly election of March 24, 1992, from which it emerged with a total of 149 out of 299 seats, one vote short of a majority. In the December 1992 presidential election, DLP candidate Kim Young Sam won with a 42 percent plurality. Known as the New Korea Party since January 1996. In the April 11, 1996, National Assembly elections, the DLP experienced a slight decline, but with added members from other parties, it holds a majority position in the assembly.

Democratic Party (DP). Established in early 1990 as an opposition party after two of the three former opposition parties had merged with the ruling DJP to form the DLP. Its leader is Lee Ki Taek. In 1991 it merged with the Party for Peace and Democracy, headed by

Kim Dae Jung, and in the March 24, 1992, National Assembly election it won a total of 97 of the 299 seats. In the December 1992 presidential election, DP candidate Kim Dae Jung drew 34 percent of the vote. Following June 1995 election success, Kim Dae Jung withdrew and the DP collapsed.

Democratic People's Republic of Korea (DPRK). Official name of North Korea since 1948.

Elections. The **13th presidential election of December 16, 1987,** was the first direct election for president in South Korea since 1971. DJP candidate Roh Tae Woo secured 36.6 percent of the vote, trailed by Kim Young Sam of the Reunification Democratic Party (RDP; 28 percent), Kim Dae Jung of the Party for Peace and Democracy (PPD; 27 percent), and Kim Chong Pil of the New Democratic Republican Party (NDRP; 8.1 percent).

Supreme People's Assembly elections took place in North Korea on April 22, 1990. Of the 687 seats, 601 (87.5 percent) were won by candidates of the ruling Korean Workers' Party (KWP).

On March 26, 1991, local elections were held for the first time in the ROK since the military coup of 1961 to elect representatives to city, county, and district assemblies. Candidates ran ostensibly without party labels, but candidates supporting the ruling DLP were seen as having won a strong majority of the races. On June 20, 1991, a second round of local elections was held for provincial and Special City (e.g., Seoul and Pusan) assemblies, in which declared party candidates ran and the DLP won 65.1 percent of the seats (564 out of 866), many more than most observers had predicted.

The 14th National Assembly election in South Korea was held on March 24, 1992. The ruling DLP emerged with 149 out of 299 seats in the national legislature, one short of a majority. The Democratic Party won 97, the new United People's Party won 31, independents won 21, and a splinter party won the remaining vote.

The 14th presidential election of December 18, 1992, brought victory to Kim Young Sam of the Democratic Liberal Party. Kim is the first nonmilitary president to be elected in South Korea in more than 30 years.

On June 27, 1995, local elections saw success for the Democratic Party, whereupon Kim Dae Jung withdrew. On July 18, 1995, he formed the National Congress for new Politics (NCNP).

National Assembly elections were held in South Korea on April 11, 1996. The NCNP suffered surprising losses in the elections; Kim Dae Jung failed to win election to the assembly. North Korean provocations in the DMZ may well have strengthened the vote for Kim Young Sam's New Korea Party.

Fifth Republic. The Chun Doo Hwan regime, 1980–88.

Foreign Joint Venture Law (1984). The first DPRK law permitting foreign investment. Updated in 1992.

Hanahoe. Unity Society. Private organization of military officers including Chun Doo Hwan and Roh Tae Woo, disbanded in 1993.

Han'gul. The Korean phonetic alphabet, promulgated by King Sejong in 1446.

Juche. Kim Il Sung's ideology, first articulated in 1955. Stresses self-reliance, nationalism, frugality, hard work, unity, and respect for North Korean revolutionary tradition. Ideological basis of the Kim Il Sung cult in North Korea. Basic texts include Kim Il Sung's collected works.

Kang Song San. Prime minister of the DPRK since 1992. His absence from public life in 1996 is said to be the result of serious illness.

Kim Chong Pil. Member of General Park Chung Hee's junta in the military coup of 1961 and founder of the Korean Central Intelligence Agency; architect of Park's ruling Democratic Republican Party (1963); key player in South Korea's normalization of diplomatic relations with Japan (1963–65); prime minister (1971–75); in semiretirement after Park's assassination, reemerged as National Assembly member and founder of the New Democratic Republican Party. After winning only 35 of 299 seats in the National Assembly elections of April 1988, Kim merged his NDRP with parties led by Roh Tae Woo and Kim Young Sam to form the Democratic Liberal Party in January 1990. In 1995 he left the DLP to form the United Liberal Democrats.

Kim Dae Jung. Co-leader and 1992 presidential candidate of the main opposition Democratic Party. A native of South Cholla Province, Kim began his career in presidential politics in 1971, when he mounted a surprisingly strong showing against then-president Park Chung Hee, winning 45.3 percent of the popular vote. After being subjected to various forms of pressure including incarceration during the 1970s, Kim was convicted of sedition in 1980, just before the start of Chun Doo Hwan's Fifth Republic, and sentenced to a 20-year prison term. Then-DJP chairman Roh Tae Woo's June 1987 Declaration restored Kim's civil rights and enabled him to establish a political party in time for the 13th presidential election of December 1987, in which he won 27 percent of the vote as opposed to Roh Tae Woo's 36.6 percent. In 1990 he helped create the Democratic Party, and he ran as its candidate in the December 1992 presidential election, drawing 34 percent of the popular vote and coming in second to Kim Young Sam. In the April 1996 National Assembly elections, Kim failed to win a seat in the assembly.

Kim Il Sung. Leader North Korea since 1945. Known as the Great Leader. Died July 8, 1994.

Kim Jong Il. The eldest son of Kim Il Sung, named to succeed him as North Korea's leader. Known as the Dear Leader. As of July 1996 Kim Jong Il still had not formally been named General Secretary of the Korean Worker's Party or President of the Government. He rules as the Supreme Commander of the Korean People's Army and Chairman of the National Defense Commission.

Kim Young Sam. As presidential nominee of the Democratic Liberal Party (DLP) in 1992, elected President of the Republic of Korea. Also head of the New Korea Party, formerly the DLP. Former co-chairman of the DLP. Former leader of the Reunification Democratic Party, which he represented in the presidential election of 1987 and later merged with President Roh Tae Woo's Democratic Justice Party in January 1990. Longtime opposition leader during the presidencies of Park Chung Hee and Chun Doo Hwan.

Korean Workers' Party (KWP). The ruling party of North Korea, usually characterized as communist or "Kimilsungist."

KOTRA. Formerly the Korean Overseas Trade Association. Renamed the Korea Trade and Investment Promotion Agency, keeping the original acronym.

Kwangju Incident. A violent ten-day confrontation in May 1980 between ROK special-forces troops under the command of Roh Tae Woo and anti–martial law demonstrators in Kwangju, South Cholla province. The death toll is still not certain; somewhere between 190 and 2,000 people were killed. Chun Doo Hwan and Roh Tae Woo are on trial for their part in the incident, which has become a symbol of the democratization movement in Korea.

Kyongsang. Refers to North and South Kyongsang provinces in southeastern Korea. Also referred to as the Yongnam region. Home area of Roh Tae Woo, Chun Doo Hwan, and many other Fifth and Sixth Republic figures, as well as of Kim Young Sam. Pusan and Taegu are major cities.

Law on South-North Exchange and Cooperation. Promulgated in August 1990 by the South Korean government in order to promote and regulate South-North exchange and cooperation; revised in December 1992.

Lee Ki Taek. Democratic Party chairman.

Liberation Interval (1945–48). The period between Liberation in 1945 and the installation through UN-sponsored elections in 1948 of the separate political regimes in the North and South. Viewed as the brief period following Liberation before Korea was completely divided.

March First (1919) Independence Movement. The spontaneous popular uprising against Japanese colonial rule that erupted with the reading of a Korean declaration of independence during preparations for the funeral of the fallen monarch, Emperor Kojong. The movement, planned in part by Korean students in Japan and by religious and community leaders in Korea, was the biggest outbreak of resistance to Japanese rule during the entire colonial period (1910–45). As it spread across the nation and continued into 1920, it provoked severe repression from the Japanese, who took an estimated 7,000 Korean lives in the process of quelling demonstrations.

Most modern political movements in Korea claim some connection to the March First Movement.

Ministry of National Unification (MNU). South Korean ministry having planning oversight and evaluation responsibility for all contacts with North Korea. Known as the National Unification Board before 1995.

National Congress for New Politics (NCNP). The new political party of Kim Dae Jung.

National Security Law. Enacted in 1948 to control the activities of "anti-state" organizations. The law's ostensible purpose is to protect national security, but it has frequently been applied selectively to punish domestic dissidents. The law was amended in May 1991 to limit offenses to those that would "endanger the security of the nation or basic order of liberal democracy."

New Korea Party (NKP). ROK government party, headed by Kim Young Sam. Formerly the Democratic Liberal Party.

Nordpolitik **(Northern Policy).** A term to describe the Roh Tae Woo government's diplomatic strategy to initiate détente with North Korea and to establish economic and diplomatic relations with other countries of the former Soviet bloc when they were still under communist rule.

P'anmunjom. Originally a village south of Kaesong in what is now the DMZ; site of the truce talks at the end of the Korean War. Since 1953 it has been the primary point of contact between the United Nations (South Korean) side and North Korea.

Park Chung Hee. Leader of the military coup of 1961; president of the ROK from 1963 to 1979. In 1972 Park instituted the Yushin Constitution, under which he became the first indirectly elected president of South Korea, chosen by an electoral college, and ruled by decree through most of the 1970s. Park was assassinated by the Korean Central Intelligence Agency director Kim Chae Gyu on October 26, 1979.

Rajin-Sonbong Free Economic and Trade Zone (FETZ). An area bordering China and Russia in the northeast corner of the DPRK. In 1991 it was declared a zone for joint-venture and other international enterprise operations.

Republic of Korea (ROK). Official name of South Korea since 1948.

Reunification Democratic Party. The political party created when Kim Young Sam and Kim Dae Jung joined forces in the 1987 presidential election. Following the 1987 election, the party merged with Kim Jong Pil's New Democratic Republican Party and Roh Tae Woo's Democratic Liberation Party.

Rodong Shinmun. "Workers' Newspaper" in P'yongyang. The organ of the Korean Workers' Party.

Roh Tae Woo. President of the Republic of Korea, 1988–93. Having risen from the military with Chun Doo Hwan, he served as minister of home affairs, minister of sports, chairman of the Seoul Olympics Organizing Committee under the Fifth Republic, and chairman of the ruling Democratic Justice Party from 1985 to 1987, when he became the DJP's candidate for the presidency, which he won by a plurality of just under 37 percent in the December 1987 election. As president, Roh worked to ease authoritarianism, open a dialogue with the former socialist bloc, and rectify the imbalances in the Korean economy. Though he was largely successful in setting the stage for "democratization" in South Korea, he never completely escaped the taint of association with Chun Doo Hwan and the Fifth Republic. On trial beginning in December 1995 for his part in the Kwangju Incident of 1980 and other charges, he was found guilty and sentenced to prison.

Sampoong Department Store. Luxury goods store that collapsed, killing over 650 people, in Seoul on June 29, 1995.

Segyehwa. Globalization, the theme of the Kim Young Sam government in the mid-1990s.

Status of Forces Agreement. The agreement covering U.S. military facilities and jurisdiction over U.S. military personnel suspected of crimes committed in South Korea, signed in 1966. In 1990 the agreement was modified to give the Korean side more latitude in the arrest and prosecution of U.S. military personnel charged with crimes in the ROK.

Super 301 provision. Section 301 of the U.S. Omnibus Trade Act of 1988 designed to discourage unfair trading. Countries found to be trading unfairly or discriminating against U.S. goods may have preferences canceled for their goods and restrictions such as special duties imposed by way of retaliation.

Team Spirit. Annual ROK-U.S. joint military exercise between 1976 and 1991. In the 1980s it usually involved about 140,000 South Korean soldiers and 60,000 Americans, many of whom were flown in from outside Korea. In 1991 the exercise was scaled down in light of the Persian Gulf War and U.S. defense budget cuts, and in 1992 Team Spirit was canceled in the interests of promoting North Korean cooperation on nuclear inspections. However, with the impasse that was reached over the North Korean nuclear program, the exercises were resumed in March 1993, but canceled in 1994, 1995, and 1996.

Three Ds. A term of the 1990s referring to the dirty, difficult, or dangerous jobs that Korean workers no longer want. By implication, the term suggests a labor shortage in Korea, as well as a reason for the increasing numbers of South Asian immigrant workers.

Three Kims. Kim Young Sam, Kim Dae Jung, and Kim Chong Pil. Used especially with reference to the 1987 presidential election and the idea that there were "too many Kims."

12/12 Incident. Military coup orchestrated by Chun Doo Hwan on December 12, 1979, to remove rivals for power.

United People's Party (UPP). Also known as the Unification National Party. Founded by Chung Ju Young in 1991.

Yongbyon. City north of P'yongyang; location of North Korea's nuclear facility, which is suspected of being capable of producing nuclear weapons and to which, until June 1991, the DPRK refused to permit access for international inspection. In 1992 the P'yongyang facilities were opened to inspection by the International Atomic Energy Agency, though the course of the inspections has been extremely problematic. The October 1994 Agreed Framework between the United States and North Korea froze the operation of these nuclear facilities.

Suggestions for Further Reading

Introduction

Myers, Bryan. *Han Sorya and North Korean Literature: The Failure of Socialist Realism in the DPRK* (Cornell East Asia Series). Ithaca, N.Y.: Cornell University, 1994.

Shorrock, Tim. "Ex-Leaders to Go on Trial in Seoul." *Journal of Commerce* (February 27, 1996).

The Politics of Transition in North and South Korea

Bedeski, Robert. *The Transformation of South Korea: Reform and Reconstitution in the Sixth Republic Under Roh Tae Woo, 1987–1992.* New York: Routledge, 1994.

Clifford, Mark L. *Troubled Tiger: Businessmen, Bureaucrats, and Generals in South Korea.* Armonk, N.Y.: M.E. Sharpe, 1994.

Eberstadt, Nicholas, and Judith Banister. *The Population of North Korea.* Berkeley, Calif.: University of California Press, 1972.

Koo, Hagen, ed. *State and Society in Contemporary Korea.* Ithaca, N.Y.: Cornell University Press, 1993.

Scalapino, Robert, and Chong-Sik Lee. *Communism in Korea.* Berkeley, Calif.: University of California Press, 1972.

Yang, Sung-chul. *The North and South Korean Political Systems: A Comparative Analysis.* Boulder, Colo.: Westview Press, 1994.

The Problem and Promise of Inter-Korean Economic Cooperation

Eberstadt, Nicholas. "Inter-Korean Economic Cooperation: Rapprochement Through Trade?" *Korea and World Affairs,* Vol. 18, no. 4 (Winter 1994), pp. 642–661.

Hwang, Eui Gak. *Pukkhan kyungjeron: Nam-Pukkhan kyungjeui hyunhwanggwa pigyo* (The North Korean Economy: Current Situation and Comparison with South Korean Economy). Seoul: Nanam Publishing, 1993.

Lee, Doowon. "The North Korean Economic System: Historical Analysis and Future Prospects." Paper presented at the conference A Comparative Study of the System of Market Economy and Land Ownership/Use, East-West Center, Honolulu, Hawaii, August 7–12, 1995, pp. 1–56.

Tongil Paekso 1995 (Unification White Paper 1995). Seoul: National Unification Board, 1995.

Yoo, Jang-Hee. "South-North Economic Relations in the Korean Peninsula: A Complementary Hypothesis." *Korea and World Affairs,* Vol. 14, no. 3 (Fall 1995). Also published in the ROK Ministry of National Unification's Information Service, Vol. 5, October 31, 1995, pp. 30–42.

Young, Namkoong. "A Comparative Study on North and South Korean Economic Capability." *Journal of East Asian Affairs,* Vol. 9, no. 1 (Winter/Spring 1995), pp. 1–43.

Why the Cold War Persists in Korea:
Inter-Korean and Foreign Relations

∨ Cotton, James, ed. *Politics and Policy in the New Korean State: From Roh Tae-woo to Kim Young-sam.* New York: St. Martin's Press, 1995.

Eberstadt, Nicholas. *Korea Approaches Reunification.* Armonk, N.Y.: M.E. Sharpe, 1995.

Kihl, Young Whan, ed. *Korea and the World: Beyond the Cold War.* Boulder, Colo.: Westview Press, 1994.

✓ Mazarr, Michael J. *North Korea and the Bomb: A Case Study in Nonproliferation.* New York: St. Martin's Press, 1995.

South Korean Teachers' Struggle for Education Reform

Committee for Publishing Minjung Kyoyuk, ed. *Minjung Kyoyuk 1* (People's Education [Minjung Education] Vol. 1). Seoul: Silchun Munhak, 1985.

Committee for Publishing Minjung Kyoyuk, ed. *Minjung Kyoyuk 2* (People's Education [Minjung Education] Vol. 2). Seoul: P'urun namu, 1988.

Kim, Shin-il. "Korean Education Past and Present." *Korea Journal,* Vol. 27, no. 4.

Korean Teachers and Educational Workers Union, ed. *Hankook Kyoyuk Undong Baekso* (White Paper on the Korean Education Movement). Seoul: P'ulpit, 1990.

McGinn, Noel, et al. *Education and Development* (in the series Studies in the Modernization of the Republic of Korea: 1945–1975). Council on East Asian Studies. Cambridge: Harvard University Press, 1980.

Office of Planning for Publishing Educational Books, ed. *Kyoyuk Nodong Undong* (Educational Labor Movement). Seoul: Sokt'ap', 1986.

Rhee, Mok. *Hanguk Kyowon Nojo Undongsa* (History of the Korean Teachers Union Movement). Seoul: P'urun namu, 1989.

Life After Death in North Korea

Kim, Il Sung. *Reminiscences with the Century.* P'yongyang: Foreign Languages Publishing House, 1992.

Linton, Stephen W. "North Korea Under the Son." *Washington Quarterly* (Spring 1996), pp. 3–17.

Linton, Stephen W. "Patterns in Korean Civil Religions." Ph.D. dissertation, University Microfilms, Ann Arbor, Mich., 1989.

Merrill, John. *Korea: The Peninsular Origins of the War.* Newark, Del.: University of Delaware Press, 1989.

Suh, Dae-sook. *Kim Il Sung: The North Korean Leader.* New York: Columbia University Press, 1988.

Yi, Kibaek. *A New History of Korea.* Cambridge: Harvard University Press, 1984.

Language, Politics, and Ideology in the Postwar Koreas

Coulmas, Florian, ed. *Language Adaptation.* Cambridge: Cambridge University Press, 1989.

Joseph, John Earl. *Eloquence and Power: The Rise of Language Standards and Standard Languages.* London: Francis Pinter, 1987.

King, Ross. "Korean Writing," in Peter Daniels and William Bright, eds. *The World's Writing Systems.* New York: Oxford University Press, 1996, pp. 218–227.

Kumatani, Akiyasu. "Language Policies in North Korea." *International Journal of the Sociology of Language*, no. 82, pp. 88–107.

Sasse, Werner. "The 'Cultured Language': Implementation of a Policy in North Korea." *Korean Linguistics*, 2, pp. 647–676.

About the Contributors

Charles K. Armstrong is Assistant Professor of History at Columbia University. He received his Ph.D. in East Asian history from the University of Chicago and has taught Korean history and politics at the University of Washington in Seattle and at Princeton University. He has published articles on contemporary Korea in a variety of journals and is currently working on a manuscript on the origins of the North Korean state.

Young Whan Kihl is Professor of Political Science at Iowa State University at Ames. He served in the ROK Marine Corps (1950–1955) and the Ministry of Foreign Affairs (1956–1957) before coming to the United States, where he received a B.A. from Grinnell College and an M.A. and Ph.D. from New York University. His books include *Politics and Policies in Divided Korea: Regimes in Contest* (1984), *Political Change in South Korea* (coeditor, 1988), *Korea and the World: Beyond the Cold War* (editor, 1994), and *Peace and Security in Northeast Asia: The Nuclear Issue and the Korean Peninsula* (coeditor, 1996).

Ross King is Assistant Professor of Korean at the University of British Columbia. Dr. King earned his B.A. in linguistics and political science from Yale University in 1983. He completed his Ph.D. in linguistics (major field Korean linguistics and philology, minor field Altaic comparative philology) in 1991 at Harvard. From 1990 to 1994 Dr. King was Lecturer in Korean Language and Literature at the School of Oriental and African Studies, University of London. His research interests include the history and prehistory of the Korean language and script, the language and culture of the Korean minority in Russia and the former USSR, and the sociology of the Korean language.

Stephen W. Linton was born in the United States and grew up in Korea, where his father was a third-generation Presbyterian missionary. Dr. Linton received a B.A. from Yonsei University, an M.Div. from Korea Theological Seminary, and an M.Phil. and a Ph.D. from Columbia University in Korean ethics and ideology. Dr. Linton served for three years as Associate Director of Columbia University's Center for Korean Research and is still an active Research Associate. Dr. Linton currently chairs the Eugene Bell Centennial Foundation (EBCF), a not-for-profit organization whose mandate includes educational, humanitarian, and religious programs related to North Korea. The EBCF works with nongovernmental organizations interested in developing relationships with North Korea.

David R. McCann is Professor of Korean Literature at Cornell University. After service in the U.S. Peace Corps in Korea, he undertook graduate training at Harvard University, receiving M.A. and Ph.D. degrees in Korean literature. He has published many translations and studies of Korean literature, including *Form and Freedom in Korean Poetry* (Brill), *Winter Sky: Selected Poems of So Chongju* (QRL New Poetry Series), *The Middle Hour: Selected Poems of Kim Chi Ha* (Human Rights Publishing Group), and *Prison Writings by Kim Dae Jung* (California). He received the 1995 Korea PEN Centre Prize for translation and the 1973 *Korea Times* Translation Prize for Poetry; his own poetry has been published in *Poetry* magazine and *Ploughshares* and is included in the 1978 *Pushcart Prize Anthology*.

Kongdan (Katy) Oh is co-principal of OH & HASSIG, Pacific Rim Consulting, specializing in policy research on the two Koreas. A native of Korea, she received her B.A. at Seoul National University. She subsequently earned an M.A. and Ph.D. in Asian studies at the University of California at Berkeley. She was an international policy analyst at RAND from 1987 to 1995 and has taught at Dominican College and at the University of California at San Diego. Dr. Oh's recent publications include *The U.S.-Japan Security Relationship After the Cold War* (co-authored with Francis Fukuyama, 1993; and in Japanese, 1994), and *Restarting the Peace Process on the Korean Peninsula* (senior editor with Craig Coleman, 1995).

Sang Duk Yu is Vice President of the Korean Teachers and Educational Workers Union (Chunkyojo). A principal leader of the Korean teachers movement from its inception in the 1980s, Mr. Yu went on to become one of the union's founders. He is a graduate of Seoul National University's College of Education. Mr. Yu taught secondary-school geography for several years until he was dismissed by the military government for organizing teachers. He has been imprisoned twice as a result of his activities in the teachers' movement.

Index

UNDP (UN Development Program), 64
Unesco Recommendation on the Status of
    Teachers, 80
Unification
    of Germany, 25-26, 29, 51-52, 55
    inevitability of, 23-24
    North-South dialogue and, 28-30, 103-109,
        159, 168, 170-171, 174, 175-176, 181,
        182, 187, 189, 204-205
    Reunification Democratic Party (ROK) and,
        6, 215
    under Roh Tae Woo, 26
    ROK costs of, 165
    scenarios of, 2-3, 65-67
    See also Inter-Korean economic
        cooperation: DPRK *and* ROK;
        Language, politics, and ideology:
        DPRK *and* ROK
Unification National Party (UNP, ROK), 208
Unified Democratic Republic of Korea
    proposal (ROK), 26, 65
Unified Han'gŭl Orthography (Korean
    Language Society), 111, 117, 120-121
Unified Spelling, 121, 122, 123, 139
United Liberal Democrats (ULD, ROK)
    Kim Chong Pil of, 11, 178, 184, 211
    local elections (1995) and, 11-13, 184
    National Assembly elections (1996) and, 204
United Nations (UN)
    Children's Fund of, 193
    Department of Humanitarian Affairs of, 66
    Development Program (UNDP) of, 64
    DPRK nuclear weapons issue and, 60, 157,
        158, 160-161
    DPRK participation in, 27, 58, 64, 174
    Korean War soldier remains and, 151, 152,
        153
    ROK participation in, 53, 58, 194
    World Food Programme of, 1, 17, 18, 64,
        97, 106, 197, 200
United People's Party (UPP, ROK), 7, 149, 216
United States
    DPRK policy of
        1953 Armistice Agreement and, 62-63,
            159, 202, 203, 204-205, 207
        aid to, 1, 66, 85, 97, 164, 193
        diplomatic relations with, 60-61, 62-63,
            85-87, 94, 99, 170, 174, 175, 179
        DPRK missile exports and, 205
        espionage incident and, 172-173
        Kim Il Sung and, 100-101
        Korean Americans and, 100-101
        nuclear issue and, 28-29, 34-35, 57,
            59-61, 85, 94, 105, 175, 176-177,
            178, 179, 180-182, 183, 192, 196,
            198-199, 200, 201, 207

    trade with, 33, 175, 178, 179, 182
    global nuclear nonproliferation
        activities of, 29, 33, 59
    on human rights, 155, 179-180
    Korean War and
        1953 Armistice Agreement and, 62-63,
            159, 202, 203, 204-205, 207
        soldier remains from, 166, 182
        Veterans Memorial from, 186-187
    language policy of, 115-116, 131-134
    ROK policy of
        Combined Forces Command and, 57-58,
            149, 154, 169, 193, 208-209
        Hwarang Drill exercise with, 150
        investment in, 158
        Korea Energy Development Organization
            and, 174
        Kwangju massacre and, 76
        military crimes and, 3, 199
        missiles to, 154, 155, 156, 177
        Record of Understanding Concerning
            Market Access for Cigarettes,
            190
        security alliance with, 57-58, 208-209
        Team Spirit exercise with, 34-35, 149,
            152, 155, 156, 159, 177, 201, 216
        trade with, 190-191, 215-216
    Status of Forces Agreement and, 3, 215
    Super 301 provision and, 191, 215-216
    Truman's containment policy and, 50
UNP (Unification National Party, ROK),
    208
UPP (United People's Party, ROK), 7, 149,
    216
U.S.-Japan Foundation, 178

Vietnam
    economic vs. political changes in, 24
    ROK investment in, 38, 39

With the Century (Kim Il Sung), 88
Wonsan, 37
Woo Myung Kyu, 167
Woolsey, R. James, 151, 154, 156
World Advertisement Congress, 58
World Food Programme, of UN, 1, 17, 18, 64,
    97, 106, 197, 200
World Trade Organization, 58, 172
Wulf, Norman, 168, 183

Yi Hŭi Sung, 112, 114, 115
Yi Kung No, 112, 114, 115, 124
Yi Man Gyu, 112, 114, 125
Yi Sŏn Gun, 120
Yi Song Nok, 30
Yi Song Tae, 30